Along Navajo Trails

Will Evans, 1925, at the height of his career as owner of the Shiprock Trading Company.

Along Navajo Trails
Recollections of a Trader, 1898–1948

by
Will Evans

Edited by
Susan E. Woods and Robert S. McPherson

Foreword by
Charles S. Peterson

UTAH STATE UNIVERSITY PRESS
LOGAN, UTAH

Utah State University Press
Logan, Utah 84322-7800

Photographs are from the Will Evans Collection in possession of his family unless otherwise noted.

All drawings are based on original art by Will Evans.

Cover painting by Kelly Pugh.

Cover photography by William Pennington.

Cover design by Dan Miller.

Manufactured in the United States of America.
Printed on acid-free paper.

Library of Congress Cataloging-in-Publication Data

Evans, Will, b. 1877.
 Along Navajo trails : recollections of a trader, 1898-1948 / by
Will Evans ; edited by Susan E. Woods and Robert S. McPherson ;
foreword by Charles S. Peterson.
   p. cm.
Includes bibliographical references and index.
 ISBN 0-87421-605-2 (hardcover : alk. paper) -- ISBN 0-87421-606-0 (pbk. : alk. paper)
 1. Navajo Indians--New Mexico--Shiprock Region--History. 2. Navajo Indians--New
Mexico--Shiprock Region--Social life and customs. 3. Navajo weavers--New Mexico--
Shiprock Region--History. 4. Trading posts--New Mexico--Shiprock Region--History. 5.
Indian traders--New Mexico--Shiprock Region--History. 6. Shiprock Region (N.M.)--History. 7. Shiprock Region (N.M.)--Social life and customs. I. Woods, Susan E. (Susan Evans),
1952- II. McPherson, Robert S., 1947- III. Title.
 E99.N3E93 2005
 979.1004'9726--dc22

     2005001650

Contents

Foreword xi

Acknowledgments xiv

Introduction
Will Evans, Trader to the Navajos 2
Starting Along the Trail 36

Events
Views of History around the Four Corners 52
    Agapito Remembers the Old Days 53
    Yellow Horse and the Long Walk 59
    The Establishment of Trading Posts 74
    Harry Baldwin and the Hogback Post 82
    Redrock Trading Post 86
    Little Singer and the Beautiful Mountain Uprising 91
    Prosperity in Reverse 104
    Oil and Gas on Navajo Land 108
    A Christmas Eve in Navajo Land 110

People
Navajos I Have Known 116
    Costiano 117
    Black Horse 122
    Bizhóshí 126
    Ugly Man 132
    Fat One and Son of Fat One 136
    Faith, an Episode 140
    Tragedies in Navajo Land 143
    Sandoval 145
    Slim Policeman 152
    A Dedicated Medicine Man 158
    Dan Pete 162

Culture
Daily Life and Customs of the Navajo People 180
    Daily Life in a Hogan 183
    Navajo Hospitality 187
    Trading with the Navajos 190
    Navajo Blankets 193

Silversmithing. 197
Cleanliness, Clothes, and Manners. 198
Hairstyles 202
Tobacco, Alcohol, and Morality 203
Navajo Marriage Customs and Family Life. 206
Divorce 210
Tribal Traditions and Lore 212
Sandpaintings. 214
My First Fire Dance 222
Squaw Dance (Enemyway). 227
Death, Witchcraft, and Skinwalkers. 228
Navajos and Animals 233

Postscript: The Death of a Man, the End of an Era. 235

Appendix: Publications by Will Evans. 239

Notes 242

Index 259

List of Photographs

Will Evans, 1925 . . . . frontispiece

Fruitland Trading Company, 1908–1911 5

Traders to the Navajos, 1912 6

Traders to the Navajos, 1930 8

Thomas Evans and sons 9

Building "Grandpa" Pipkin's house, 1897 12

Will, Ralph, and Sarah Evans, 1910 13

Will Evans and Dominick Rooster, 1920s 15

Evan Smith 17

Will Evans in his den in Farmington, New Mexico, 1950 18

Eddie Lake Trading Post 18

Missionaries, Young Stake Lamanite Mission 19

Painted book cover 20

Sarah and Will Evans holding wooden cross 23

Will Evans studying petroglyphs 28

Will Evans surrounded by art and collections 32

Claude Youngblood and Will Evans, Fruitland Trading Post 38

Will Evans, wedding photo, 1902 39

Sanostee Trading Post 41

Ch'įįdii hogan 42

Painting of Navajos and Will Evans trading inside his post 46

Trade tokens 47

Wool bags, 1908 50

Agapito family 55

Agapito, 1951 55

Yellow Horse 60

Navajos at Shiprock Agency, 1910 61

Old style hogan 63

Hastiin Deshnod 64

Mr. Mustache 66

Tocito Trading Post 75

Friends and traders 80

Shiprock Trading Company 81

William and Mrs. Shelton 85

Red Rock Trading Post, 1912 88

Little Singer 92

Shelton and Navajo police 93

Crowd at Sanostee Trading Post 95

General Hugh Scott 101

Robert and Asenebá Martin 102

Jacob C. Morgan and John Collier 105

Lukachukai Mountain gathering 111

Howela and Ruth Polacca 112

Costiano 118

Curley Jim 120

Two Grey Hills Trading Post, 1910 121

Black Horse 123

Bizhóshí, 1930 127

Little Singer 130

Bizhóshí and Little Singer at Sanostee Trading Post 131

Fat Medicine Man and son 137

Navajo rug 139

Hastiin Dáábali 141

Walker family 142

Sandoval 146

Hans Sandoval Aspaas 151

Slim Policeman or Siláo Ałts'ózí 153

Dan Pete 163

Shiprock aerial photo 167

Mother Earth and Father Sky 169

Shiprock Trading Company, 1925 182

Storm God with arrows mural 183

Stone hogan 184

Watering trough and sheep 186

Navajo madonna and baby 188

Judge Clah and two wives 192

Navajo weaver at work 194

Weaving a Navajo blanket 196

Navajo silversmith 197

Navajo sweat lodge 199

Harding Yazhi family 201

Water Under Oak Tree 202

Navajo children 208

Navajo cradle board 211

Storytelling 213

Making a sandpainting 215

Joe Redcap demonstrates sandpainting . . . . 216 and 217

Monster Slayer mural 221

Navajo ceremonial gathering, 1910 227

Will Evans with Navajo women 231

Will Evans in the mountains, 1952 236

Will Evans holding painted items 237

Will Evans looking over the Grand Canyon, 1926 238

Foreword

In 1948 Will Evans closed his trading post at Shiprock, New Mexico, for the last time. In leaving its "bull pen" trading room, he walked away from a half century as a Navajo trader, from a fraternity of businessmen who lived more intimately than perhaps any other European Americans with the Navajos, during one of that remarkable people's most challenging and successful periods. Like others of the trader fraternity, Evans was confident he knew "his Indians"—the families and clans that traded at his post. Moreover, he almost certainly shared the opinion commonly held among traders that anything important in the way his patrons felt, or in what they were doing, surfaced sooner or later in the bull pen and, from that vantage point of the white man's world, made its way around the larger trading community.

In this book, Evans's response to the Navajos, ably illuminated by editors Susan Woods and Robert McPherson, adds a welcome and enlightening chapter to the story of Indian trade in the Four Corners region. Written initially while Evans was on the job, his narrative focuses on the cultural exchange that took place between him and the Navajo men and women who lived within accessible distance of the Shiprock Trading Post, which to Evans was the heartland of the Navajo world. Masters of survival's give and take, the Navajos of the Evans era had been back for three decades from the terrors of their own "Babylonian Captivity," at Fort Sumner in eastern New Mexico. In the first half of the twentieth century they were fully engaged in an astonishing period of population growth and selective adaptation that ultimately served their cultural survival so well.

In reading *Along Navajo Trails,* it is well to note that Evans was a Mormon—part of a group which was also proving to be a surviving people. He had emigrated from Wales with his parents and, following the promise of a coal mining job, ended up at Fruitland, New Mexico. Corresponding closely in time to the Navajo return from Fort Sumner, the Mormons had colonized a vast, disjointed Four Corners Indian country, which included the Navajo and Hopi Reservations as well as Paiute, Ute, Apache, and

Zuni tribal lands. Eastward from Utah's Dixie on the Virgin River, a broken line of Mormon colonies could be traced through Kanab, Utah, and then southward and counterclockwise from Lee's Ferry and Tuba City, Arizona, through the lower and upper Little Colorado Basin towns, to Ramah, New Mexico, and north to the San Luis and San Juan Basin communities in Colorado, New Mexico, and Utah. This thrust to extend the Kingdom of God to the remnants of Book of Mormon people was at first largely preempted by Mormon preoccupation with desert survival and then reemerged, though as less of a priority, in a period that culminated in the appointment of Arizonan Spencer W. Kimball to the top levels of Mormon leadership after 1943.

During Will Evans's time the line between Indians as spiritual duty and as commercial prospect was at best blurred. The particulars of Mormon belief colored both the relations between Indians and LDS traders and the way other whites perceived the latter. Their distinctiveness complicated working the Mormons into the trader culture and their role into literature of the Navajo trade. Perhaps helpful in understanding this is Edward Hall's 1994 *West of the Thirties: Discoveries Among the Navajo and Hopi.* Hall divides Navajo traders of the era into three categories: those who worked for the Babbitt Brothers of Flagstaff, who were narrowly interested in business; independents like the Hubbells and the Wetherills, who he sees as sensitive, broad-gauge liberals; and Mormons, who looked to Salt Lake City and followed aggressive trade practices, including peddling that ignored other traders' rights.

The Four Corners loop also encompassed burgeoning industrial, transportation, government, and ranching communities, as well as world-class prehistoric culture sites and stunning natural beauty. It is not surprising that combined with Native Americans, polygamist Mormons, cowboys, and freewheeling archaeologists, these had a magnetic effect, drawing tourists, scientists, journalists, artists, as well as Hollywood and other myth makers. All together they molded the Four Corners into a cherished national cultural property.

Among the myth makers were many who wrote about the Navajo people and Indian traders. Their literature is various. Much of it is fascinating. Some of it is romantic and misleading. But like most stories in a free society, it is unfinished. As we advance, our capacity for comprehension grows, as should our taste for fuller, more useful interpretations. So it is in the case of Indian traders. Certainly the story of the Navajo capacity for adaptive survival is not complete. The success of Tony Hillerman's novels, for example, suggests that new and unexpected adaptations and interpretations continue.

In a different way the New Mormon History has poured out in a veritable stream of information. Much of it is narrowly crafted, aimed mainly at Mormon consumers, among whom self-indulgent tastes are creating viable markets for popular art, movies, and retold stories. Amidst this trend, scholarly work on the Mormon past continues to have an active, though limited appeal. With the possible exception of the stereotyped fiction of Gerald Lund (*The Work and the Glory*) there has, however, been a retreat from the social and cultural history of colonization. As Mormons sweep into their awareness of their church as a worldwide institution, work toward understanding the Mormon West remains unfinished. Although the first admiring Mormon expression of interest in Navajo Indians dates to 1831 and an occasional record of intercourse with Indians has followed the church's entire western career, next to no effort has been made to understand the role of Mormon Indian traders of the Four Corners or elsewhere. Neither Mormon nor Four Corners historians nor the myth makers have taken their measure, much less done justice to the social tension that has made western writers and publishers reticent to address the topic.

In Will Evans we see a Latter-day Saint who had the opportunity to observe the still preliterate generation of Navajos who returned from the Long Walk. In him stirred the need to collect and record. He was a man of his times and of his people. Both his biases and his strengths were apparent in his friendships with his trading post patrons and in his determination to observe the character and daily course of their lives. This was true also of his extended attempt to capture for posterity the nearly ethereally creative artistry manifested in sandpaintings—created at night as extended rituals reached their climax and then erased before morning.

It has been more than fifty years since Will Evans left his trading post. May we continue to find interest in the things that stirred him so.

April 2005

Charles S. Peterson
Professor of History Emeritus
Utah State University

Acknowledgments

Those who have traveled unknown trails are familiar with surprise, exhilaration, and occasional disappointment encountered along the way. The evolution of this book has followed such a path, spanning eighty years and three generations of the Evans family to reach its final goal. The time may seem excessive, but the trail has led to something important—the preservation of a piece of Navajo history otherwise forgotten. The path began in the Shiprock area, long before Will Evans put pen to paper. He began his journey through Navajo culture and history in 1898 but did not begin recording experiences until December 17, 1924, when the painted cover of "Navajo Trails: Being a Collection of Stories, Legends and Records of the Navajo People" emerged. Thirty years later he died, leaving his book unpublished except for excerpts in scattered newspaper articles.

Before Evans departed this life on a different trail, he charged his son Richard to see that the manuscript reached the public eye. Richard took the responsibility seriously, retyping the stories on a manual typewriter and photographing Navajo people who had worked with his father to preserve their legacy. Richard, however, never completed the project before he followed Will in death. Richard's daughter, Susan Evans Woods, next took to the path and invited Bob McPherson to accompany her. And now the final destination has been reached.

Many have assisted during stops along the way. In keeping with the personal, familial nature of the undertaking, we express appreciation to David J. Evans, who urged that the journey of his father and brother Richard reach fruition, while Robert Doyle reminded the family of the value of Will's collections. Harvard Heath and Brad Westwood accepted this collection on behalf of the Special Collections Department, Brigham Young University, where it is housed today. Liesl Dees and the Farmington Museum, New Mexico, have helped preserve Will's folk art and have featured it in a four-month exhibition at the museum. Will and Richard would be happy to know that the fruits of their journey now reside where they may benefit future generations.

In preparing this manuscript we are indebted to many for their help. Thanks to Anna and Jimmy Benally and Linda Keams, who assisted in

standardizing Will's spelling of Navajo words, which he attempted pho-
netically before there was a regularized form. Tom Wells and Russ Taylor
shared photographs from the Frank L. Noel Collection, housed at Brigham
Young University, while the Noel family graciously gave permission to
use them. This cemented ties forged between two trader families, whose
friendship began with Will and Frank close to a century ago. Evans, if
able, would also express appreciation to William Pennington, with whom
he became friends in the mid-1920s. Will served as his guide and interpreter, as the photographer traveled about the Navajo Reservation. Bart
Wilsey of the Farmington Museum, Eunice Kahn of the Navajo Tribal Museum, the Museum of Northern Arizona in Flagstaff, and the Sharlot Hall
Museum of Prescott graciously granted permission to use photographs
from their collections. All of these associations with the resulting photographs enrich this book and give faces to otherwise forgotten individuals.
A special thanks to John Alley, editor, Utah State University Press, for
shepherding the two authors through the brambles of publication.

We express our gratitude also to family members who have assisted
either with information or patience. Those in the former category include
Richard B. Evans, Alene Evans King, Pamela Evans Whitmer, Juliette Evans Probst, and brother-in-law Allan Whitmer, who has served as an important source for names and events associated with life in the trading
posts. In the latter category, we appreciate our spouses and families. Susan's husband, Bob Woods, and sons Aaron and McKay patiently allowed
her to become hypnotized by the work and provided editing and digital
photography skills. Bob McPherson appreciates the continuing support
from his wife, Betsy, and his children as he spends his free time in learning about the Navajo people. This is a gift more precious than gold.

As you, the reader, start down the trail with Evans, we hope you enjoy
sharing his view of the world of a trader and the people of his time. Although strenuous efforts have been made to maintain his initial thoughts
and voice, just as much effort has been taken to improve the spelling and
enhance the style. Any errors that have crept in are unintentional. The
authors hope that your journey with Will Evans, trader to the Navajos,
enriches your life as much as it has ours.

April 2005   Susan Evans Woods
                                                      Provo, Utah

                                                 Robert S. McPherson
                                                   Blanding, Utah

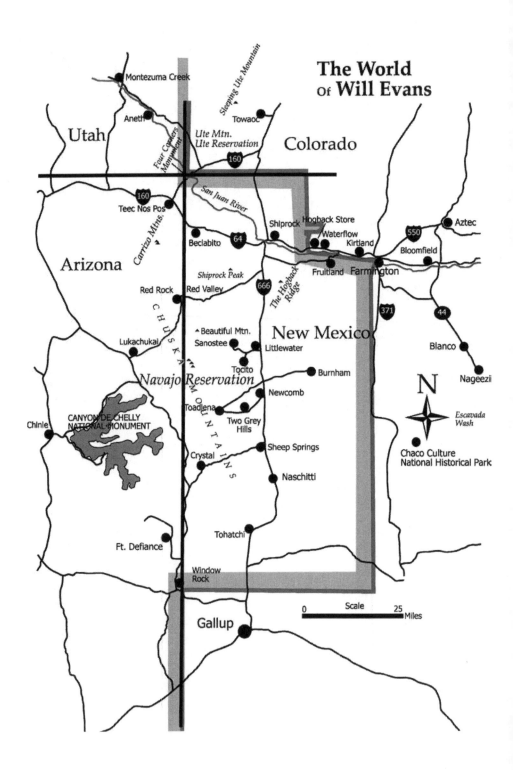

The World
Of **Will Evans**

Montezuma Creek
Aneth
Utah
Towaoc
Sleeping Ute Mountain
Four Corners Monument
Ute Mtn.
Ute Reservation
Colorado
160
160
Teec Nos Pos
San Juan River
Shiprock
Hogback Store
Aztec
Beclabito
64
Waterflow
Kirtland
550
Bloomfield
Arizona
Carrizo Mtns.
Fruitland
Farmington
Shiprock Peak
666
The Hogback Ridge
Red Rock
Red Valley
C
H
U
S
K
A
Beautiful Mtn.
New Mexico
371
44
Sanostee
Littlewater
Blanco
Lukachukai
Tocito
Burnham
Nageezi
Navajo Reservation
Newcomb
N
M
O
U
N
T
A
I
N
S
Toadlena
Two Grey
Hills
Escavada Wash
Chinle
CANYON DE CHELLY
NATIONAL MONUMENT
Sheep Springs
Crystal
Chaco Culture
National Historical Park
Naschitti
Tohatchi
Ft. Defiance
Window
Rock
Scale
0   25
Miles
Gallup

Introduction

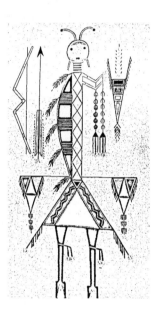

Will Evans, Trader to the Navajos

Mormon Traders in the Southwest

The American Southwest has been a place of sharp images and contrasting cultures. Starting with the prehistoric then historic Native Americans, moving to Spanish *entradas* and settlement, continuing through the Mexican period with the entrance of the Anglo-American, and ending with today's metropolises, a colorful saga of expansion and growth has played against a backdrop of antiquity and stability. Indeed, one of the most prominent appeals used in tourism and sales promotion is to call upon lingering, romanticized notions of yesteryear. Stagecoaches sell banks; rabbits and Monument Valley monoliths market batteries; and Indian tribal names denote sport utility vehicles. Image sells.

One enduring and often romanticized image is that of the Navajo trading post. Frank McNitt's classic, *The Indian Traders,* provides a broad survey of this fascinating phenomenon, where two cultures exchanged products and fostered a series of social as well as economic changes.[1] Following a brief chapter that combines the Spanish and Mexican eras and a cursory nod to Charles and William Bent's establishment in southern Colorado, the book launches into a detailed exposition of trade with the Navajo in New Mexico and Arizona, with less information on activity in Utah and Colorado. Not surprisingly, the majority of its pages focus on the last quarter of the nineteenth and first quarter of the twentieth centuries, encapsulating the most formative period and a good portion of the "golden years" that ended in the 1930s. Readers are indebted to the author for his excellent overview of a complex period.

Although McNitt is very thorough in some aspects of this overview, there is one topic that did not receive its due, and that is the role of the Mormon traders in the Southwest and especially in the Four Corners area. While Jacob Hamblin and John D. Lee were two dramatic figures who belonged to the Church of Jesus Christ of Latter-day Saints (LDS or Mormon), many others escaped McNitt's attention. Hardly mentioned are the large families and numerous individuals who spread throughout the region, creating extended social and economic networks that fed the posts and energized the trade. This is not to suggest that the LDS Church took an active role in directing this economic system; rather, those involved chose trading as their occupation because of individual circumstances.

The LDS Church from its inception has fostered expansion. By 1877, "more than 300 settlements had been established in the present states of Utah, Idaho, Wyoming, Arizona, Nevada, California, and Hawaii."[2] Church missionaries encouraged converts to gather to "Zion" and build a physical Kingdom of God on the earth. The pattern of growth continued into the early twentieth century as the church's population swelled due to high birthrates. Many members came from the British Isles and northern Europe, where land, freedom to worship, and a desire to commune with the Saints proved to be powerful inducements to migrate.

As the Great Basin filled with small communities, expansion pushed into Nevada and northern Arizona. Many of those people who settled on the Little Colorado River were called by church leadership to take their families, apply their skills, and create a community of Latter-day Saints on the borders of the "Lamanites," a term from the Book of Mormon denoting ancestry for some of the Native Americans in North America. Beginning in the mid-1870s, planned settlements on the Little Colorado sprang up along the banks of its usually torpid brown waters.[3] Cameron, Sunset, Saint Joseph, Woodruff, Taylor, and Saint Johns were just some of those early settlements where Mormons went to practice church programs of communal living. While they never achieved the ideal state of equality taught in church doctrine, the people in these towns persevered by means of a more economically viable system.

As the tentacles of expansion shifted out of the Great Basin and into the Southwest, they placed Mormons in more direct and continuous contact with southwestern Indians such as the Navajo. Other settlements along the periphery of the Navajo domain followed the Little Colorado settlements. During the 1880s, the Four Corners region experienced a flurry of town building in Bluff and Monticello, Utah; Fruitland, Farmington, Waterflow, and Kirtland, New Mexico; and Mancos, Colorado. Each of these towns struggled economically to survive in the austere environment of the northern Colorado Plateau.

All were initially based on subsistence farming and animal husbandry. Eventually, other people joined the original pioneers and furthered specialization in trades and services supporting the small but growing communities. Still, the question persisted as to how a small settlement, removed from efficient transportation and faced with small-scale production, could enter into the economic mainstream of the late nineteenth century. Part of the answer arose in the trade of wool and blankets sold by the Navajo.

Mormon traders brought some important features and effective skills to this trade. Considered by outsiders to be somewhat clannish, church members enjoyed the advantage of both an official and unofficial "grapevine" that made possibilities and options available. Some LDS members were "called" as part of their church responsibility to go and settle an area. They remained until "released" from their time of service and then were free to go wherever they wished. When converts from the East or from foreign countries arrived in Salt Lake City, church officials might direct them to areas where specific talents could be used in an existing community. Others went where members who shared a similar heritage lived.

The more informal grapevine existed for those mobile seekers of opportunity. As new lands opened and local economies developed, word spread. While individuals were certainly involved, entire households might transplant to an area of enterprise. Families, Mormon and non-Mormon alike, who lived in rural America, tended to be large. Thus family networks often lived in the same area, shared in a supportive economic endeavor, and prospered or failed according to their fortunes. This was particularly true of those who settled in the Four Corners area and traded with the Navajo.

Take, for instance, Joseph Lehi Foutz.[4] He spent his younger years exploring and working with Jacob Hamblin among the Paiute, Hopi, and Navajo tribes. Beginning in the 1870s, he started a career in trading that did not end until his death on March 19, 1907. In the meantime, his family of sons and daughters had become entrenched in the business so that by 1940, an army of thirty-seven relatives, all of whom were LDS, were involved in trading.[5] What follows is a brief synopsis of some of this activity. It reads like a directory of posts on or near the Navajo Reservation, illustrating the pervasive nature of the Mormon trader.

In 1878 Joseph Foutz moved to Lees Ferry in Arizona to escape persecution by federal officials against Mormons practicing polygamy. Shortly

Fruitland Trading Company, 1908–1911, owned by Frank L. Noel and a Mr. Cline.

after that, he began trading at Moenkopi then moved to Moenave on the periphery of the Hopi Reservation. Joseph Lee, son of John D. Lee, opened two posts to the Navajo—Red Lake and Blue Canyon—where Foutz worked before moving to Tuba City to trade. In 1900, the federal government bought the lands from the settlers in this community and made it part of the Navajo Reservation. Foutz arrived in Kirtland, New Mexico, where opportunity encouraged the expansion of his trading business, which was now joined by his six sons. Add to them sons-in-law and their families—three of the most prominent names being Tanner, Dustin, and Powell—and there appears a far-flung network of social and economic relations spread across the Navajo Reservation.

Those familiar with this area will realize that the following list of posts served by this net of relations is only indicative and not comprehensive. In New Mexico were Gallegos, Beclabito, Tocito, Sanostee, Smith Lake, Burnham, Bisti, Whitewater, Pinedale, Shiprock, Sheep Springs, Tó Łigaai, and Coyote Canyon. Arizona posts included Keams Canyon, White Cone, Redrock, Teec Nos Pos, Red Mesa, Dinnehotso, Piñon, Sawmill, Wide Ruins, Hunter's Point, Tuba City, Moenave, Moenkopi, Greasewood, and Cedar Ridge. Located in Utah were Aneth, Bluff, Mexican Hat, and Blanding, while in Colorado there was the Mancos Creek Trading Post.

Traders after a meeting with Superintendent William T. Shelton at the Shiprock Agency in 1912. Half of the traders identified are Mormon (M). *Top row, left to right:* Sheldon Dustin (M), John Walker (M), Jesse Foutz (M), Ike Goldsmith, Bert Dustin (M), Frank Noel (M), Alphonso (Fonnie) Nelson, June Foutz (M), Bruce Bernard, unidentified government employee. *Third row:* Herbert Redshaw (government farmer), "Al" Foutz (M), Olin C. Walker, Will Evans (M), John Hunt (M), two unidentified. *Second row:* [James M.?] Holly, Frank Mapel, Edith Mapel, Crownpoint agent Samuel B. Stacher, George Bloomfield (M), Mrs. Ed Davies, and Ed Davies with daughter Mary. *Bottom row:* Unknown, Arthur J. Newcomb, Supt. Shelton, Joe Tanner (M), Louisa Wade Wetherill, John Wetherill.

For well over a half century, this family, sharing either blood or conjugal ties, had a significant impact on the Navajo trade.

Other Mormons and their families also played an important role in the posts. Ira Hatch, like Foutz, began his official interaction with American Indians under the direction of Jacob Hamblin while serving a mission, as early as 1854. He also became conversant in Paiute, Hopi, Ute, and Navajo and eventually moved to Fruitland in the Four Corners region. With the assistance of family members, he became extensively involved in trade with the Navajos. Other LDS families who figured prominently in this enterprise during the last part of the nineteenth and first half of the twentieth centuries in the Four Corners area included Hunt, Hyde, Stolworthy, Ashcroft, Burnham, Kennedy, Arrington, Bloomfield, Washburn, and Blair. An informal survey among relatives in Will Evans's family listed by name over fifty individuals with LDS connections involved in the trading business.[6]

Many non-Mormon traders also operated posts. It is almost impossible to determine what percentage of traders over a broad period of time was LDS because of the high turnover in posts and the comings and goings of the various owners. Many stores changed hands a dozen or more times within as many years, and so an in-depth owner genealogy of each post would have to be performed—an almost herculean task. Also, there were some posts that may have started with an LDS trader, such as Charles Nelson, who later sold his business to non-LDS Arthur and Franc Newcomb in 1913. The post became famous because of Franc's work in preserving various aspects of Navajo culture, while Nelson is relegated to the mists of history.[7] The only people who really kept track of post ownership were the traders themselves, and most of them have passed away.

What is needed is a snapshot of a certain period of history to determine trader percentages. Fortunately for our purpose, just such a photograph is found in McNitt's *The Indian Traders*. In 1912, William T. Shelton, superintendent of the Northern Navajo Agency located in Shiprock, held a meeting with the traders under his jurisdiction and had a picture taken. There are nontraders pictured in the photo, as well as some family members of participants. Once those who were not traders or who have not been identified are removed and families are counted together, twenty traders or trading families are depicted, half of whom are LDS. No doubt, not all posts were represented in the meeting, but this gives a good indication of the prominence of the Mormon faith among the traders of the Four Corners region at this time.

Another means of quantifying the extent of the trading industry in this region is with a quick perusal of a local history compiled by Rosetta Biggs in 1977.[8] Entitled *Our Valley,* this hefty tome is primarily an account of the people in and near Farmington, New Mexico, from the town's inception to the time of publication, although the majority of the work centers on the earlier years. In this book, the author identifies 150 families that range from single individuals to groups of a dozen relatives. It is not an economic history and follows no particular format, some of the entries, which were submitted by family members, are as short as a paragraph and others a half-dozen pages. Fifty-nine of the 150 families, or 40 percent, mentioned being involved in some aspect of trading, either

Traders with Shelton (retired) at Shiprock Fair, 1930. Ten of the thirteen traders identified in this photo are Mormon (M). *Front row, left to right:* Asenebá Martin, Arthur J. Newcomb, Deshna Clah (one of the first chairmen of tribal council), William T. Shelton, Bert Dustin (M), Carlos Stolworthy (M), Roscoe McGee (M), unknown. *Back row:* Walter Gibson, Don Smouse, Asa Palmer (M), Roy B. Burnham (M), Shiprock agent Evan W. Estep, Luff Foutz (M), Elmer A. Taylor (M), Richard P. Evans (M), Will Evans (M), Charles Ashcroft (M). Cline Library, Special Collections and Archives, Northern Arizona University.

as a trader, bookkeeper, freighter, or clerk. This figure does not include individuals whose families were well known as traders if the individuals did not mention their own involvement. Fourteen families also wrote of their service as missionaries to the Navajos.

What was different, then, about these LDS traders? In some cases probably nothing. Trading, as an occupation, did not require any special religious attributes, just a basic understanding of traditional Navajo beliefs that might have had an impact upon sales and courtesy in the store.[9] On the other hand, those who believed and practiced LDS teachings had a theological underpinning to their relations with Indians not found among other traders. Their beliefs derived from the origin of the church rooted in the Book of Mormon.[10]

Briefly, the Book of Mormon is a religious history of a group of Israelites who journeyed from Jerusalem to the Americas around 600 B.C. During the approximately one thousand years covered by this text, the

Four of the eight children of Thomas and Jane Ann Coles Evans. *Back row, left to right:* Wilford, Edwin (Ted) C. *Front row:* William, Thomas (father), and John.

group divided into Nephites and Lamanites, who warred against each other and became spiritually distant. The Lamanites are portrayed, generally, as a fallen race, while the Nephites maintained more of their spiritual purity but struggled to keep a proper religious perspective based upon the teachings of prophets who foretold the coming of Jesus Christ. At one point in the book, Christ visits the Americas, spends time teaching the people, and leaves them with a renewed faith and understanding of the gospel of salvation. Eventually, the Nephites depart from their ways and, by 421 A.D., have become so wicked that the Lamanites destroy them. According to LDS beliefs, at least some of today's American Indians are a remnant of the Lamanites. They have lost much of the once powerful Christian teachings held and shared by the Nephites.

When Joseph Smith received this history on gold plates, he translated the story and later, as the founder and prophet of the LDS Church, directed missionary efforts to the Indians to restore what they once had. Thus, as traders and missionaries, Jacob Hamblin, Ira Hatch, Joseph Foutz, and Thales Haskell attempted to return what had been lost. Haskell, like the others, gained his Indian experience during the settlement of the Little Colorado area, before moving to Bluff, Utah, in the early 1880s. These men and many of the traders descended from them shared a belief about these Indians' origins and their destiny.

Will Evans's Biography

William "Will" Evans in some ways is a representative figure of the Mormon experience, in general, and of the settlers in the Four Corners area, specifically. Much of the following overview of his life is based upon the research of Liesl Dees, who gathered information for an exhibition of Evans's art in Farmington in August 2001.[11] Dees's contribution through oral interviews and written sources is particularly effective in summarizing the broad range of Will's endeavors.

Evans was born in Pontypridd, South Wales, Great Britain, on March 14, 1877, to Thomas and Jane Ann Coles Evans. His father and grandfather were coal miners, and William, upon completing three years of formal education at the ripe age of nine, joined family members in the depths of Wales's coal mines. Danger of rockfalls from the roof of the shaft, fear of the "black damp"—natural gases that seeped into the corridors and ignited with a terrible explosion—and the darkness found 2,500 feet below the earth's surface created an environment the boy dreaded.

Thomas and Jane Ann initially belonged to the Methodist Church, attended services regularly, and even brought Will as a baby to the meetings. An incident occurred concerning their crying baby and their treatment in church that turned them away from that faith and toward a fellow miner and member of the Church of Jesus Christ of Latter-day Saints. Thomas wrote,

> I went to the mine the next day to work with my partner. It occurred that he was a Latter-day Saint. I told him what happened the night before. He said "Why don't you come to our meeting; it is down the road below the mine along the side of the highway." I told my wife and she thought it would be alright. The man who took us out was named Robert Bishop. In the course of time we joined. Jane was baptized eleven months before me, in the month of November 1880.[12]

Held back by his fearful stammering, Thomas made fast friends with the Mormon elders who labored in Wales. He could be found with them on a Sunday, walking from village to village, attending up to eight meetings a day. He bore frequent testimony of the knowledge that came to him through this activity. Finally, urged by his wife and encouraged by his missionary friends, he was baptized in October 1881. He recorded in his journal that as he came out of the water, he began to speak clearly, his stammering vanished, and never again did his speech falter.

Persecution followed, embroiling not only the parents but also Will and his three brothers and two sisters. Townspeople railed against the family and their newfound faith. Thomas wrote, "Wherever we went, the children were egged on by their parents to shout, 'Old Saints of the Devil go to Salt Lake.'" It even cost Will his front tooth in a scrap with some neighborhood boys. Years later, the Navajos gave him the name Awóshk'al'ádin, "Missing Tooth in Front," based on this characteristic.[13]

The family left their home in Wales on August 27, 1892, and three weeks later, along with 130 other Mormon emigrants from the British Isles, stood on American soil. In another month, they were in Salt Lake City hunting employment. Temporary work, including a short stint of coal mining in Scofield, Utah, by Thomas and fifteen-year-old Will, did not bring much satisfaction. An economic depression rendered any lasting benefit elusive.

Following a series of layoffs, Thomas received an offer from John R. Young, nephew of Brigham Young, to come to Fruitland, New Mexico, to work as a coal miner. The family accepted. They took the train to Thompson, Utah, continued by wagon through Monticello, on to Cortez,

Joe Hatch, Sr., Lude Kirk Hatch, and Will Evans building James "Grandpa" Pipkin, Jr.'s house, June 1897 in Fruitland, New Mexico. This was shortly before Evans's initial trading experience at Sanostee.

Colorado, to Farmington, and then west twelve miles to Fruitland. By September 4, 1893, the Evans family began life anew in the Four Corners area. Both father and sons again worked in the mines, but Will supplemented his income by assisting others in farming and construction. He was not enamored of either. He wrote, "Late in 1898, I decided that coal mining and farm labor ran into too much work. I was offered an opportunity to go on the reservation and assist in erecting the first trading post within the confines of the Northern Navajo Reservation. This trading post was located at Sanostee Valley."[14]

Evans tells the rest of the story later in this book. But for the remainder of his life, he was intricately connected to the Navajos as a Mormon trader and student of their culture. An overview of his experiences illustrates the powerful impact of these two cultures upon him, as they met over the trading post counters and circulated within the "bull pen" of the posts in which he worked.

Evans began as a trader in 1898 with the building and operating of the Sanostee Trading Post in partnership with Joseph Wilkins and Edwin Seth Dustin (Mormon). He assisted in shipping supplies to other posts located in New Mexico and to stores in Snowflake and Taylor, Arizona. During this time he met Sarah Luella Walker, who belonged to a trading family that had lived in Taylor before moving to Fruitland in 1896. Evans married her

Evans, son Ralph, and wife, Sarah, 1910.

in 1902 and eventually had four children—Ralph, Gwendolin, Richard, and David. The couple spent their lives together working in their posts and the trading business before retiring in 1948.

In Evans's early years in Fruitland, he put his building skills to work by constructing the Two Grey Hills and Fort Defiance trading posts, as well as erecting a Methodist mission for Mary Eldredge and Mrs. H. G. Cole near Farmington.[15] He also ran the post office in Fruitland from 1904 to 1909 and edited a short-lived newspaper, the *Fruitland Tribune,* in 1906.[16] For the next few years he put in stints at Two Grey Hills, Sanostee, and other posts; he worked as well for the C. H. Algert Trading Company in Fruitland as a bookkeeper.

Following a two-year respite from the trading business when he served a mission for the LDS Church in Portland, Maine, Evans returned to the Algert Company, where he worked until 1917.[17] This enterprise figured heavily in the Navajo trade of the Four Corners region. It took its name from the original owner, who, although not a Mormon, worked with them in the Tuba City area until that land became part of the Navajo Reservation in 1900. When the settlers moved to Fruitland, Algert followed and established his company. The business, "a wholesale trading store housed in a two-story building constructed of brick, adobe, and cement," was purchased within a few years by four traders.[18] Junius (June) and

Al Foutz with their two brothers-in-law, Bert and Sheldon Dustin, each paid $4,000, renamed the business the Progressive Mercantile Company, and offered goods appraised at $10,000.[19] All four of these owners were Mormon, again illustrating the influence that church members had in the trading business of this region.

In 1917, Evans purchased from Junius Foutz the Shiprock Trading Company, located on the reservation, and began his own enterprise. The post stood across a wash, about 125 yards southeast of its present location. The business shifted to today's site following the construction of a new road in 1925.[20] Evans remained there for the next thirty-one years.

Like most traders, he encouraged Navajo weavers to create rugs and blankets that would sell. In his early years at Shiprock, he fostered in his clients the idea of incorporating sacred figures into their work, popularizing a style of rug often identified with this region. Not all Navajos and non-Navajos favored the use of sacred images in this way, and to this day there are some who oppose it.[21] Evans was very aware of the dangers foretold in Navajo traditional beliefs surrounding this practice and also of the cost of protection provided by medicine men to avert risks in creating such weavings. While the growth of the "Yé'ii" rug industry has spread to many parts of the Navajo Reservation, most art historians agree that it had its birth in the Four Corners region; and while Evans was not the first to initiate such practices, he certainly knew those who did and aligned his weavers to follow suit.[22]

Regardless of the subject matter, Evans loved the beautiful products fashioned from materials of this high desert environment. When one considers the simple things used to create art—sand, wool, wood, and a little silver—the beauty and variety of the finished products are astounding. Evans recognized the skill involved and paid homage to his customers and friends: "The handling of Indian-made products is a source of great pleasure. The artistry of the Navajo blanket, which is the chief product of the tribe, grows on one. I believe that I get as much of a thrill out of buying a Navajo blanket as I did on that day way back in 1898 when I traded for my first specimen."[23]

The study of Navajo ceremonial art became another all-encompassing passion. Most white men were either not interested or did not have the trust and respect of Navajos necessary to view these holy images. Evans obtained both, was intent on preserving this aspect of culture, and was fascinated by their intricate beauty. He explains,

> I acquired the hobby of collecting copies of sandpaintings and the stories that go with them. So, for years, I have been watching the making

Evans with his prized Dominick rooster, 1920s. Behind is the original Shiprock Trading Post. The tin shed stored pelts, oil, and other inventory. Family living quarters were at the rear of the store; east of the trading room were rental rooms, while next to the porch was a cooling room to hang beef and mutton. At far left is the Old Bond Lodge Hotel.

of these beautiful works of art, have sketched them while the medicine men worked, later making copies of them in oil paints so as to preserve them. Today, the Navajos marvel at the collection I have. At times, someone will come in to the store and ask me to let him see a certain sandpainting. He wants to make one and has forgotten some detail or other and wishes to see my copy so that he can get the items. I am only pleased to do this because he will some day reciprocate. I am satisfied that the art of sandpainting will become extinct and a collection of them will be priceless, not only in a monetary sense but from their value as study material for research into the religion of a native people.[24]

These early years in Shiprock were a time of exploration in other areas for Evans and his family. Will's son, Ralph, recollected infrequent trips to Fruitland but remembered more frequent times spent with the Navajos, attending ceremonies, or "sings," and Squaw (Enemyway) Dances, watching pony races, and hunting jackrabbits. Will's daughter, Gwen, wrote of her father's love for the mountains, enjoyment in wildflowers, and ability as a camp cook. He was known for making a slumgullion stew with canned tomatoes, corn, green beans, and corned beef—or whatever else happened to be on the shelf at the time.[25]

Evans, although living in a land where isolation was normal, was not a recluse. He was civic minded, playing the violin in the Shiprock Band as the only white man in the Navajo orchestra. At one point he encouraged local citizens to establish a historical-scientific society and dedicated a room in his post as a museum for Navajo blankets and art work.[26] In 1929–1930, Evans traveled often to Aztec, Farmington, and Santa Fe to fulfill his responsibilities in the New Mexico State Legislature as a Republican representative. He served on agriculture, judiciary, and mining committees, reflecting his regional and personal interests.[27] Three pieces of legislation that he was particularly proud of championing were a bill that granted the state the right to retain half of the archeological materials excavated within its boundaries, a law that penalized individuals who sold liquor to Indians on the reservation, and the initial survey of the San Juan River for the Navajo Dam, which was later constructed outside of Farmington.[28]

Evans, even with his desire to encourage positive innovations for the Navajo, was also a preservationist. His time in the posts saw change— sometimes slow and inexorable, other times rapid—which affected the culture. Among the milestones passed by the tribe during this time were the opening of the Shiprock Agency (1903); the first Shiprock Fair (1909); World War I (1917–1918); the influenza epidemic (1918–1919); the introduction of the automobile (1920s); livestock reduction (1930s); the beginning of the wage economy (1940s and 1950s); expansion of the coal, oil, and gas industry into the reservation (beginning around 1900); and World War II (1941–1945).

Evans realized that the older forms of Navajo practices were changing and so set about to record what he could. How he became interested in preserving sandpaintings and the teachings behind them he will explain later. But he attempted to accurately capture many of these visual images. He attended numerous ceremonies and was allowed to make sketches of the designs—images that are generally not recorded by Navajos. These religious symbols are sacred and powerful and are to be viewed only by those initiated into the ceremonies and beliefs of the People. Evans compiled a "library" of at least sixty images, which he kept in the Kiva Room of the Shiprock Trading Company.

In the late 1930s, Evans observed difficult times for the Navajo, due in part to the government's livestock reduction program. He suggested a plan for economic development in which the Navajos could build and decorate furniture as a local craft—an idea that, by this time, he was implementing himself.[29]

Evans incorporated into his own artistic endeavors visual images from the sandpaintings he recorded. He designed and built simple furniture, such as tables, chairs, and picture frames, which he painted with Navajo

Evan Smith, Navajo employee at the Evans store, 1937–1949, in front of pictures of Navajo rugs painted by Evans.

art. He also decorated other items, such as bottles, trays, metal cans, and even Pepsi signs. A niece, Florence Walker Cluff, remembered that "someone was always being surprised at what turned up newly painted after a few days absence, the mantel clock for instance."[30]

By the late 1930s, Evans had painted the exterior of the Shiprock Trading Company with geometric designs and ceremonial figures.[31] In 1941, the interior of Harry's Place, a Farmington restaurant, had similar wall coverings. Other large-scale murals included ceremonial art on the trading posts at Hogback, Waterflow, and Mancos Creek. Larger-than-life figures from Will's brush enlivened the interior of Farmington's Totah Theater. The local Avery Hotel and Stalling's gas station also sported his art.[32] His enthusiasm for Navajo iconography seemed boundless.

The end of the Depression and the beginning of World War II left the store short of funds. In 1943, Evans wrote to his son David, who was serving an LDS mission, that he had sold $160 worth of pieces that he painted—funds that allowed Sarah to have dental work and helped pay for the mission.[33] This was while Will and Sarah served as the first mission president and matron of the Young Stake Lamanite Mission (1941–1943), a proselytizing effort that covered a good portion of the northern Navajo Reservation. Roy B. Burnham, stake president of the Young Stake, and Evans divided the mission into six districts. Not surprisingly, Burnham

Evans in his den, Farmington. Sitting in a love seat he built and painted, he is applying the finishing touches to a table painted in Navajo sandpainting designs. Photo by Charles Dustin.

Eddie Lake Trading Post, Waterflow, New Mexico. Painted by Evans using sandpainting figures and designs. The abandoned building still stands as of 2005.

Missionaries Will Evans, Lucy Bloomfield, Ralph Evans, Clyde Beyal (interpreter), and George Bloomfield of the Young Stake Lamanite Mission, preparing to baptize Navajo converts at Crystal, New Mexico.

descended from a trading family and was himself a trader, as were five of the six missionaries presiding over their districts.[34]

Although he continued to work in the store, Evans served diligently and traveled constantly as the first person to hold this position. Daughter-in-law Beth Evans remembers that he used his knowledge of Navajo ceremonies to explain the connections he saw between Navajo tradition and Mormon beliefs, drawing figures from sandpaintings in the dirt floors of Navajo hogans.[35] The drawings also may have assisted in overcoming limitations of his "trader Navajo" language, which did not have the capacity to translate deeper religious beliefs. He often took a native speaker, Evan Smith, with him.[36]

In 1924, Evans began writing essays, which he called "Navajo Trails." This inaugurated a series of articles published in the *Farmington Times Hustler* (later *Farmington Daily Times*), which continued until his death in 1954. He also published a number of articles in other journals and a small book on sandpaintings, illustrated with his drawings. As old age sapped his strength, Will eventually turned the "Navajo Trails" manuscript over to his son Richard to bring it to completion.[37]

In June 1948, Evans sold the Shiprock Trading Company to Vernon W. Jack, another Mormon trader, allowing Will and Sarah to move to Farmington.[38] He continued to paint in his new house, ornamenting the

Navajo Trails

Painted by Evans, "Hogan Gho" was to be the cover of "Navajo Trails, Being a Collection of Stories, Legends, and Records of the Navajo People," the compilation of which began December 17, 1924.

porch light with a Navajo figure and the garage door with a large sun symbol. The local newspaper reported a visit to the Evans's home, saying,

> In the kitchen there is one chest of drawers painted only a severe, plain white. When Will Evans was asked why there were no figures on it, his wife answered the question before Will could get his mouth open. "Will Evans," she said, "you just leave that alone—there's going to be one thing here that doesn't have Indians all over it."[39]

In 1952, the voters of Farmington elected Evans on the Greater Farmington ticket as the city police judge for a two-year term; and in true Evans fashion, he decorated the interior of his office at the police station.[40] As judge, he emphasized fair treatment for all and, drawing on his experiences as a trader, allowed Navajos to use jewelry as security against fines assessed in court.[41]

Sarah Walker Evans's journal records that Will occasionally sold his hand-painted pieces, but the vast majority of his work he gave away to friends and relatives. As his health began to fail, one of Sarah's journal entries commented that "Will had a very dizzy spell pass over him, his head fell against a jar he was painting and the brush fell from his hand."

He ran for police judge a second time in 1954, but lost. His health continued to fail until he passed away on December 6, 1954.[42]

Evans's Views of Navajo Religion

In one sense, Evans is a representative figure of the class of traders who lived and worked in the Navajo posts during the early twentieth century. He was hardworking, interested in profit, attentive to customer likes and dislikes, and rooted in the daily life of the Navajo community. On the other hand, he was unique. He is the only Mormon trader who recorded traditional Navajo teachings with an eye to correlating them with LDS beliefs and practices. Certainly Jacob Hamblin had earlier intellectually aligned Hopi and Navajo teachings in accordance with his understanding of Mormon views, but like so many other missionaries of his era, never recorded for publication his thoughts.

Not so with Evans. He was very public in his views on how these two differing faiths coincided. While these thoughts are not discussed in the main part of this book, it is worthwhile for the reader to understand the context within which his writings are framed.

Today, Evans would be considered an apologist. He was deeply entrenched in Latter-day Saint theology, and so his main goal was to show how Navajo beliefs connected to church dogma. He superimposed his scriptural knowledge over what he encountered in Navajo ceremonies and oral tradition to provide proof of his own beliefs and justification for theirs. This is not to suggest that he intentionally distorted what he found but only that he was primed to interpret his findings in a particular vein.

Evans was adamant that the origin of the American Indian had nothing to do with the prevalent belief of Mongolian-type peoples crossing a land bridge during the Ice Age. The Book of Mormon mentions a number of transoceanic crossings, which Evans accepted as true. By examining contemporary Navajo practices, he believed one could find proof. In "Indian Culture," an article written for a church publication in 1938, he outlines some of his basic tenets.[43] In accordance with the general story in the Book of Mormon, "as early as the fourth century, B.C., native Americans had a good working knowledge of steel and copper" and "when Caesar was invading Britain, ancient America was looking forward to the coming of the Redeemer."[44] The fall of the Nephites at the end of the book signaled the loss of a written language; and so Indians went to a form of picture writing, proof of which the Spanish destroyed during their conquests in South and Central America. The pictographs and petroglyphs etched into the rocks and alcoves of the Southwest are a remnant of this knowledge and mark the farthest advance of Central American Indian expansion. Evans wrote, "This spread of colonization reached its last great wave on both sides of the southern boundary lines of the modern states of Utah and Colorado."[45] The religious beliefs of the Hopis and Navajos are the same as those of the Ancestral Puebloans (Anasazi), who were the descendants in that region of Book of Mormon peoples. Within these Indians' oral tradition could be found stories that "to a startling degree [parallel] those recorded in the ancient Hebrew record."[46]

A number of similarities served, in Evans's mind, as proof of this history. The creation of the four worlds that occurred before and beneath this world, according to the Navajo account, was similar to what was described in Genesis and the Latter-day Saint scripture entitled the Pearl of Great Price. The correlations included the placement of the heavenly bodies by a number of Holy Beings; the separation of waters and appearance of land; the creation of plant life, animals, and man; and a snake that walked and talked like a person. Just as the Lord spoke to Job out of a whirlwind, so is there a Navajo being, Dinay-De Ginnie [Dinééh Diyiní (Holy Young Man)], who has a similar experience. He also raises the dead as did Christ. Another Holy Being is swallowed by a great fish, as is Jonah.

Sarah and Will holding a framed cross found in a cliff dwelling near Shiprock. To Evans, this was proof of the Ancestral Puebloans' (Anasazi) tie to the Book of Mormon. Photo by Richard P. Evans.

First Man and First Woman, comparable to Adam and Eve, are never portrayed in sandpaintings because of their sacredness. In the Yé'ii Bicheii ceremony twelve ancestors assist with the creation; and the name of the ceremony can be "interpreted as the Great Ancient One, The Ancient of Days," in parallel to Adam and others in the Christian pantheon.[47] There is a worldwide flood similar to the one encountered by Noah. A Moses-like figure strikes a rock and water gushes forth, is concealed by a cloud as on Mount Sinai, and crosses a place called Red Water.[48] Another Holy Being has a rod that shoots forth buds as did Aaron's. There are proscriptions against handling the dead, which would otherwise cause one to become unclean. Similarly, ceremonial purification for such contact is outlined by Hebrew law in the Old Testament.[49]

Evans also had a cross, which came from an Anasazi dwelling he believed to be from the eleventh century, that he saw as iconic evidence that long before Columbus ever set sail, Indians practiced Christianity in the Americas. He also believed that the ingestion of corn pollen during a ceremony was comparable to partaking of the sacrament. The washing and anointing described in the Old Testament are similar to the washing done in a medicine basket with yucca soap.[50] All of these practices confirmed what Evans believed to be true.

What, then, was his attitude toward the customers he faced every day across the counters? Was he a tight-fisted pragmatist, waiting for the dollars to follow the Navajos' rugs and wool, or a saintly man, so caught up in intellectual study that he missed opportunities to prosper? Probably Evans shared a little of each quality. He certainly reflected the thinking of his times. He held a deep respect for Navajo traditions but at a time when most outsiders did not understand or consider beneficial these ceremonial practices. He was also somewhat skeptical of the methods, if not their ultimate efficacy. An important glimpse into his private views is found in personal correspondence with a man named B. H. Reddy, who lived in Long Beach, California.

Reddy's relationship with Evans began in July 1939, when Reddy inquired about the possibility of a "Navaho Medicine Man [holding] a healing dance or ceremony for one who is having a great deal of trouble with their gall bladder, liver, and stomach."[51] Reddy was referring to his wife, who apparently shared with him "considerable faith" in native practices.

Though somewhat leery, Evans responded immediately to one of "the strangest requests that has come my way."[52] Writing of the Navajos' ability to heal, he noted that he "respect[ed] them as far as their knowledge is concerned; but there is a greater Power which can come to our rescue whenever sought. . . . He [Navajo medicine man] knows nothing of pills, soothing syrups, or drugs. . . . He uses fetishes of extremely doubtful value and his appeals are mainly to the ancient ones of their legendary lore." In Evans's mind, it was the faith of the patient that did the healing and "many cures are wrought." This was in keeping with the miracles of the Old Testament and practices explained in the Book of Mormon.

He next inquired if Mr. Reddy's patient intended to come to the reservation for the ceremony or have it performed by "remote control." This question was not facetious. Evans understood the principle of what anthropologists call synecdoche, using a part to represent the whole, as practiced by Navajo healers.[53] He concluded by saying that he had "followed the Navajos in their religion, their religious legendary history, and their ceremonies during 45 years. I have learned to respect them in their religion as I do any other race of people."

A week later, Reddy responded. He compared the British attitude toward the natives of India to those of Americans toward the Indian, who know far more about the "Book of Nature than those same Americans will ever dream about."[54] The contention of Anglo superiority ignored the reality of healing by nature. "There is no doubt but that the Indian Medicine Men have contacted that Higher Power" that only a few whites ever had. Reddy, obviously enamored of Native Americans, next pointed out that "one cannot deceive a real Medicine Man as to one's thoughts and intents" and that "Indians and other primitive tribes are the original

Spiritualists. Medicine Men are all psychics, else they would not be Medicine Men." He closes by calling them "seers."

The Californian had provided Evans with a perfect opportunity to burst an idealistic bubble. While he perhaps shared some romantic notions, as a trader operating for years on the Navajo Reservation, Evans felt he held a much firmer grasp of actual conditions. Evans responded at length. Asserting once again his credentials, he informed Reddy that Protestant missionary friends accused him of being a "lover of Indians and their ceremonies" and of "committing a sin when he attended these ceremonials."[55]

Evans believed that "the white man is superior in many respects to the colored races. In the arts and sciences he has proven that, overwhelmingly. At best, the colored races are but copyists. . . . I have learned that the white man has a mysterious something . . . which the Indian has not . . . [that] will carry him on when the Indian would falter and lag." Having thus shown he shared some of the racist attitudes of his times, he still asserted that the Indian has been "in touch with that 'Higher Power' for many, many generations. . . . They have a definite appeal to a definite individual—one of the ancient medicine men of the past." No doubt, Evans was referring to Jesus Christ, based upon his Book of Mormon orientation, yet he did not explicitly say so. As for Indians being the "original Spiritualists" and "Psychics", he believed that a real medicine man would "laugh" to be called such. He had taken the time to ask a medicine man about Reddy's situation and inquired into the possibilities of serving as a proxy. The singer told Evans that although some things could be done at a distance, better results would be obtained through actual presence. Evans closed his letter by opening his home to the Reddys if they chose to come to New Mexico.

Reddy's final letter came a week later. He told of being under the tutelage of Tibetan lamas and pointed out that if the white man had to undergo what the American Indian had, very few would have survived. He agreed with Evans's assessment of a "Higher Power" and added his own international twist from various faiths. Next he explained what had prompted his correspondence. The previous year he had stopped in Gallup and been referred to the trader Roman Hubbell as a possible facilitator of a healing ceremony. Hubbell's response made Reddy realize something to which Evans had earlier alluded. Reddy wrote,

> Inasmuch as I did not have access to the pot of gold reposing in the concrete vault underground back in Kentucky, I could not quite reach the astronomical heights to which I could visualize the expenses would

mount to. It was not exactly clear to me just why I should have to go way out in the desert, nine miles from nowhere, live among the natives (although I have done so in the past), pay about $2 per day for a car standing idle while my own car was costing storage. I was also told the ceremonies were from five to nine days long; that the fee of the Medicine Man was from $30 to $75 depending upon the kind of ceremony. Then there was that little matter of feeding an undetermined number of relatives, etc. No, not just yet![56]

What happened to Mr. Reddy and his ailing wife is unknown. Whether they ever met Evans on an anticipated trip back East was never recorded. Evans's way of representing the Navajo to the outside world is clear in this correspondence. Having worked out a system of explanations about the efficacy of Navajo ceremonialism, he saw its healing power and did not deny it. Obviously he assumed a Mormon view of the means by which it occurred, working from his own scriptural interpretation and also asserting white racial superiority. His was not a heavy-handed approach or explanation though. Being a person who went on two proselytizing missions for his church, he presented his beliefs in a manner that was palatable to the dominant white culture, while also showing respect for Navajo beliefs. Many Navajos accepted him. He could claim never having been denied access to Navajo ceremonies and was often encouraged by medicine men to record aspects of them.

A Contemporary View of Evans's Contributions

Where, then, does Evans fit in the broader context of American historiography and, more pointedly, that of Native Americans in the West? Are his writings so imbued with Mormon beliefs that they have little value? And if not, how should they be approached? Perhaps the best way to answer the first question is to turn to Sherry L. Smith's *Reimagining Indians: Native Americans through Anglo Eyes, 1880–1940*.[57] In this work, Smith examines how George Bird Grinnell's extensive writings about the Cheyenne, Frank Bird Linderman's work with the Crow, George Wharton James's study of the Navajo, and Mabel Dodge Luhan's interest in Taos Pueblo were bearing fruit at the same time that Evans recorded information about the Navajo.

All of these writers were from the East, Midwest, or England. They viewed themselves as a voice for the Native American to the dominant culture with the intent of explaining the misunderstood. While they lacked the sophistication of the professional anthropologist, they nevertheless provided a sympathetic view to the general public.

Smith argues that

> For approximately fifty years, the period roughly between the Dawes Act of 1887 and the Indian Reorganization Act of 1934, these writers produced books for popular audiences that offered new ways to conceptualize Indian people, alternatives to the images that had transfixed Americans for centuries. Simply put, these writers asserted Indians' humanity, artistry, community and spirituality.[58]

These writings came at a time when the country was reevaluating its own history and values, questioning the past and present behavior of dominance over less-sophisticated cultures. In a very particular way, this is in keeping with what Evans set out to do by preparing his "Navajo Trails" manuscript.

One of the most important motivations for his work was an "intense fascination" with Navajo thought and character. He recognized early in his career that Navajo culture was a stimulating philosophical venture far different from what he had encountered in his own world. Their culture was very much intact at the beginning of the twentieth century, not having been seriously damaged by inroads of white culture. Will stood at a vantage point, seeing that change was inevitable and there was much to be recorded. As author and friend John Stewart MacClary wrote of him, "The 'intellectual storekeeper' role does not fully portray the character of the man. Yes, he is a storekeeper. His trading post provides home and livelihood. Intellectual by nature and by self-development, Will Evans has vision far beyond the side-meat and beans of his business enterprise."[59]

In a letter dated October 16, 1938, Evans wrote of his very specific intentions to preserve the culture. A few months before this, he had taken an old loose-leaf ledger lying around his trading post, had covered the worn leather with muslin, then had drawn on the front a picture of Shiprock and an old Indian woman walking with her dog. He named his collection of materials, then an inch thick, "Navajo Trails." The manuscript started with Navajo biographies then went to "legendary lore" and "everything connected with Indians." He mused, "When this thing is completed, it will be one of the most valuable collections of Indian and Book of Mormon subjects in existence."[60] While much of his Mormon theology and comparisons have been left out of this work, his experience with the Navajo and their teachings are included intact.

Evans studying petroglyphs, which he saw as the remnants of ancient writings from a fallen people.

Evans's sense of urgency in obtaining a full record of the Navajo people is mentioned later in the same letter. After writing about obtaining an interesting story from "old Salow-Elt-Socie [Siláo Ałts'ózí], who was born during the captivity [Long Walk era] on the Pecos River," Will noted,

> I must get real busy on the biographies of the older Indians who had much to do with shaping the destinies of the tribe. They are passing quickly and I must get the job done soon. Old Fat Medicine Man passed away last week, and one more tribal historian is gone. Soon, the material I have been fortunate enough to get will be well nigh impossible to obtain.[61]

How prophetic. Much of what is contained herein would now be lost if it had not been for his efforts.

The primary means that other writers of this period used to achieve the ring of authenticity was to use the Native American voice. Although a great deal had been written about Indians, only a feeble attempt had been made to incorporate their perspective. Now there were those who insisted on it. These white authors "exuded great confidence about their abilities to serve as purveyors of truth about Indians."[62] How effective they really were at doing this is another story. Little internal or external evidence remains to document the interview process; nor is it known what the interviewee intended beyond what the author provided through translation and the writing style he or she adapted to the material.

Few readers doubt these authors' sincerity. They did not dabble in the extremes of nobility or savagery but concerned themselves rather with the humanity of Native Americans, providing a much-needed antidote to previous portrayals. Still there were problems. The cultural perspective of an outsider, no matter how well intentioned, still too easily missed the mark. "To acknowledge that they often failed to grasp the complexities of Indian peoples; that they often failed to transcend their own ethnocentric and even racist assumptions; and that early twenty-first century Indian and Anglo readers might find their works sentimental, romantic, and simple-minded does nothing to negate their cultural power."[63]

This is also true of Evans's writings. He worked at portraying what he learned from his Navajo friends, although often he was unable to leave behind his own biases. When one considers the fairly good collection of autobiographical writing by traders about the Navajo, Evans holds his own.[64] Many of these books are of recent vintage, and most of them discuss the life of the trader during the first half of the twentieth century. They also tend to follow a pattern of interesting episodes that took place between store owner and customer, difficulties of life on the reservation, and insights concerning Navajo culture.

Very few traders, Louisa and John Wetherill, Gladwell Richardson, and Franc Newcomb excepted, labored to record and preserve the culture for future generations; and even they, like Evans, only partly succeeded. The Wetherills published relatively little, while Gladwell Richardson was more prolific but aimed his writing toward the tourist trade. Franc Johnson Newcomb, however, parallels closely Evans's work. During her stint as a trader, she collected over 450 sandpaintings, many of which today reside in the Wheelwright Museum of the American Indian. Some of her published works include *Navaho Neighbors,* which discusses her life as a trader; *Hosteen Klah,* which chronicles the life of a powerful medicine man; and *Navaho Folk Tales,* a collection of traditional stories.[65] Whether Will and Franc ever compared notes is not recorded. But she certainly shared a common acquaintance: Lucy G. Bloomfield, whose husband, George, ran the Toadlena Post and served in the Young Stake Lamanite Mission with Evans. Lucy wrote the foreword to *Hosteen Klah.*

Evans, like Newcomb, was embroiled in the business of the trading post yet spent hundreds of hours on his "avocation" of interviewing and recording Navajo life stories, historical events, and cultural insight. Indeed, his collection of materials concerning the 1913 fracas at

Beautiful Mountain provided him with regional recognition as one of the most knowledgeable about the incident. His interviews with some of the main participants captured details that would otherwise have been lost. The same is true of the life histories that provide family and local insight, which by now would be forgotten.

Evans faithfully recorded this information. Through it all, he had only "pleasant memories and no regrets. The many years spent as neighbor to and among the Indians in Navajo land are certainly not counted as lost, but as a privilege and as an integral part of a life-time education."[66] Intellectually, he was engaged. When asked what some of the reasons were that kept him in the "desert," he responded, "In dealing with the natives, I like to match wits with them and that, sometimes, is no small task. One has to be on his toes all the time and that also keeps [me] interested."[67]

This is a telling comment. In spite of his intense interest in Navajo culture, he was still an outsider. His comments about racial superiority, that "mysterious something" that white men had that prevented them from "faltering" and "lagging" as Indians did, speaks of underlying cultural assumptions. Stereotype is not too strong a word in some instances. No matter how honest and straightforward his evaluation may be, there is no missing that he is a white man of the early to mid-twentieth century. While this does not negate his work in the following pages, the reader needs to be aware that those times were very different from the present.

Here are a few examples. At one point, while discussing the culture, Evans writes, "Navajos do not have double standards of morality. In fact one might say that in the past there was little standard at all and that being found out [in some type of transgression] was the only sin." This is difficult to understand, given his depth of knowledge of Navajo practices. The entire Navajo universe is saturated with laws and penalties established by the Holy Beings. Indeed, the ceremonies and sandpaintings with which he was so fascinated were performed or created because of a transgression of one of these laws. What Evans fails to recognize because of his own belief system is that Navajo religion emphasizes a different set of values that, given their basic teachings, is just as "correct" and rational as his own. The only time he reaches a point of agreement on this is when the two sets of values coincide based on LDS beliefs.

"Matching wits," which keeps him "on his toes," could take a similar course. When he tells Slim Policeman that owls have told him about a coming eclipse just before it happens, he is amused at the amazed and subdued response. The Navajo is portrayed as being naive and mystified by the information this white man has, playing off an implied ignorance. Navajos were very aware of what an eclipse was and employed a series of traditional practices to counter any effects derived from the experience. Evans, whose conscience spurred an editorial apology to Slim Policeman, realizes that he had taken advantage of the situation and a friendship.

With others, there was no apology. Bizhóshí, a man with whom Evans had a direct confrontation over the building of a post and whose two sons physically fought with Evans, receives a number of well-placed jabs. The old medicine man carried the title of "Missing Link" because he looked Mongolian in appearance and seemed to Evans to be like a relic from the past. Three of his four sons acquired the epithets of Big Link, Middle Link, and Little Link because of their family connection. And when the events of the Beautiful Mountain Uprising came to a close, Bizhóshí and his fourth son, Little Singer, were described as sitting before General Scott "weeping when the General lectured them as only an army officer can." This, to Evans, is a fitting reproof of a man who is pictured as a tough stalwart resisting the change fostered by white culture. Evans gives qualified respect to Bizhóshí in spite of the conflict, but it definitely appears grudging.

Today's reader may also be offended by some less dramatic forms of ethnocentrism. While lice were a very real problem on the reservation—exacerbated by lack of soap and water and an overabundance of poverty—Evans's discussion with Dan Pete, who is trying to rid his clothes of the creatures, is instructive. At one point the Navajo receives a lecture about cleanliness that ends with a reminder that the whites at the post "get them [lice] only when they crawl off you fellows in the summer time." No subtlety there.

Another example is found when Evans discusses the loss of traditional practices. In addition to the changes in sandpaintings and diminishing ceremonial knowledge, he is also concerned that the younger generation is losing the spirit of what both should be. His attendance at an Enemyway ceremony prompted the following observation: "Now, squaw dances are held when the weather is warm enough in the spring and into the summer. These have degenerated into an arm-in-arm crow-hopping exhibition to cadences of the singers and the tom-tom, à la Hollywood barn dances."

A final question needs to be asked about his use and exploitation of Navajo ceremonial figures in art. Was he being presumptuous and offensive by taking this sacred iconography and putting it on every piece of furniture, object, and building he could? What would he have said if sacred Mormon art had been treated likewise? As mentioned previously, he was neither the first nor the only one to be doing it. Hastiin Klah, with the encouragement of Franc Newcomb, provided the basis for her collection. No

Evans surrounded by his artwork with his trademark designs and colors. Note the arrowhead collection on the shelf above his head. Photo by Charles Dustin.

criticism or boycotting of Evans's store because of his gathering practices is recorded. Indeed, he mentions in a number of instances that medicine men came to him to refresh their memory of some of the designs. He emphatically states he obtained the information with permission and a clear understanding of its use from the medicine men.

Still, it does not appear totally right. In a society where a sandpainting has to be destroyed before the sun either sets or rises (roughly twelve hours), to portray one on a table or to place a Holy Being on a Pepsi sign is, for at least some Navajos, desecrating the sacred. Placing a Heinz catsup bottle over an image of Black God and setting a drinking glass on the symbol of Mother Earth would have been disrespectful to the believer, just as putting Christ's face on a footstool would be to a Christian.

Evans was obviously not a believer. While faithful to his own religion and respectful of some aspects of Navajo beliefs, he did not make the transfer of power and sacredness between the two differing systems of symbols. Navajo paintings were only art. Today's society shows a greater concern for such matters. Never before has there been so much controversy over issues of cultural sensitivity, ranging from the use of Indian names as team mascots to labels on beer to visiting sacred geographic sites to attending dances and ceremonies. These feelings have derived from very real issues and a greater need for respect of people's values.

In Evans's day, collection and preservation of the objects were the important points. Very much in keeping with both past and present periods of history, if the unique and powerful can be turned into an economic venture, so much the better. Encouraging Navajos to make furniture with sacred symbols on it may have helped feed some people, but it also encouraged profaning the sacred, which was probably why this plan never came to fruition.

This concern was not as prominent then as it is now. Those medicine men who allowed Evans to copy the designs did so willingly, showing not only their trust in him but also their fear of having treasured teachings and ceremonies lost. From the vantage point of hindsight, this has proven to be the case. The number of obsolete or extinct ceremonies has grown. Of twenty-four chantways that are known to have existed among the Navajo "only eight were well-known and frequently performed in the 1970s."[68] Although the copying and use of sandpaintings may be questioned, it is highly doubtful that Evans ever did it in a secret, malicious manner. He never related what he was doing to his own religious beliefs, but he was true to his friends.

In spite of the preceding examples, Evans expresses far more often his appreciation and love for, and his faith in, the Navajo people. He is genuine in his respect and established lifelong relationships during his work with them.

What of the origins and motivation behind his "Navajo Trails"? Evans began his recording at the very beginning of his trading career with an eye toward publishing. Unlike many traders who share their memoirs after the fact, he intentionally collected material on a daily basis. His son Richard recalled how he worked at it "with two fingers in the hunt-and-pick style . . . on an old typewriter when alone at a trading post at Little Water and later Sanostee and other reservation locations."[69] Between 1924 and 1954, he frequently contributed to the local paper, *The Farmington Hustler*. He persisted for years, recording lore, biography, history, and observations as he went.

Although he worked on this manuscript for eight years, he was never able to bring it to fruition. In 1945, he bequeathed all of his materials to Richard, who showed more of an interest in it than the other children. A witnessed statement charged him to "protect and preserve" what he received so that he could "correlate and develop the above material for eventual publication, to the end that a true knowledge of these things might be made available to the world" and "be preserved for the Navajo people themselves in future generations."[70]

Richard took his charge seriously. For thirty years, he safeguarded and performed light editing by shortening some of the longer sentences and removing some of the anachronisms in the writing style. He, like his father, never completed the task. His daughter, Susan Evans Woods, next assumed the responsibility. She continued the light editing process and helped organize the materials into a sensible scheme. She estimates, when comparing the original to this manuscript, that 95 percent of the writing remains in Will's voice and that all of the content is present.

Today, Evans's materials reside at the Brigham Young University Library. This includes over sixty sandpaintings of various sizes, the "Navajo Trails" manuscript, approximately one hundred pages of Navajo folklore and teachings, and all of Evans's other writings and correspondence. Still in the possession of his granddaughter is a large collection of photographs. His goal of preserving elements of Navajo culture for future generations has been achieved.

What the reader encounters in the following pages is a "period piece." The work has not been "sanitized" to fit in with twenty-first-century values, but rather serves as an expression of a white trader living in a Navajo world. While sensitive and genuine in his respect, he framed everything that he saw and was told within his own worldview. He lived at a time when tremendous changes and some dramatic events were occurring with the Navajos. As a conscious recorder of this history, Evans provides a fascinating glimpse into the lives and world of the People.

This book is divided into three sections—starting with the historic events, then moving to the people, and ending with the culture. This sequence provides a context for the actors. There has been a liberal amount of grouping of materials on the authors' part and a moderate amount of editing to make the text flow. The generous inclusion of photographs throughout gives an unparalleled opportunity to put a face or place with a life history or story. Few white authors during this period were as conscientious about giving their native informants so much credit. Again, Evans was true to his friends.

The most valuable section of his writing is the historical. Evans spent days recording events on the reservation and became an expert on the Beautiful Mountain Uprising. By capturing firsthand accounts, especially from the traders intimately involved in the incident, he provides not only detailed information that parallels the official accounts, but also a texture in the lives of the participants. Other sections provide a loose chronology of some of the major events in Navajo history. Starting with the struggle of life before the Long Walk period, the incarceration at Fort Sumner, the establishment of early trading posts on the northern part of the reservation, livestock reduction, and the expansion of the oil and gas industry, Evans provides personal insights from those who lived through these events. The history section concludes with a Christmas celebration that serves as a point-counterpoint to his first Christmas spent at Sanostee, forty-four years earlier. The warmth that emanates from this experience captures Evans's own feelings toward those he was working with as a Mormon missionary.

The biographical section contains elements of fourteen life histories that parallel the events in the preceding section. More importantly, these accounts are personalized, the characters real, and the tenor of life for the Navajo more explicit. While Evans selected some of the most prominent individuals to interview, he allowed them to tell their own story. This is an invaluable service not only to family members now, who want to learn about those who have gone before, but also for the Navajos as a whole, who have an oral history committed to paper so that it will not be lost. Starting with Costiano and Black Horse and ending with Dan Pete and his stories, the reader has wonderful slices of life to draw upon in understanding the Navajo experience.

The final section on culture is a potpourri of customs and beliefs, ranging from birth to death. Although Evans viewed these practices as a white trader, he has a depth of understanding that is both sympathetic and highly observant. He does not approach the topics as an anthropologist would, with detailed questions, but rather as he understood things from his world of the trading post or as he sat observing Navajo ceremonies. Some of his longer sections are on trading, blankets, silversmithing, sandpaintings, and the rituals. These were familiar or dramatic events. But there are also some interesting glimpses into family life, marriage and divorce, hairstyles and cleanliness, morality and witchcraft, and general hospitality. He has preserved observations of Navajo life as it existed in the 1930s.

There is one last thought concerning Evans's writings. Anyone who has had the pleasure of listening to an "old time" trader (and that opportunity is fast disappearing) knows how interesting the experience can be, in spite of, as well as because of, the "flavor" of the time from which the trader comes. So as you settle down in the "bull pen" to listen to Will's experience, enjoy not only what the Navajos are saying but also our narrator's voice. Traveling "Navajo Trails" is an opportunity to visit the past, without the discomfort and problems of that bygone era, and to meet some colorful personalities along the way. Let Evans be a guide, with all of his strengths and weaknesses, into the past of a trader on the northern Navajo Reservation.

Starting Along the Trail

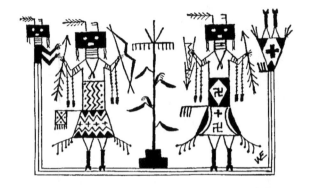

From start to finish, Will Evans was proud of being a trader and liked to talk about it. He wrote in the style of his times, using descriptive phrases and colorful detail to create an image of life in a trading post, the people who frequented it, and the events of his day. Lengthy sentences and a certain amount of repetition were also common fare. Not long on analysis, Evans was a storyteller and a good one at that.

In keeping with this style, this introductory chapter is framed in a fictional setting that encloses two accounts by Evans. The first is one of his most widely publicized articles on his entrance into the trading business. This was a formative experience that describes the founding of the Sanostee Post and a lonely Christmas in the midst of Navajo land. There is no missing the isolation this young man felt, surrounded by a strange culture, cut off by winter storms, and short on basic amenities. Yet it was a deeply moving experience that he often referred to in later life. He grew to love and understand the Navajo, as what at first seemed foreign became customary.

The second piece is Evans's description of a typical exchange in a trading post. He provides detailed context that seems simple and yet creates a vivid impression. For instance, the dialogue between the trader and customer is basic and so slow that the reader begins to feel how time-consuming and elementary these transactions were. A sense of the realities of this workaday environment is clearly related.

What follows is context. While Evans often wrote about the dramatic and colorful, his daily life was much more like what is described here. And since these days are now gone forever, the reader can catch a glimpse of yesteryear, when wool and blankets spelled survival for both customer and trader in the Navajo world of the first quarter of the twentieth century.

Imagine. It is December 1917. By obscure starlight, you thread your horse along a trail over a sage-covered plain. Shiprock, framed against the Carrizo Mountains, is dark, darker than you remember from the last time you passed this way, but a thin shaft of light in the distance serves as a pole-star for your journey. A few wisps of snow swirl about your horse's hooves before sifting through the brush on their way to an eddy at the base of a pinyon tree. The freezing wind at your back causes a shiver and gives one more reason to adjust your coat's collar.

You have been riding now for two long hours, and the cold has numbed toes and fingers. As you draw closer to the light, pungent smoke from a juniper fire fills your nostrils. The hitching rail outside the trading post is visible now, its worn surface ready to hold your horse's reins. Pushing the heavy wooden door open, you fumble for an instant to unhook your coat sleeve from the door latch. Senses are jarred by the onrush of light, heat, and smells of the store. Blinded momentarily, you squint. A wave of warmth radiates from the potbellied stove, providing welcomed relief from the winter cold.

Loosening outer clothing, you sit on a bench and begin to notice details. The stove rests in the middle of the "bull pen," surrounded by three high, wide counters running along the perimeter of the room. A middle-aged man stands behind one of them with his elbows propped against the well-worn boards. His once curly hair is beginning to gray and recede, but his blue eyes have the glint of youth and he is trim for his age. Checked shirt, wool pants, and a wide belt show signs of daily wear from a business that demands lifting and handling.

Behind the counters against which Will Evans rests are sacks of Arbuckles Coffee, flour, sugar, tubs of lard, and rounds of cheese, whose aromas blend. Canned goods with brightly colored labels and dry goods— work pants, shirts, harnesses, ropes, saddles, wash tubs, axes, and a variety of other tools—line the shelves and hang from the ceiling. The dirt floor is swept clean except for a small wooden box holding the residue of chewing tobacco and spittle from the day's customers. Everything else is tidy.

Evans, known to the Navajos as "Missing Tooth in Front," draws a deep breath and welcomes you to his domain. A trader of nineteen years, he invites you to hear about his life and the people with whom he trades and lives. His reputation as a well-known raconteur is second only to

Claude Youngblood and Evans behind the counter at the trading post
in Fruitland, New Mexico.

his reputation for honesty. He does not realize it now, but he will spend
another thirty-one years in this line of business before finally hanging his
hat on a different peg. A person does not remain as a trader in isolated
posts unless he is accepted and trusted by his clients. Competition with
other stores is growing now.

Unlike many other traders, who are just as fair and responsive, Evans
has one characteristic that makes him different. He enjoys writing. Few,
if any, of these other men take the time to record their experiences and
those of the Navajo with the detail he musters. He realizes now, and will
continue to realize for the remainder of his life, that Navajo culture is
dynamic and is moving increasingly into the white man's world. Even the
trading post, which allows Navajos to remain on the reservation to shop
and sell their wares, is an institution of change. Evans, with urging from
Navajo elders, wants to record what they tell him for their own people in
generations to come.

With a small sigh and twinkle in his eye, he presses his waist against
the counter, reaching for a leather-bound book with black pages. On each
sheet are two or three black-and-white photographs of the land, the people, and events that have formed his world for years. He is proud of the
fact that he has had the foresight to take pictures of those he works with,
since many are old and some have passed on. Few traders had the ambi-
tion to record the faces of their daily customers. Not so with Will. He is a
"shutterbug."

Coming around the counter, he puts another cedar log in the stove,
adjusts the vent, and sits down on a wooden chair before you. The faint

Wedding photo of Evans
before his marriage to Sarah
Walker, May 11, 1902.

smell of sweat mingled with oil from wool and freshly chopped wood gives a pleasant odor in this warm environment. He offers a quick glance, insures you are comfortable, then tilts back his chair to inspect the ceiling, as if his stories hang next to the harnesses and washtub above. He begins his story softly.

"Late in 1898 when I was twenty-one years old, I decided that coal mining and farm work were simply too much labor. I received an offer to assist in building a trading post in the northern Navajo Reservation in New Mexico and gladly accepted. On December 7, 1898, Joe Wilkins, old-time wagon freighter, and Indian trader Edwin Seth Dustin, pioneer teamster and freighter, and I set out from Fruitland, New Mexico, with two wagons, each drawn by a four-horse team. One wagon was loaded with lumber, roofing materials, nails, and other construction supplies, a tent and poles, a kitchen range, and a small heating stove. The other wagon held various groceries and dry goods to stock the shelves of this new store.

"After fording the San Juan River, our party topped the rock-covered hills and headed southwest. We followed a horse trail, then waded the muddy Chaco Wash that flows through a gap in the great Hogback Ridge. We then left the wash and returned to our course on a series of horse trails marked with water holes and Navajo camps. Late in the afternoon we reached Barber Spring and camped for the night. Our destination lay twenty or more miles ahead in the Sanostee [Tse''Al na'ozt'i'i', anglicized to Sa-Nos-Tee, meaning 'Overlapping Rocks'] Valley, where Joe Wilkins had a permit to open a store.[71]

"I enjoyed the trip and the changes of scenery along the northwestern side of the Hogback. What a country we had crossed that day, so different from the green hills of Wales, where I was born. The Navajos had few, if any, wagons at that time, so there were even fewer roads to travel. We simply set our course and moved on. The two wagons traced the first wheeled tracks in that wilderness, making a primitive road that was traveled for years and still exists, though it is now used only as a camp-to-camp trail by Navajos.

"We could not help discussing the plight of these people as we sat around our campfire that night. The government in Washington had given them a large slice of country for a reservation. I had often looked over the arid hills and flats, waterless save for an occasional spring, and had thought, 'What a worthless stretch of country. What a shame to relegate human beings to such a life! The government has again given the Indians the short end of the stick!' Many white men who visited Navajo land in the early days believed Uncle Sam had treated them badly by shoving them into the confines of this reservation, then practically deserting them to shift for themselves.

"Late in the evening of December 10, 1898, three weary travelers arrived on the banks of Sanostee Wash, in the central portion of the valley near Little Water [Tó 'álts'íísí]. I estimated that Navajos had farmed this area, whose name meant 'Valley Surrounded by the Great Rock Fence,' for about three hundred years. Abundant evidence of earlier populations still existed, too. Ruins of cliff dwellings and other remains of this ancient culture were found along the arroyo.

"A small stream of clear water meandered through the wash, even in dry weather, from the mouth of Sanostee Canyon, one of the beautiful spots on the Lukachukai range of mountains. Several miles from the canyon's opening stood an immense natural bridge of red sandstone. The surrounding hills were covered with evergreens.

"We chose a campsite in the shelter of a high bank a short distance from the stream, believing it would be a good spot for the trading post. A storm had been brewing all that day. Darkness fell shortly after we made camp and with it came a steady snowfall. I was chosen to remain on watch for the camp that night, while Wilkins and Dustin rode upstream to stay with the well-known Bizhóshí clan beneath the rimrocks of the valley. Bizhóshí was an old medicine man, who led his clan with force.

"When I awoke at daybreak, I shook almost twelve inches of snow off my bedroll before arising. Wilkins and Dustin soon rode back to camp, and we set to work shoveling snow to clear a spot, erecting the tent, then bringing in the table and chairs. This was to be my home for the balance of the winter.

"With the lumber and other materials, we hastily built the walls and roof of a small, temporary building. We applied battens over cracks in the upright plastering, spread heavy tar paper over the roof, and installed a half-window and door. The result was a 16 x 20 foot building, the first store opened in the northeastern foothills of the Lukachukai Mountains.

Sanostee Trading Post, where Evans began his career. This
post was also the home of the Frank L. Noel family for ten
years. Frank L. Noel Collection (P-166), L. Tom Perry Special
Collections, Harld B. Lee Library, Brigham Young University,
Provo, Utah.

"After shoveling six inches of snow from the interior and setting up
the heating stove, we spent most of the evening placing shelves on one
side of the shack and making a high, rough counter over which to trade. I
was to measure, weigh, and sell directly from the sacks of sugar, potatoes,
onions, and beans.

"Next day we opened the case goods and placed them on the shelves;
then came the small stock of dry goods, shirts and overalls. By the second
evening of our arrival, the Sanostee Trading Post, J. R. Wilkins, owner, was
launched. Meanwhile, the storm slackened, so Ed and I took a team and
wagon into the foothills and hauled a load of cedar [juniper] for firewood.

"On the third morning after our arrival the storm began to intensify.
Joe and Ed decided to return to the San Juan and bring another load of
goods and building material once the storm was over. So I was left alone to
trade the meager supply of goods for pelts, blankets, and what little cash
the Navajos had.

"Snow continued to fall until twenty to thirty inches lay on the level
ground. I had taken over the jobs of cook, dishwasher, bed-maker, and
trader. During the day business was mildly brisk though the Navajos were
afoot. Loneliness, especially in the early evening after their departure,
settled down like a pall. Christmas was less than two weeks away, adding
to my feelings of isolation.

· "The Big Snow had taken a terrible toll on Navajo livestock. Many
horses died from the cold and lack of forage, which was plentiful but
could not be uncovered. Sheep, the main source of meat, lay in pitiful

A ch'įįdii hogan located southwest of Shiprock. Believed to be inhabited by the spirit of the person who died inside, these structures are either deserted or destroyed. Photo by Richard P. Evans.

heaps, victims of the bitter northwest winds and snow. I knew that when spring came there would be thousands of carcasses huddled in the gullies. The ghostly remains of animals, frozen where they stood, were now completely covered by drifting snow.

"Before long, trading stock of the most vitally needed supplies was gone. I was forced to close the store, saving a supply of food to sustain myself until relief arrived. The long winter of loneliness and inactivity dragged on. I had an old Hammond typewriter and a supply of paper so I tried my hand at composing poems and essays. This helped a little to pass the slowly moving time.

"Because of the shortage of food and supplies in the area, dinner at my camp attracted many hungry Navajos who eagerly accepted a small handout. When I ran short of firewood, I knew it was vitally important to locate a new supply. My search was limited to a very small area because of the deep snow, so I ventured a short distance up the creek and found the crumbling remains of a 'Cheendy' [ch'įįdii] hogan on the bank. This is a home in which a Navajo has died and so use of any part of it is taboo.[72] Taboo or not, here was firewood I badly needed, so I carried a log from the old hogan back to camp, then continued to use this source of wood. In a day or two the 'handout gang' failed to show up at noon. The dangerous wood had done the trick. No Navajo would eat food cooked over a 'tabooed' fire like that.

"Christmas arrived after endless days and nights of utter loneliness. I was not above a tinge of despair, wondering when my friends with their wagons would arrive. I found myself in an interesting situation that Christmas Eve, living in a world rigidly circumscribed by a waist-high blanket of white. My domain, if it can be called that, was a few hundred feet of narrow trails through the snow, the longest extending from the store door to the edge of the stream, which was now frozen solid, forcing me to melt snow.

"There were rough, snowy trails from the scattered hogans to the store, but I had no means of travel other than on foot, not even a burro and a sharp stick to make him go. There was no telephone line to the outside world, not even along the San Juan River, at this time. I had no access to newspapers or the few magazines available in those days. I had brought along some books for diversion and they helped, but I truly missed reading and learning about the day-in, day-out world.

"That year, 1898, was eventful. The Spanish-American War had been fought and won in short order. Even as late as December, the names of Teddy Roosevelt, Admiral [George] Dewey, General [William R.] Shafter, Admiral [William T.] Sampson, and others were prominent in news dispatches. When I left Farmington, New Mexico, and the San Juan River behind, all national news ended for me.

"The Indians began to make inquiries as Christmas Day approached. Early missionaries had spread the story of the Christ child and Christmas traditions. Word traveled quickly on the reservation that this was a day of presents passed around by the white brothers. The early traders at places like Round Rock, Hubbell's at Ganado, and posts near Ft. Defiance, Arizona, handed out gifts to their customers on Christmas Day. The Navajos' main question was 'How many days to Christmas?' My answer was 'Tomorrow is Christmas.' 'It is so,' they replied, and went away satisfied.

"Evening came and loneliness bore down more heavily than ever, as I thought of Christmas in the San Juan Valley. There would be a Christmas tree at the meetinghouse and a profusion of parcels for everyone, then a dance, perhaps until the late hours of the night. There would be violin music possibly accompanied by a guitar, this meager orchestra adding to the joyfulness. I tried to push these reveries from my mind and picked up a copy of Dickens'[s] *A Christmas Carol*. The kerosene lamp was all I had to light my tent, but it was enough. I finished the story and dreamily allowed the book to slide to my lap. I thought of the words 'Twas the night before Christmas and all through the house, not a creature was stirring, not even a mouse. . . . '

"I became fully aware of my situation and surroundings. 'Why,' I said to myself, 'there is no house here, just a snow-banked tent and a small slap-sided store in a sea of heavy snow!' The house that was home to me was fifty miles away in a trackless white wilderness. As for a mouse, none would approach my humble quarters in such a cold setting! I picked up the water pail and walked into the night to get a breath of fresh air, traveling the narrow frosty trail to the stream that was frozen solid. I had to dip a pail full of snow that could later be melted for a cheery cup of Adam's clear, pure ale.

"While standing on the frozen path I scanned the heavens with a feeling of awe. From zenith to horizon and every point between, a myriad of little diamonds twinkled and glittered in the sky. To the north the stars of the Big Dipper shone brightly, making their circuit around the North Star. The Evening Star shone well above the westward horizon this night, reminding me of the Star of Bethlehem.

"There were no angels singing, yet in the distance I could hear the voice of a Navajo lad raised in an old tribal song. The snow-clad heights of the Lukachukais gleamed in the brilliant starlight. Enchantment is not the proper word to describe my feelings as I stood there; loneliness was lost for the moment, carried away by this indescribable night and the spirit and romance of the season.

"Christmas Day dawned clear and cold. When the sun had risen high in the sky, groups of Navajos trooped toward the store. A few wore shoes, most had none, their feet and lower legs wrapped in burlap or pieces of Navajo blanket which they later dried over campfires to make ready for their next trip.

"My friends smiled as they recited their well-practiced singsong greeting of the day: 'Melly Ke'eshmish, Melly Ke'eshmish!' They expected gifts, which posed a problem since my stock was practically gone. Fortunately, in the sweets department there was a pail of old-fashioned barber-pole striped stick candy. I also had a box of cookies with a hole in the center and covered with coarse, multi-colored sugar. There was also a box of small cull apples called Indian Apples. I decided to share what I had for as long as it lasted.

"The children came in with their feet wrapped in rags, their thinly clad bodies shivering with cold, and their noses running. I gave each a stick of candy and cookie. The older people happily accepted an apple. Their shy smiles showed that my small gifts were genuinely appreciated, knowing as they did of my limited supplies. The last of my calamity-stricken neighbors came in just as the sun dipped toward the western mountains. Once they left, my stock of apples, candy, and cookies was gone. What remained around the stove was an aura of peace on earth and goodwill to men. Their expressions of thanks, which I felt really came from their hearts, awakened in me a feeling of warmth that combined both happiness and pity. How such a small gift could bring forth such hearty expressions of gratitude was one more evidence of the power of the spirit of Christmas.

"My neighbors might not have accepted my small contribution. They could have easily destroyed me and taken everything. But the spirit of the day prevailed, and thankfulness and good will rested over the little snow-bound valley of Sanostee. So ended my first Christmas in Navajo land. My loneliness, profound and painful, has become a memory of one adventure amid a host of experiences over a lifetime. Every year as the Christmas holiday arrives, I remember the gentle message from my friends, 'Melly Ke'eshmish, Melly Ke'eshmish.'

"My lonely isolation ended with the advent of spring [March]. Joe Wilkins came in with a load of building material for a permanent store. Ed Dustin also brought in a wagon load, and the day after his arrival we began work on the new building."

Evans pauses. He shifts his boot to the side of the wood box and pushes his chair up on two legs. A deep sigh and he continues.

"That is how it all began for me, how I got into the trading business. Now the Navajos are highly dependent on this economic system. A trading post, by necessity, is a department store. Away from towns served by the railroad, I have to stock a variety of supplies for my customers. A trader and his post are the center and heart of the Navajo community. He is their creditor, advisor, and at times, their midwife and undertaker. He supplies them with flour and coffee, sugar and salt; he measures out their cloth, fits their feet with shoes and stockings, clothes them with shirts and trousers, shades them with hats and umbrellas, protects them with coats and shawls, dispenses their medicine and soft drinks, satisfies their sweet tooth, weighs their nails and bolts, and supplies their tools. Very little money enters into these transactions.

"Let's say a Navajo woman has woven a blanket or rug. When she comes to the store, she has already set a value on the rug, somewhere in the neighborhood of what she thinks the trader will offer for it. She enters the post with the rug enclosed in a used flour sack and conceals it under the trader-supplied Pendleton shawl she wears summer and winter.

"Shyly, she sidles over to the counter and places the flour sack on it. The trader walks over to where she stands and, if she is a visitor from an outlying district, extends his hand and shakes in the loose, brief motionless handclasp of the Navajo. In quiet low tones they converse.

"'Hello, my cousin.'

"'Yes, my friend.'

"Although obvious to both, the conversation continues.

Painting of Navajos and Will Evans trading inside his post, by Kelly Pugh.

"'Where did you come from?'

"'Beyond Shiprock.'

"'Unh.' This grunt is used in the tone and meaning of 'I see.'

"'On what day did you come?'

"'Yesterday, by horse; I came alone.'

"'Yes, that is good. Is that a rug that you have brought in? I will look at it.'"

"The trader unties the rag-string that binds the gathered end of the sack and grasps the folded rug, his trained fingers at the same time recording the feel of the rug to see if it has a coarse or fine texture. She takes hold of the bottom of the sack and holds it as the trader pulls the rug out and places it, still folded, on the counter scales. Having weighed it, he carries it into a room reserved for rugs and spreads it out on the floor. Swiftly, deftly, while she is on her way into the room, his fingers have pulled the wool or yarn apart enough to reveal the warp. This is examined

Trade tokens used by the C. H. Algert Co. of Fruitland in place of cash.

for the spurious, oft-rejected twine warp used in place of the native spun wool which denotes a genuine, totally handmade rug. While she waits shyly by the doorway or examines the select rugs he has hung on the wall, the trader stands off a short distance from the rug spread on the floor, his eyes taking in its design, weight, quality of weave, and size.

"'How much do you want for it?'

"'That is for you to say; you are buying it.'

"'It is not straight; that end is wider than this one. Nine pesos and four bits ($9.50), I think.'

"'Nine and four bits. I thought it was worth at least eleven.'

"'No, it is narrow at one end and there is a mistake in the border in that corner.'

"'I will take the blanket. Perhaps the white man at the Hogback will pay more. I will leave it for ten, my friend. Ten is good. I have come from far away and weaving is hard work.'

"'All right, ten.'

"'All right, my friend.'

"The rug is left upon the floor, and the two return to their places in the store. The trader draws from his shirt pocket a small notebook and pencil, opens to a page, and writes down the amount of the rug, then leans back against the shelves, waiting. It is good to create a spirit of patience and endurance for Navajos are very slow 'trading out a rug.' Minutes drag by between orders no matter how small the transaction. Conversation about goods during a purchase is endless.

"'How much is the flour?'

"'For money, one peso and nine blues.' (The Navajo word for blue denotes ten cents and yellow means five cents.)[73]

"'The little sack is how much?'

"'One peso.'

"'Bring me a big one and some baking powder for one blue.'

"The sack of flour is carried in from a nearby storeroom and laid on the counter. The can of baking powder is placed on the flour, the trader draws a line with his pencil through the $10 and writes directly below it $7.90.

"Navajos invariably standardize their purchases by buying first flour, then baking powder, sugar, salt, coffee, potatoes, lard, bacon, cloth, thread, bias tape, and last of all, when there are only about two "blues" left, soda and candy for the children. They are a frugal people. Purchases are made carefully and wisely, stretching the trade to the limit.

"While the trader has been recording the deal, the woman's fingers have been deftly counting, lips moving silently. Under her breath she whispers to herself the results of her subtraction. Aloud she asks the trader for verification.

"'How much left?'

"And so it goes. Each purchase brings forth questions about price, what kind, how many, how much? Each purchase must always be subtracted and the balance announced to the buyer. The storekeeper's notebook records it all. Traders have found that to rush the process creates confusion and suspicion. Navajos feel that by putting the transaction on paper, it is insurance against making an error.

"Cash purchases are also long drawn-out affairs. Each article is paid for and change given individually. A Navajo comes to the counter and with a loud 'Ssssss!' engages the attention of the trader, who says 'What?' inquiringly.

"'Soap.'

"'What kind?'

"'Shirt-washing soap.'

"'How many?'

"'Two. How much?'

"'One blue.'

"The bars of soap are tied together with string and placed before the customer. He fumbles slowly in one pocket. Empty. The other pocket is carefully, slowly searched. The trader waits silently. Unconcernedly, when minutes have slipped by in the treasure hunt, the Navajo's brown fingers bring forth a very aged and faded dollar bill. The trader gives him change from the register and stands waiting without a word.

"'More soap.'

"'What kind?'

"'Hand-washing soap.'

"'What color?'

"'White. Strong, good smelling soap. How much?'

"'One blue.'

"A fifty cent piece is given in payment, rung on the register, and change returned.

"'Tobacco.'

"'Chewing or smoking.'

"'Chewing.'

"'What kind?'

"'Horse shoe.'

"'How much?'

"'Just cut one yellow's worth.'

"The five cents is paid and registered and the trader stands waiting. Thus it goes, ad infinitum. Why doesn't he pay for all of this in one lump sum? A Navajo would answer, 'It is not done that way. The white man might cheat on the amount. In this way, he does not cheat. He gives me the right change and I know how much money is left to draw from.'"

"Confidence engendered by circumspect dealing and honest treatment does not in the least alter this mode of business; it is just the Navajo's way, guided by tradition and careful parental advice. For instance, John Kee would come into the store and order a quarter's worth of potatoes. His eyes follow the trader's hand reaching up toward the hanging rack which holds the paper bags.

"'That paper is too small. It will short weigh me.'

"'No. It is large enough,' replies the trader. He dumps potatoes into the sack, John intently watching every move as though he suspected cobblestones interspersed with the potatoes. The trader puts the filled sack on the scales. John is waiting, eyes focused upon the indicator, checking to see if the weight corresponds to 'last time,' or his last purchase of potatoes. If the white man has missed his estimate in filling the bag and the weight was short, John watches every ounce as the trader drops in more potatoes. If the bag was filled beyond the proper weight, suspicion flames in his dark eyes as potatoes are removed and returned to the bin.

"John Kee, like many of his fellow tribesmen, has not yet been to school, but he can read the scales and, perhaps by laborious practice in writing numerals under the tutelage of some school boy, has learned to read numbers and price tags on merchandise. He can even write his name, a clumsy almost unintelligible scrawl of letters, learned perhaps by

Unidentified man and Evans surrounded by a load of wool at the C. H. Algert Store in Fruitland. The heavy, cumbersome bags are burlap, six to seven feet long, stuffed with uncleaned wool.

tracing and retracing, times without number, the name someone has written out for him. He does not recognize the marks as letters. He has only memorized by repetition a strange design or scrawl which is accepted by the white man as his name on paper. And like many Navajos, he is adept in the use of the simple arithmetic he needs to get along. He can add, multiply, and subtract in a queer, intricate, self-taught system, which is nevertheless an efficient one that he knows and uses thoroughly.

"That is how trading with the Navajos has been for years."

Evans shifts his weight and pauses for a response. He sees your interest and knows there is much more to tell. Rising, he reaches across the counter for a manuscript he calls "Navajo Trails" resting by his photo album.

"Here. If you want an idea of my life...and...the stories I have heard, you can read this and look at these pictures." And so you will. You have been drawn to this friendly gentleman whose words are tinged by a slight accent he says comes from his Welsh upbringing. The typed pages, though overwritten with notes in a flowing script, have an impressive neatness and volume. A few customers have begun to trickle into the store, dividing Evans's attention, and you ask if there is some quiet place where you can read uninterrupted. Evans excuses himself from his customers and opens the door to his Kiva Room, a mini-museum and rug room, draped with rugs, saddle blankets, and Pendleton shawls. He motions you toward a padded bench, painted with designs similar to figures woven into the rugs. He quietly closes the door and you begin your journey into the printed pages that represent the recollections of Will Evans, trader to the Navajo.

Events

Views of History around the Four Corners

Will Evans's life as a trader spanned some of the monumental events in Navajo history. For more than fifty years, he shared an insider's perspective with the Navajo people as these events unfolded. He also recorded the reminiscences of elders whose experience hearkened back to the early to mid-1800s. Up-front and personal, these stories, even though filtered through Evans's eyes, are an invaluable source to the Navajo past.

Take, for instance, the events leading to, comprising, and following the Long Walk period. This episode is one of the most traumatic and important mileposts for the People. It has been heavily studied by scholars and almost mythologized by the Navajos. The further one is removed from the time and events, the easier it is to generalize and offer facile explanations. Evans provides eyewitness accounts by men who were there. They point out that raiding by the Navajos was, at least in part, a reason for the devastating "Fearing Time," when surrounding tribes and the United States military wreaked havoc on them. The mistreatment of those who went to Fort Sumner is also addressed.

For those who want to believe in the ease of life before the white man became prevalent, there are some points to consider. Food was scarce; danger from competing tribes and the constant pressure to survive provided challenges. Agapito and Yellow Horse testify that perhaps "the good old days" may not have been that good.

Evans also provides a wealth of information concerning the establishment and ownership of trading posts in the Four Corners area. His anecdotal information gives a feeling for the hardships and bright spots of this life and what it meant to the Navajos. Traders were instrumental in improving local economies. From introducing new strains of sheep to marketing a finished blanket, these men and women fostered craft development and offered products that dramatically changed a way of life. The Navajos willingly embraced a good part of this change or else the posts never would have had their characteristic appeal. This symbiotic relationship prodded and enticed the People into the market economy of the twentieth century.

Still, conflicts arose between customer and trader, which Evans duly notes. Nothing provides a better symbol of the tension that accompanied change than the episode at Beautiful Mountain. With strong personalities like Agent William T. Shelton, Bizhóshí, and Little Singer, something like this was bound to happen and not just there. The Tol Zhin (Tó Łizhini) Affair (1905) in Arizona and the Ba'illi incident (1907) at Aneth, Utah, provide two other examples where challenges to traditional practices and conflicts over the authority of government agents erupted into armed resistance. Evans's contribution is one of a local perspective that emphasizes the role of the trader in quelling the discontent. Absent or barely mentioned in official reports, these men provided a peaceful link between warring factions and probably saved lives on both sides.

Loss of livestock in the 1930s was one of a number of culminating events in the transition of the Navajo from traditional ways into midcentury American culture. Second only to the Long Walk period, Livestock Reduction is still a hated symbol of government intervention and insensitivity. By reducing sheep, goats, cattle, and horses as much as 50 percent, in some instances, the dominant society redirected Navajo lifestyle forever. While Evans discusses some of these events, he is surprisingly kind to the government programs and Commissioner of Indian Affairs, John Collier, who is blamed by the Navajos as its evil architect. Considering the impact of Livestock Reduction on the posts, the entire episode is treated mildly.

Of all of Evans's writings, his recording of events is probably the most significant. As a participant or willing listener, he provides an unparalleled view on a local level that will benefit generations to come. Observant and interested, Evans offers rich detail found in few other traders' accounts.

Agapito Remembers the Old Days

On a long, low, arid ridge near the south bank of the dry Escavada Wash, there stands a small, male-Navajo hogan. The humble home is about seventy-five miles south of Farmington and a few miles east of the ancient ruins of Pueblo Bonito in Chaco Canyon. The structure is surrounded by a dry country of rolling hills and waterless arroyos. Desolation encompasses the region from horizon to horizon no matter the direction one travels in the penetrating waves of summer heat.

The hogan is the home of a toothless old Navajo man, who is near-sighted and well-nigh deaf. With him live his aged wife and two grandchildren, a boy and girl, who assist in tending his pitifully undernourished sheep and goats.

Thousands of acres of soil bore lush grass when the rains came and the snow fell deep; abundant clumps of brush sustained the animals when rain did not come plentifully. That was in the old days. Though the Navajos are great lovers of home, family ties, and their native soil, today the rich grass no longer grows. A vital cycle has been broken, and the dead and dying grass seems beyond resurrection from the parched earth.

Water for the family's needs is obtained by scraping a shallow hole in the bed of the wash near the bank, into which an old rusty tub, its bottom beaten out, has been placed to prevent caving. A battered metal pail fastened to a short rope draws the water. Two other battered tubs lie near the primitive well, providing water for the sheep, goats, and bony, sore-backed horses. When water for washing is needed, these old horses pull a battered wagon with a 50-gallon wooden barrel. It takes time to fill the barrel when the tub is empty because the water has to seep into the "well."

Inside the hogan, the beds—sheepskins which are rolled up during the day and laid down at night—are spread on the earthen floor. Cooking utensils consist of a cast-iron frying pan, enameled coffee pot and cups, a few plates, and silverware. Meals are cooked over a central pit, the smoke from the fire rising through a hole in the roof. The room has no partitions; the open space serves as kitchen, dining room, bedroom, weaving and sewing room. Usually there is very little to eat. Bread and coffee are staples with an occasional sheep sacrificed for food, hide, or a bedroll. Leanness is the rule, and want is everywhere. The people hope for a better way of life.

Each day, the old patriarch, Agapito, calls his grandchildren, then helps them drive the grazing sheep and goats to water. The animals browse along the banks of the dry wash, where underground moisture beneath a fine cover of windblown sand has forced green buds to appear on small clumps of greasewood. This plant cannot be called handsome, but in this sea of sand and desolation it seems lovely. The small animals nibble the tender shoots and obtain a degree of sustenance. What the frail

Agapito and his family outside their hogan.

Agapito at Escavada Wash in 1951, when Evans and friend John Arrington interviewed him. Photo by Will Evans.

horses live on is a mystery; their jutting bones testify of a life-and-death existence.

The struggle is not an isolated case in the drought-stricken wastes of Navajo land. Efforts are continually made by government and tribal workers to develop sources of water, but this work needs to increase.

John Arrington, from Farmington, and I visited the Escavada camp on July 7, 1951. We sought Agapito who, we had heard, was probably the sole survivor on the reservation of the eight thousand or more Navajos rounded up by Kit Carson and his troops, then marched to Fort Sumner in 1864 for four years of incarceration.

The roundup and exile occurred because the Navajos were making frequent raids upon white and Mexican settlements, robbing and kidnapping individuals, and destroying property.[1] Complaints poured in to Washington; so Carson, after being commissioned, exerted disciplinary action upon the tribe.

Agapito was born on the Escavada Wash and had lived there continuously except for the Fort Sumner period. He was three years old when he made the trek and seven when he returned. Although he has little memory of the experiences of that arduous period, his recollection of stories related by family elders is keen.

We found Agapito and his small granddaughter herding sheep across the arroyo from his makeshift well. The boy was drawing water for the famished horses, when his grandmother sent him to tell the old man that visitors had come to see him. Agapito, with crude staff in hand, hobbled across the sandy wastes towards us. His niece by marriage, Ella Cly, was with us and served as interpreter when difficult phrases had to be shouted in his ear. Ella—very intelligent, pleasant, and obliging, and a former school girl—lives about five miles from her uncle.

After he extended his hand to the visitors and his niece in a very gentle clasp, he asked what we wanted. Before answering, we moved into the shade of a six-foot-high bank with a clump of greasewood growing above. There the four of us sat or squatted, sheltered from the blistering sun. Once seated, Ella answered the old fellow's question, carefully telling him that we were there to listen to his story about the Fort Sumner days. We also wished to look over the land to see if there was sufficient water underground to provide a better water supply for his family. John Arrington was a trader in this area years ago and was convinced that there was plenty of water below the ground's surface. We would do all we could to inform the proper authority.

Agapito's eyes lighted up as he quietly listened, filled with hope. Once he launched into his story, however, his words and phrases came in such abundance that Ella frequently had to restrain him while we made notes. His parents and their peers had told him, as a young man, of their experiences at Fort Sumner. Every family received a small ration of corn and -flour, each of which would probably fill a one-pound coffee can. Sometimes there was meat, a small chunk of sowbelly, and perhaps a few beans. This was the ration for one day. Navajo clans and families were usually large so this food did not go far, and it was customary to eat only two meals a day. "Just enough," said Agapito, "to keep them alive." The small amount of coffee given them was in bean form, so they roasted it in a skillet, then ground it on a metate used for corn.

The people received a little seed corn at planting time, "Very little," said Agapito, but the scant crop of roasting ears tasted sweet when they were ripe, satisfying, for a while, the Navajos' craving for green food. A ration of buffalo meat sometimes eased their desire for meat.

The soldiers allowed the Navajos to keep what few rifles and bows and arrows they owned. Occasionally, Navajo hunting parties drifted over the Texas border into Comanche territory where bison were plentiful. Once they killed a buffalo, they brought back every edible part and the heavy skin to tan in camp; I knew one or two individuals who owned buffalo hides which came from Fort Sumner. The flesh of a buffalo meant that the clan members who formed the hunting party and their families, who camped in separate groups, would feast for a while.

When Navajos went afield to hunt buffalo, they sometimes met Comanche war parties determined to keep Navajos away from their herds. Battles became inevitable. Agapito recalled one hunting party that encountered Comanches; and after a protracted battle, the Navajos fell back, having had a pair of youthful twins killed. There was great mourning over them, because twins are a rarity and loved by the Navajos.

The exile at Fort Sumner was marked by mourning on every side. Smallpox laid its spotted hand upon the people, with so many dying that the living could not bury the dead fast enough. Some were thrown into unused ditches or arroyos and buried in mass graves.

Once the pestilence finished, the survivors felt time hanging heavily over them. They began to chafe and cry aloud the names of localities they called home, then tearfully begged their captors to let them go. I asked Agapito and others I knew if any escaped from the camps and made their way back to their homeland. I did not find any survivors who recalled this.

At long last the government and Navajos signed the Treaty of 1868.[2] The tribesmen symbolically laid down their arms, signifying they would not take them up against the government and "Wááshindoon." Agapito's family returned to the Escavada, where he has been ever since. The return trip was by way of Fort Defiance, Arizona, where the government gave each Navajo two sheep. A few plows, harrows, horse-drawn scrapers, grubbing hoes, shovels, and axes were also issued to people from each locality. Then the families departed to where they formerly lived.

We asked Agapito if there were any white people in the area. He replied that there were none except at Forts Wingate and Defiance. "How did the Navajos manage to survive on just two sheep for each individual?" He replied that during the years preceding this time, and also within his own memory, great herds of deer and antelope roamed through the Four Corners region, especially in the San Juan and Animas River valleys. Even bighorn sheep were occasionally seen on the Hogback.

Those were the days of venison and antelope steaks, and although there were no firearms, snares captured these fleet-footed animals. The people made these traps of yucca fiber cord, then killed the deer with arrows or clubs, cutting the animal's throat with an obsidian knife. A genuine feast followed the snaring and killing of a deer. The Navajos also used the blood from the animals. Deer and antelope were so actively hunted that they eventually disappeared. Agapito said that throughout his homeland, grass grew stirrup-high to a horse. Plentiful brush retained snow and rain, and there were only a few deep arroyos. The people lived on the fat of the land until their flocks multiplied.

In the past, when Manuelito was a leader, Navajos warred against Apaches.[3] One day a government representative from Fort Defiance called a meeting with Manuelito and his Navajos. The official asked them to take up arms against the renegade Apaches. Agapito quoted Manuelito: "You surely know that we laid down our arms, our guns and bows and arrows at Fort Sumner before we came back home and promised never to take them up again in war?" The government man replied, "Will you not take them up for the sake of the government and benefit of the settlers? The Apaches are killing too many settlers; when they rush back to their hideouts in the mountains, we need good trackers to find them."

Navajos are some of the best trackers in the world. I have heard it said that they can track a deer and strangle it. Some people believe that a Navajo could identify most of his acquaintances by their footprints. This is generally true in the case of family members and of his horses.

Finally Manuelito agreed. A group of young Navajos set out for north-central Arizona under his direction. In due time, they came close to the hostiles. When they reached the area of the Apache hideout in the timbered foothills, Manuelito told his men to tie their horses and seek the Apaches on foot. They spread out, kept in close touch, eventually surprised the Apaches, and captured their leaders. The Navajos killed some and took others prisoner, tying their hands with rope, then walking them down the mountain to be turned over to the Army. Agapito had suffered loss of memory, so he could not recall the names of the captors or captives.

He did, however, tell us that the representative of the government promised them an extension of the reservation lands in return for their assistance against the Apache. This extension was to cover a considerable amount of land including the Escavada and Pueblo Bonito area. The promise was never kept, like many other agreements made by "Wááshindoon." Some allotments of land have been made to individual families on the eastern edge of the Navajo country; however, these are not worth much without additional water resource development.

Yellow Horse and the Long Walk

Yellow Horse was a man of great power amongst his people for many years. When he was approximately ninety years old, bent and infirm, he could still hitch his ponies to his rickety old government-issue wagon received at Fort Defiance and drive in to the Shiprock Agency. He was a frequently honored visitor to my trading post and always carried an old butcher knife in a scabbard of rawhide looped to his belt. This old man had graying shoulder-length hair, bound about his brow by a rolled kerchief. His laugh was gruff but ready.

In his youth Yellow Horse was a warrior by inclination, a hunter by necessity. In his later years he was a herald of peace between his tribe and the whites. One day, during one of our frequent conversations, I asked him if he considered the coming of white settlers a calamity or a benefit to his people.

In his rough but kindly voice he replied: "There is no argument, no use in asking that but let me tell you what I think. In the old days we knew nothing about comfort and luxury. Our food was wild animals caught in a snare or trap or shot with a bow and arrow. We ate corn cakes when rain and snow came to the land and our crops did not fail.

"When I say that we snared larger game animals, I mean that we could not kill them with our pointed arrows. We set snares with cords made from yucca fiber. When the animals did not break away, we cut their throats with knives chipped and ground from obsidian. I inherited my obsidian knife through my father from his father. We always had a basin made of burned clay to catch the animal's blood, which was an important food used in many ways. We skinned the animals for badly needed clothing, bags, and other items.

Yellow Horse at William Meadows's Trading Post, northwestern New Mexico, early 1900s. Meadows commented on Yellow Horse's wealth and his strong character, derived from an adventurous life. Courtesy of Museum of Northern Arizona Photo Archives, Earle R. Forrest Images (MS 43, Neg. #521).

Navajos at the Shiprock Agency, 1910. This photo was taken at the east end of the agency where the carpenter-blacksmith shop was located.

"We really feasted when we killed a deer or antelope. In those days many antelope and deer roamed hills and flats of the San Juan Valley where there was plenty of feed. The grass and high brush held the rain around the roots, and there were few deep arroyos like there are now. Though game was plentiful, snaring the animals was very difficult, and we went hungry for long periods of time. Between the killing of large animals, we survived on rabbits shot with arrows.

"We had no furs to furnish winter warmth, because tradition told us not to slay coyotes, wolves, or bears.[4] We did not know what shoes were, so we either went barefoot or in moccasins. Most of the tanned animal skins went for leggings, which we used in our ceremonies and wore with moccasins. We had very few buffalo robes and were told that buffalo did not live on the sunset side of the Rio Grande. Few of us ever reached the river's sunrise side, so we did not hunt this animal, which would have been useful as food and shelter.

"Sometimes we outfoxed a few prairie dogs when they were away from their burrows or drowned them in their holes by turning torrents of water into them when it rained heavily. If their burrows were close to water, we carried enough in vessels to pour down their holes, forcing them out so we could club them. This was always a lot of work. Think about it: a bunch of youngsters running to the hole and pouring water down it then dashing back for more water. We whooped and yelled as we ran and yelled even louder when they came out and we clubbed them. The older people kept a fire burning nearby so that when the coals were glowing and ashes all around, we stuck the animals in to roast until done. We put them into the coals whole so the meat was very tender, juicy, and nutritious. Very little went to waste.

"Our ancestors taught how to turn water from the streams running off the mountains onto patches of land where corn, squash, and beans were planted. We relished melons for their sweetness. We had no implements of iron, so our ditches were small and the land was not deeply worked; we used bare hands and pointed sticks to dig and turn the soil. When we planted our crops, we loosened the dirt with these wooden tools and dropped the seeds into the small pockets of earth.

"When the ears of corn were ready for roasting, we feasted, danced, and chanted our prayers of gratitude. With toil and skinned fingers we dug a deep, round pit into which we built a roaring fire of juniper wood. Once this had burned down and only ash remained, we placed the un-husked ears into the pit, covered it with a slab of sandstone, and let the corn rest in the radiant heat until tender and delicious.

"Then, loading the rest of the harvest into our deerskin bags, we car-ried it to our hogans, where we husked the corn, stripped off the kernels, ground them into paste on our metates, then added a little charcoal to give it a blue-black color. Once we had this paste, we mixed in water, cre-ating a thick batter that we spread onto a heated, smooth stone slab. The warmed rock toasted the mixture, making a sweet thin, papery bread, which we rolled up and hungrily ate. Some corn kernels were dried in the sun, parched on a cooking stone, then carried in a deerskin pouch. This was nourishing food to sustain us during a hunt.

"We also harvested pinyon nuts [Pinus edulis], which we ground, shell and all, to a fine paste before baking it into a sweet, nourishing rich bread. We were careful not to eat too much because it was very strong food and could make us ill.

"At this time we did not have fruit such as apples and peaches un-less we obtained some from the Hopi. Usually we had to be content with what we had. There were wild raspberries and strawberries growing on the mountainsides, but we ate few of them because we would have eaten the food of our brother, Bear. The little reddish-orange berry called squaw berry was plentiful everywhere and made a good food. The berries were

Old style Navajo Hogan.

dried, ground into a flour, cooked in water until they became a paste, then spread on corn bread like white people use butter and jam.

"We knew nothing of coffee, but for tea we used the stems of a shrub which is plentiful in Navajo country. This served as a drink and medicine.[5] We had no sugar, with only an occasional beehive loaded with honey as our sweetener. Salt was very hard to find, so used sparingly. A salt lake was a long distance to the south, and it was difficult to transport the salt.[6]

"We knew nothing of matches and were glad to get them when the white settlers came to our country. The old way of making fire was by striking two pieces of flint together, setting fire to a small bundle of tinder made from the fine inner bark of either the juniper or cottonwood. We also rolled a round stick, sharpened on one end, between our hands. The point was placed into a hole in a slab of soft wood and, when twirled long and hard, created a spark that lighted the tinder. This was hard work.

"We made our beds from thick heaps of cedar bark. Sometimes we had only a well-worn deer or antelope skin between us and the hard ground, but we had warm hogans of wood and mud, without which we would have suffered greatly during the cold winter months. For cooking utensils we either traded or stole pots when we raided the pueblo settlements. Only a few of our women knew how to make crude cooking pots.

"A great change has come about since those early days. We saddle our horses with strong leather saddles, guide them with leather reins and iron bits, and ride in comfort. Wagons and cars allow us to travel away from home to buy what we need, to sell or trade our products for things the white man has brought to us. In the heart of the reservation we can

Hastiin Deshnod and family driving wagon away from the Shiprock Trading Post, 1942. Photo by Richard P. Evans.

get salt, flour, and matches, all the things we went without or worked so hard for when I was a young man. We are shown how to build better homes and plant better farms. Your question is useless; we all know we are better off."

Yellow Horse was a native of the Four Corners region. He was born near Table Mesa in the early 1840s and always lived near his birthplace. From the heights above his hogan he could see the mountain ranges of his homeland: San Juan, LaPlata, Sleeping Ute, Abajos, and in his backyard, the Chuska range. He often rode his cayuse into their foothills but called Table Mesa home. He desired no more than this panoply of mountains; what lay beyond was of no interest.

He often gazed into the heavens, skies, and at the stars he had known from boyhood. The great arch of blue was the ceiling of a hogan and held a pathway for the sun, moon, or stars that journeyed over trails at their appointed times. He noted the short trips of the Sun in winter months and his longer trip in the summer. The Sun simply walked a shorter trail when it was cold, a longer one when weather permitted. Yellow Horse knew the names of the greater stars of the night, committing them to memory. He also knew when each would be prominent in the summer or winter, how the Big Dipper led him to the North Star, and the creation story about the formation of the sun, moon, and stars.

Until the great march to Fort Sumner, he never knew what lay beyond the four sacred mountains. As a lusty young warrior, he was fond of raiding other tribes. The elders remonstrated against this, but their words had little force, since they too were raiders in their youth.

One day Yellow Horse and his friends crossed the San Juan River and rode to Mancos Creek, the traditional boundary between Utes and Navajos.[7] A band of Utes was camped on the creek, but most of the warriors were away hunting in the Gallina Mountains, southeast of Mancos Creek near present-day Cuba, New Mexico. The raiders had easy pickings, killing a number of Utes, including women, and driving off their horses in retaliation for raids and horse stealing against them.

A Ute runner went after the hunters, who returned in a hurry. Their route took them through what is now Farmington, across the Meadows north of Waterflow, skirting Mesa Verde, to Mancos Creek. They quickly organized a small army and started on the trail of the Navajos who had killed their people.

Learning that the Utes were in pursuit, the Navajos turned towards the San Francisco Peaks, arriving there as quickly as possible. The Utes gave up the chase and returned home. When they had crossed the San Juan in pursuit of Yellow Horse, nearly all the Navajos in the San Juan area fled, fearing retaliation. They headed into the Lukachukai Mountains with only a few concealed men remaining behind. Eventually the Utes won the battle because the refugees lost many people to starvation before spring arrived.

The young Navajo renegades made their way back to the Fort Defiance country and remained there until Kit Carson took them to the Pecos River region. By then, Yellow Horse and his companions were starved, nearly naked, and had to recuperate for some time after they arrived at Fort Sumner. If they had not been hardened to the trail, used to little water and scanty rations, they would have died.

Once the imprisoned Navajos reached Fort Defiance, they passed the Hay Stacks[8] and went on to where Gallup now stands. This permitted them to march in a great file along the vermillion cliffs which today see so much traffic. They then went past Wingate, Bear Springs, to Cubero, past what is now Bluewater, then to the Laguna pueblo lands and the Rio Grande. They traveled over the mountains east of the river and marched down the plains until they reached the Pecos River; the entire trip took over eight months.

As Yellow Horse traveled to Fort Sumner, he joined his uncle's party. He said that he was about nineteen or twenty years old at the time and his parents were dead. The caravan was ragged and unkempt, becoming more so as the journey advanced. The Navajos took their horses, sheep, and goats, not many to each family, but all went with the caravan.

The captives had none of their own wagons, but the government furnished a few. The people dragged along, day after day; some of the older ones and the ill rode in army wagons. A number of them rode their gaunt ponies while the rest went afoot. These were the ones who suffered the most.

Yellow Horse said that at times the march almost turned into a drive. The troopers yelled, "Hurry. Hurry. We want to get to Hwééldi [Fort Sumner]." He knew of no whippings, but the troopers rode among the scattered groups, cracking their mule train whips, urging them to get along. This was especially true after seemingly endless days and nights on the march.

One night, after a long, hard day's horseback ride, his aunt gave birth to a baby boy. The camps during the journey were strung along

the trail, with each family picking out the spot it wished to use. Yellow Horse's uncle's camp was on the outer fringe of this night's area, allowing some privacy during the birthing event. Next morning the mother wished to stay a day or two, to rest before resuming the ordeal of carrying the infant on a

Men like Mister Mustache (Hastiin Dághaa') survived the Long Walk era and were the type of people Evans preferred interviewing. Mister Mustache of the Hashtł'ihnii (Mud People) Clan was a noted medicine man in the Teec Nos Pos area and worked for Wilford Wheeler at the Hogback Trading Post for many years.

jogging pony. But the guards would not listen to it. The party had to go on, and all must be in the ragged line of march.

She wept and pleaded, told them she was tired and ill, but to no avail. The husband helped her on the pony, tenderly handing her the hours-old son, and the march continued. After two or three days of this jarring ride over rough country, the mother became inured to it, but the babe became ill and began to fail. For the next day or two, the mother rode the pony while the father walked beside her and carried the ailing infant in his arms. The second evening, a medicine man performed his ritual until long after midnight to heal the child.

As morning came, it was apparent the baby could not go on. The mother and father pleaded anew for the privilege of staying behind and nursing the infant back to health, promising to catch up with the main body even if they had to ride day and night to do so. They met the same negative response and had to go on.

The mother saw that the child could not live through the day unless it had rest and proper care. While the father and the remainder of the family gathered the camp equipment, she wrapped the baby carefully in all the blankets she could spare, then carried it a short distance to a clump of cedars and pinyons and placed the infant under a large sagebrush. She knelt and offered a prayer to the Holy Beings according to Navajo custom, returned to camp, climbed on her pony, and joined her family on their weary way. Yellow Horse told me that while the infant could not cry loudly, its piteous wails were heard for some distance. This was not an isolated case either, since he knew of a number of other families in similar circumstances.

The plight of those on foot was pitiful. The few who had moccasins when they started soon found them slashed to ribbons. Their feet were sore and bleeding from the sharp rocks and prickly brush. As they went on, day after day, with little chance for recuperation, the condition of many became critical. Some hung on the shoulders of the stronger as they limped on their tired way, while others got an occasional lift from those riding horseback. Others climbed on the stronger horses and rode double with the owner, but this too was only a temporary respite.

Those who did not go on the Long Walk had their troubles too. The Utes sensed their weakness and made raid after raid in the northern Navajo country, placing their enemy at their mercy. Bows and arrows were no match against Ute rifles. The raids provided ponies, many of which the Navajos themselves had stolen in raids on the Mexican settlements.

Yellow Horse tried to give me a description by drawing an oral picture of what the caravan looked like. He said that thousands of Navajos, along with their armed captors, did not travel as an ordinary column of people. They were scattered over the country at great length, stumbling through desert or wooded country. One could stand on a hill and watch the motley crowd below, appearing as a colony of ants on the march. In dry weather dust arose as if hundreds of whirlwinds were netted together, raising clouds of dry Mother Earth towards the heavens, her mate, Father Sky. That was the way the old man said it, in his own poetic way. In wet weather the people floundered through muck and mire. At night, no matter how big the fire they made, sleeping and rest were miserable because of wet clothing and bedding.

This method of scattered marching was necessary because of the sheep, goats, and horses accompanying the people; the separated camps at night became the downfall of many Navajo women—young and old. Old Hastiin Nez, a medicine man who was well into his eighties, told me his version of what happened. "The troopers treated the women very badly. They attacked any woman that was old enough. Much of this was done at night when the women in scattered camps became the prey of their captors. If a woman was caught alone, away from the main body, she was violated." Yellow Horse commented on a lot of the soldiers, saying, "They were not men; they were billy goats."

Once Yellow Horse arrived at Fort Sumner, the old restless spirit took hold of him. He would summon his friends at night and steal away from the guards, bound for west Texas, where they raided Comanche villages, "stealing whatever they could lay their hands on." The Navajos did this several times. Once Yellow Horse's brother stole two fine Comanche horses while Yellow Horse got two more on another foray, and his entire group escaped with ten good horses.

Some raids were bloodless, others were not. One time a serious battle developed with a Comanche band, angry at the loss of their stock. Yellow Horse paused at this point in his narrative, saying he wished to not only tell the part he played in the raid, but also what a swift runner he was in his younger days. He continued, "I was never afraid in all my life!" He had no fear of arrows or guns, because in earlier years, he looked upon the aged with pity; it was better to die young than to grow old and dependent. He, therefore, was among the most eager of the fighters when someone proposed riding towards the rising sun to do battle with roving Comanche bands.

The first day out from the Pecos River the war party crossed a low range of hills and made camp that night on the banks of a small creek where grass was plentiful; the following night they camped at another stream. The party traveled on and crossed a range of low hills where they camped again. At daylight the next morning they could see no mountains so they knew they were inside the western edge of a great plain. Pressing onward all day, they camped in a shallow depression at the foot of a very low hill.

One of the party killed an antelope, so they prepared a feast to stay their ravenous hunger. With difficulty they built a fire in a shallow hole where the blaze could not be seen. When they were ready to broil the antelope over hot coals, a terrific windstorm came up and scattered the joints of meat and embers all about. The feast was ruined. They gathered their possessions as best they could, rolled up in their robes, and slept uneasily as the cold and wind assailed them as never before in their own lands. The wind blew all that afternoon and night without cease.

Before daylight, a cry awakened the dusty, begrimed men, who thought the Comanches had discovered them. But the shout of pain had come from one of their own men, who fingered a burned place on his scalp. Another felt the sting on his arm, spotted with aching blisters. One man found a burnt place on his leg, another a hole burned in his scabbard, but Yellow Horse was untouched. He told them that they had lain amongst the live coals the wind had scattered but had not felt the burns because of the slap of sand and gravel upon their unsheltered bodies.

The injured fellows thought the burns confirmed an ominous foreboding they had sensed the night before, and so they wished to return to the Pecos. In spite of arguments and pleading that they would be outnumbered, placing both groups in jeopardy, these men turned back. The rest started east at sunrise on their journey. Several told Yellow Horse that the group should spread out and circle in at times as was done in a rabbit drive, but Yellow Horse said, "No; we'll keep together and follow this trail," a track made by Comanche buffalo hunters. He continued to lead; but the party had not gone far when someone shouted, "Wait! There are others who wish to turn back!"

As they discussed this new situation and tried to keep the group together, one man found the remains of a recent fire. Looking about, they found a hidden spring of water but shuddered when they saw a great clot which resembled blood, floating on it. The ashes told plainly that they were in enemy country. Fear gripped some, but Yellow Horse led on. They soon arrived at a small coulee in which a brook meandered and where two buffalo browsed on grass at the water's edge. The coulee would give these starving men both meat and concealment from the Comanche, but the buffalo scented them and began to move.

Some said in throaty whispers: "Let's kill the buffaloes and have a feast on that flat rock over there," but Yellow Horse disagreed. "No! We will not kill them. The Comanches will hear the shooting. We want to surprise them!"

The starving men could not bear to see the buffalo escape. One warrior raised his rifle and killed a buffalo, while a second Navajo fired at the other animal but missed. Hunger prevailed over reason; they built a fire to broil the meat and posted a watchman on the edge of the coulee. He reported that the buffalo was running away and antelope were fleeing with it. Someone suggested that the animals be followed and killed for more meat and hides. Suddenly the alarmed sentry shouted that the animals had swerved and were dashing back towards them.

The reason soon became apparent. A band of Comanches approached and circled the camp, yelling and shouting. A big fallen tree lay across the brook, where a number of Navajos sought refuge. Yellow Horse ran toward a large fork of the tree, but noted, "I did not run fast enough so another reached it before me." The circling Comanches began firing. Some of the younger Navajos were badly frightened, but Yellow Horse and three older men stood their ground. Bullets zinged near them and arrows pierced their clothing.

One Comanche leader who wore a long feathered headdress sat astride a big bay horse. He kept closing in, urging his fellows to do the same. Yellow Horse took careful aim at him and fired just as the bay leaped ahead. The leader fell. His warriors uttered a loud wail when they saw him hit the ground in a posture that told them he was dead. The group withdrew for a parlay as the clouds of dust that had filled the air from the horses' churning feet began to settle.

The Comanches chose another leader, who approached the Navajos on a white horse. Yellow Horse did not wait to learn if he came for a truce or to employ trickery; he took careful aim and killed him. More wails arose from the Comanches as they grouped together for another council, at a distance from the coulee. They set fire to the very dry grass, hoping to drive out the defenders then overwhelm them. The frightened Navajo youth still cowered under the fallen tree, but soon realized with the others that they had to fight the fire, which they did.

Comanche bullets sang around them. One Navajo shot an enemy warrior crouching by a bush, and the rest of the Navajos began to feel that luck was with them now that three enemy were dead and the grass fire out. The Comanches tried a different tactic. They dismounted, and a few began to crawl on their bellies through the tall grass. One Navajo played the same game and crawled off to one side, unseen by the Comanches, and killed the leading enemy with an arrow.

The attackers had had enough. They remounted and retreated like deer or antelope, turning some distance away to look back. They seemed to be considering another attack, so one of the Navajos fired at the closest Comanche but missed. The enemy galloped off at a run.

The victors scalped the dead and looted the bodies. To their amazement they noticed it was late in the afternoon although the battle had started early in the day. Four Comanche lay dead and several wounded with only one Navajo killed and a few slightly injured. The Navajos later learned, after returning to the Pecos, that the wounded Comanches had died on the ride back to their lodges.

Yellow Horse's group was low on ammunition and their arrows nearly spent. They turned back to Fort Sumner in a leisurely way, hunting with their arrows to obtain mountains of meat, upon which they gorged themselves at every stop. One day, a member of the party swung away from the trail to find more game and met a member from the group which had left them the day before the battle. He told of how a group of Comanches had killed all of his companions. Yellow Horse and his men grieved over this news, saying that the group should have remained together for mutual protection. He told about the successful battle with the loss of only one man, then his group began to mourn for their dead friends. The lone survivor relented and now told them the truth: all were safe and traveling a short distance ahead. "Then there was much rejoicing and feasting," said Yellow Horse. They killed several more antelope and dallied along, laughing and boasting of their exploits.

When they arrived at Fort Sumner, there was very little meat left for the people there. Still, for those who had gone on this adventure, it was an exciting respite from the confinement and privations of being prisoners. Yellow Horse preserved the Comanche scalp and tanned the buffalo hide with the hair left on. This robe became a great comfort, keeping him warm during the cold nights on the Pecos River.

The imprisonment of the Navajos at Fort Sumner became monotonous to a people who had been free to ride where they wished and do what they wanted. The water tasted bad when compared to the mountain springs and streams of their homeland. There was little wood for fuel in that open country, and so the Navajos walked great distances to get it. Insects swarmed about; lice and flies abounded. In the fields where the people tried to raise crops to supplement the distasteful rations, grasshoppers mowed down the young plants. Bands of hunters slipped away from the guards to hunt big game and raid other tribes and Mexican settlers.

Sickness was always rampant. Smallpox broke out in epidemics that ravaged and struck down the captives. When I asked Yellow Horse how many of his people died, he raised his arm and, sweeping it away from him, replied emphatically, "Many, many." He became silent for a few moments, looking down at the hearth as pain flashed across his face. Slowly he shook his head, the long hair beneath his kerchief waving back and forth. "Many. Our people died like sick sheep. There were so many that we could not prepare them for proper burial with the right chants; so many that we could not even bury them. We only carried them far enough away from the camps that they would not contaminate the rest of us. Even though we buried them in old ditches, under rocks, and in cracks in the earth, wild animals tore them to pieces.

"It was a very sad time for our people. Sometimes whole families died. Often only one or two remained alive in a family. Parents grieved because they could not properly care for their dead. This was the saddest our tribe had ever been. The people were so weak from the long march that when they got to Fort Sumner, many died; then disease came and tore us apart." The soldiers showed little mercy for the suffering people.

The survivors longed for their own land and familiar camps. They spoke of their deserted homes in the foothills of the Lukachukais, the tall cottonwoods along the river, and their idle sweat houses lying in ruins. They called out the names of their various districts—Ch'ínílį́ (Chinle); Tséhootsooí (Fort Defiance); Lók'a'jígai (Lukachukai), Tó Haach'i' (Tohatchi); T'iis Názbas (Teec Nos Pos); Bis Dootł'izh Deez'áhí (Round Rock)—begging, pleading to return to them. They begged Kit Carson to take them back or let them return without him to their mountains and plains. The men gained access to Carson, then crying and sobbing, told him how much they wished to return. The women howled as they stood in a group at some distance from the pleading men. They begged for their release from Carson, who they called "Red Clothes (Shirt)." "Oh, please, take us back."

Then, four years after their arrival in Fort Sumner, the time came when Kit Carson summoned them.[9] Yellow Horse said, "He was there with all the other officers of the Army." The following is taken verbatim from Yellow Horse's account:

"If you are permitted to go back home, will you steal and raid and kill as you did before?"

"No, no; we will do none of these things."

"Will you kill any more Mexicans?"

"No, no; we won't do that!"

"Will you kill any more white men?"

"No, no; we won't do that!"

"Will you steal any more cattle, horses, donkeys, sheep, or goats?"

"No, no, not any more; we will behave ourselves!"

"Now that you want to return to your own country, what about the size (area) of the reservation you will be placed on?"

"We will leave that to Wááshindoon."

"Before we let you go back, we want to ask you about schools. Will you agree to send your children to government schools?"

"Yes, we will agree to that!"

Yellow Horse said that a number of whites clapped their hands at these replies to Carson's questions. One of the provisions of the treaty was that all Navajo children should be sent to school as soon as they reached the required age. Yellow Horse interpreted this stipulation by saying "As soon as a child was born, it belonged to Wááshindoon."

Soon after this meeting the return march began with a second trail of hardship lying before them. The route followed the old trail to some degree; and when those who were walking came to familiar landmarks, they would break away and return to the land they had abandoned years before. Yellow Horse did not recall the time this return required, but he did remember how happy the people were to reach familiar territory.

Yellow Horse was thirty-four years of age when he returned to his beloved Table Mesa. More than sixty years had come to him as he lived and worked amongst those familiar buttes. His pony's hooves had trod thousands of times over the low hills to the east and northwest of his home. Below these hills, sometimes at depths of only 800 feet, lay millions of dollars worth of oil, the gold the white man would later tap and develop to the advantage of the Navajo Tribe, but Yellow Horse knew nothing about it.

Following the signing of the Treaty of 1868, Yellow Horse made it a daily practice to observe what the white soldiers required of the Navajo and counseled his fellows to do the same. He said, "With my own eyes I have seen what the white men are doing; they have good houses, good stores, fine animals, and productive farms. They know how to get ahead and the better ones set a good example for my people, who are taking advantage of some of these things; they even drive cars!"

In his own family life, Yellow Horse was never called upon to send a child to school under the terms of the treaty. He was married three times but sired no children, having only stepchildren. He had a humorous attitude about his inability to produce children: "I think I must be a mule," he remarked then laughed in his throaty voice. Still, Yellow Horse was an anchor to his people. His counsel and influence cooled the hotheads who stormed about and might have brought disaster to the Navajos. He was courageous, facing each dissident squarely, then stating his position.

This was the Yellow Horse I knew in the closing days of his life. He favored the old ways so had little to do with modern technology as it came along, unless he could adapt it for his own comfort. He puttered with his old wagon to keep it in repair and looked after his horses in spite of his great age. With bent back and wobbly knees he still had the will to move around and be about his tasks. He was mentally alert, had witty expressions, keen humor, and a light in his eyes. I was very interested in this man, as I watched him sit at my fireplace, drawing smoke from his hand-rolled cigarette, then talking between little puffs to tell the events of his life. I have come to realize that such opportunities come only now and then.

Yellow Horse was not a medicine man or any kind of tribal leader, but his character in later life left an impression upon his people which eased many a tense situation between Navajos and white men. A wild fighter in youth, he raised his voice for peace in his later years. I counted him as my friend and acknowledge a debt for the stories he told me about his people.

The Establishment of Trading Posts

Before the settlement of the San Juan region, over 130 years ago, the Navajos on the northern reservation had little contact with the white man. There were few traders and settlement was in its infancy. The Navajos returned from captivity at Fort Sumner in 1868 and went to their previous locations. Each family received a few head of sheep, some flour, sugar, and coffee, then shifted for itself. By the early 1890s they had large flocks and herds, which, together with blanket weaving and agriculture, became their mainstays. But even then, the effects of the commercial panic of the early 1890s were felt in the remotest sections of Indian country.

During the 1870s and early 1880s there was not a single trading post on the northern Navajo Reservation from Mexican Water, located many miles across the San Juan River, to Bluff, Utah, and on to Tohatchi, New Mexico. In 1880, a Mormon colony from southern Utah crossed the Colorado River at the Hole-in-the-Rock and established Bluff City in San Juan County, about 125 miles down the San Juan River from Farmington, New Mexico.

The Navajos at Mexican Water and Sweet Water traveled to Bluff to trade when the river was low. Those in the Teec Nos Pos country also made the long trip to Bluff or a longer one to the other side of the Car-

John Walker's Trading Post in Tocito, New Mexico, south of Shiprock. Walker was a Mormon trader and Sarah Evans's brother.

rizo Mountains, after Chee Dodge and a man named [Stephen E.] Aldrich established the Round Rock Trading Post in the 1880s. Aldrich was a brother of U.S. Senator Aldrich. The Indians of the Two Grey Hills and Toadlena districts went over the mountain to Fort Defiance, and later Crystal, after its establishment in the 1890s. These trips were very difficult during the winter. Those living farther south at Sheep Springs and Naschitti, traveled the same routes; they later traded at Tohatchi, especially during the winter, in the late 1880s.

Wool sold at four and five cents per pound, and sheep and goat skins eight to ten cents per pound. The merchandise which the few traders carried was ridiculously low when compared with today's prices. Arbuckle Coffee, the old standby, in later years retailed at 25 to 35 cents a pound, was then selling for ten cents. Tomatoes in 2½ size cans were 15 cents. Twenty-five-pound bags of flour were from 65 to 75 cents according to grade, and sugar 5 cents a pound. Prints and calicoes were three yards for a quarter, and heavy unbleached muslin was two yards for a quarter. Blue denim overalls sold for 65 to 75 cents, and good work shirts ran from 50 to 65 cents each. Everything handled in the store was similarly cheap.

Navajos received little for what they sold, including rugs, which were less than cheap and hard to sell. But at the same time, during these panic years, they managed to slowly build their flocks and get to where they could be economically independent. With the assistance of the trader, who took their "pawn"—beads, rings, bracelets, etc.—as security for provisions and clothing, they were able to get along.

The Navajos' wants were generally few; they had a carefree existence, attending the sings and dances and ceremonials. They raised corn in a variety of colors: red, white, yellow, and blue, with some ears containing all of the colors. There were two uses for blue corn. It was either ground to make piki or "paper" bread, which was eaten as a diversion or used at celebrations. This corn was finely ground, made into a thin batter, then spread on a heated rock. Once cooked, it was rolled and eaten.

Pony racing and jackrabbit drives filled a Navajo's craving for his sporting instincts, while card games occupied his lonesome hours. Monte and Koon-Kan were his favorite games, which frequently took on a phase akin to "strip poker," as frequently one or more players left the game pretty well "stripped." Playing cards were quite common until Uncle Sam decided to put a stop to them and the selling of playing cards by the traders became an infraction of reservation regulations. Much of the card playing ended, but there was always a game going on somewhere on the sly.

Everything was going well as the Navajos gained wealth when another great blow fell. The weather was the villain this time. In December of 1898, the skies spewed snow so heavily and so long on Mother Earth, that when it quit, approximately twenty-four inches covered the northern Navajo district in the San Juan region.

Navajo flocks starved to death. The government offered help, but it was inadequate. The few trading posts were not equipped to give much aid, so suffering by poor Navajos was acute. Many were reduced to spreading out their coffee grounds to dry in the sun on top of their hogans, so that the beans could be used over and over again until tasteless. Then the Navajos went without until they secured a fresh supply.

Some sheep survived, forming a nucleus for future herds. Families nursed along small flocks that gradually grew. The Navajos fought poverty any way they could, and because of their intense desire to build animal wealth again, they practiced a strict economy and careful husbandry.

One time I saw a goat walking on two legs, the front ones at that. It was in the spring at a camp belonging to a Navajo called Frank Barber, who lived in the upper reaches of Sanostee Valley. The goat was half-grown and seemed to be a pet around the camp. Frank told me that during the subzero weather of the past winter, the animal's hind legs froze so badly that they had to be amputated. The front legs had survived, presumably because they had been protected by the animal's body. By some means this intelligent creature learned to throw the rear part of its body into the air and peg around for short distances on its two front legs. Following the terrible loss of animals in the snow, a goat was a goat, so the family took care of it.

Many months after the Big Snow of 1898–1899, the Navajos still sorely felt the loss of their livestock. Sheep, goats, cows, horses—virtually all had frozen to death. The Navajos used their livestock for food and were especially fond of horse flesh. Stark and ravenous hunger was not rampant, but want and privation continued with the people for a long time.

In early April my friend, Harry C. Baldwin, known as "Hunter" to his Navajo friends, came riding into Sanostee Trading Post.[10] Harry was then a partner in the Hogback Trading Post north of the river with his Uncle Hank Hull and was on his way to Two Grey Hills. We made him comfortable for the night and had a pleasant visit. He never let the conversation lag and during the evening said to me, "Bill, why don't you ride over with me in the morning. Things are still pretty slack here, and you can be spared for a couple of days. You know the country, and I have never been over it. I want to see how Mrs. Cole is getting along."

Mrs. Henrietta G. Cole, a native of Massachusetts, was then an elderly woman, who had come out west and joined Mrs. Mary Eldridge in establishing a mission at Two Grey Hills. Eldridge was the head of the Hogback Mission at the time, and Harry thought very highly of them both. These two ladies had done a great work, unmarked by selfishness, among the Navajos. While their primary purpose was to give spiritual instruction and comfort to all Navajos they met, they also did what they could to meet the temporal needs of the people. The younger generation of Navajos knows nothing of them, but the elders had cause to bless these women to the end of their lives.

Mrs. Cole was a mother to us all. During the time I worked at Two Grey Hills for the Noel brothers [Henry and Frank], I felt that she interfered with no one but attended to her business, which was, as she stated, "teaching her Navajos the true way of life." The good she did at Two Grey Hills and Toadlena has certainly won her and Mrs. Eldridge a just reward.

Early next morning Harry and I saddled our horses and started towards Two Grey Hills. We debated about going across the flats to make a shorter trip or to just travel along the foothills. We decided to take the foothills, where huge drifts still lay in sheltered places but parts of the trail went across bare rock. In many spots the path was dim, in others completely hidden. There would be no traffic along the trail since most of the horses had perished that winter and the few survivors were too weak to travel.

We rode past the camp of old Mustache Smeller [Dághaa' Chin], his large, well-built stone house deserted. The scene was pitiful. He once owned many sheep, but now between forty and fifty of them lay dead in front of his home. On the surrounding hills, lying partly in and out of the snow, were score upon score of ewes and wethers. No one around could tell us where he or his family were. This grisly scene was repeated several times before we reached Two Grey Hills. All the camps were deserted and the ground littered with dead sheep. We knew that as spring advanced and the sun gained power and warmth, the stench in this area would be unbearable.

After a difficult trip we floundered into the trading post yard. Mrs. Cole was more than pleased to see us and prepared a wonderful dinner. Among her other fine qualities, she was an excellent cook. Fortunately, the traders at Two Grey Hills had a source of fresh meat. Hastiin Bicheii owned a large flock of sheep and was more fortunate than most in keeping them. When the snowstorm began, Bicheii herded his flock into a cove at the foot of a mountain where a wide rock wall protected them from the driving blasts of winter wind. He had cut a stack of wild hay that fall at his mountainside farm, and when this supply ran out, he struggled through the drifts to cut boughs of sagebrush, juniper, and pinyon to feed his animals. Thus his herd survived, though the lambs were born smaller than usual. His losses were nothing compared to others, who were completely ruined.

When the traders needed meat, Bicheii brought down a young wether to the pole corral behind the store, where it was butchered. This was a great event for his hungry neighbors. They scrambled for the warm innards and hurried home, cheered by the prospect of making a nourishing entrail stew for their hungry families.

One day a pitifully famished, elderly woman in the ravenous stages of starvation was at hand when the traders had a sheep butchered. The animal was skinned and the hide spread out, fleshy side up. As the entrails spilled onto the skin, she grabbed a section of small intestine then moved aside, fearful that someone might snatch it from her. Holding the gut in one hand, she stripped out what offal she could with the other and began gnawing at the still warm flesh. With her excellent teeth, which were unusual for Navajos, she devoured it all.

I was literally sick and stunned. I had seen people in advanced stages of hunger in the past weeks, but never a human with the ravenous appetite of a wild animal. I had only pity for the poor creature and hoped her meal would do her good. To this day when I look back upon those times, I feel deep sympathy for the Navajos because of the numerous trials and tribulations, many of which I have shared during long years of close acquaintance.

After a pleasant visit at the Two Grey Hills Post, we started back. The days were short that time of year, and darkness came early as we rode miles away from our destination. We could follow our trail in the snow fairly well, but the bare spots gave us trouble. We finally saw the golden light from kerosene lamps at Sanostee and arrived safely. Harry returned to his store on the eastern side of the Hogback the next day, and I returned to my lonely post on the banks of Sanostee Wash. In later years, Harry has laughed about that trip and how happy we were to see those welcoming lights. He also told me that he purchased hundreds of horsehides from hungry Navajos that spring. They were not worth much but brought enough cash for the sellers to buy a little coffee and sugar. He resold the hides and kept the wheels of trade turning.

I am reminded of another trip I took some years later, as I traveled by horseback from Tohatchi to the San Juan. A Navajo whom I knew well came onto the trail and joined me. As we rode through a fairly narrow defile, with high cliffs and rocky ledges on each side, he told me of a battle some Navajos had with a band of Utes at that place when he was a boy. The Utes were raiding the Navajos, stealing horses, and some of them were armed with rifles. The Navajos had only bows and arrows, and some of those arrows were merely sharpened sticks. The battle was a one-sided contest with several Navajos and only one Ute being killed. The Ute died when a Navajo youth shot him through the eye with an arrow. My friend pointed out the rock where the boy and his mother hid while the battle progressed, fearful they would be discovered.

Following that devastating winter, the people began again to succeed. In the following years wealth in flocks and herds returned, wool for weaving rugs was available, and trading posts sprang up on the better, more populated sections of the reservation. Eventually, there were thirteen posts in the northern Navajo area, each one of which did more business than the original single post.

Prosperous posts were located at Sanostee, Naschitti, Two Grey Hills, Toadlena, Captain Tom's Wash, and Red Rock. All of them were at the foot of the mountain range, called in some parts, the Tó Háálį [Toadlena], Chuska, and Lukachukai. Joseph R. Wilkins, who had previously owned an interest with Joe Reitz in the Crystal Post, opened up Sanostee in December 1898. Wilkins drove a large freight outfit from Gallup to Ganado and Round Rock before that time. Tom Bryan of Fruitland owned the Naschitti Post, but it was managed by Buke Maupin, an old timer on the San Juan.

Brothers Henry and Frank Noel were the first to own and operate Two Grey Hills. Henry spent his later years near Hot Springs, New Mexico, while Frank and family moved to Draper, Utah. Frank also owned Sanostee for a number of years and was there during the Beautiful Mountain rebellion with Bizhóshí and his son Little Singer.

Friends and traders, *standing, left to right:* Frank L. Noel, Henry R. Noel; *seated:* Edmund Noel, Will Evans, Cyril J. Collyer. Frank L. Noel Collection (P-166), L. Tom Perry Special Collections, Harold B. Lee Library, Brigham Young University, Provo, Utah.

Merritt Smith started the Toadlena Trading Post, but later moved to Cortez, Colorado. His father, R. G. Smith, was one of the pioneer farmers on Farmington's Peninsula, then known as Junction City. Charles Nelson started the Captain Tom's Wash Post, now known as Nava or Newcomb. Olin C. Walker established the Red Rock Trading Post. And Teec Nos Pos, situated in the foothills of the northern part of the Carrizo Mountains, sprang up during this early period and was later joined by the Sweet Water and Mexican Water posts, then finally the store at Red Mesa. Hambleton B. (Hamp) Noel, a brother of Henry and Frank Noel, in partnership with Hugh Currie, built and operated the Teec Nos Pos store. He was a resident of Fruitland for many years. John Wade launched the Sweet Water Post but later moved to Farmington. Joe Lee, a well-known character of Indian country, started the Mexican Water Post. He had a reputation for telling tall tales and was credited with the ability to speak the Navajo language better than the people themselves.

Navajos from the Red Rock country and Sanostee section crossed the Lukachukai Mountains and traded at Round Rock during the summer,

The Shiprock Trading Company constructed in 1925. Evans painted the pictures and decorations. Photo by Richard P. Evans.

but not in the winter because of the deep snows. One of the old features of the Round Rock Post was the floor of the "bull pen." It was made of pine poles covered with slats from wooden Arbuckles Coffee crates, both coffee and crates being old standbys in early trading posts. Navajos obtained a winter's supply of flour, sugar, and coffee, using wheat flour to supplement their corn meal. The two were mixed as long as the flour lasted, then it was straight corn meal bread. Older Navajos often had worn teeth from the grit in the meal, left by grinding the corn on a stone metate.

The mercantile activities along the San Juan were a boon to the Navajos, who traded pelts, wool, and blankets for fruit during the season. Apples, peaches, pears, plums, etc., were a treat to those who lived largely on mutton, coffee, and corn. The Navajos raised a few peaches before the fruit growers of the San Juan got started. At Tohatchi, Toadlena, and Teec Nos Pos there were old peach orchards which bore fruit, although it was somewhat tasteless by modern standards.

Indians living along the San Juan River and some distance to the south were isolated for a long time. Early in the 1880s Farmington, Fruitland, and the lower valley (then known as Jewett Valley) were established. Then came Olio, now known as Kirtland. Richard Simpson ran the store and post office at Olio, while Tom Bryan at Fruitland and a man named Welch in Jewett Valley operated their respective stores. Hank Hull and Tom White's post at the Hogback later became known as Hull and Baldwin, after Harry Baldwin, who came from New York to visit his uncle, Hank, and decided to go into business with him.

With the establishment of the Shiprock Agency in 1903, two posts opened. Matt Hubbard owned one and [Robert S.] Baker the other. I bought the Shiprock Trading Company in 1917 and remained there for thirty-one years, until Sarah and I moved to Farmington in 1948. In the early 1930s, a Mr. Mayer operated a small post at the Four Corners proper, but it was not successful; and today only a few piles of stone mark the site.

The period of Navajo prosperity in the first third of the twentieth century was largely the result of assistance given by individual traders. The government suggested there be an infusion of high-grade bucks, which would result in the production of better wool, better prices, and more prosperity. Officials said they would provide such animals, but the Indians would have to place the cash on the barrel head. These bucks were priced at an average of $35.00 each—a very high price for those days.

Few Navajos could buy these bucks on a cash basis; and so the traders stepped in, each one signing for a certain number of animals, which they later issued to their customers. The cash outlay was carried on each trader's books. Sometimes he got his money back and sometimes he did not, but the system of improving the herds continued for some time. The end result: the Navajos had better sheep, larger lambs, and a higher grade of wool.

The majority of the People in the 1920s were prosperous and happy, with only a few events to mar progress. In 1922, the wool market took a serious flop, hitting the traders more than the Navajo. Post owners paid an average of 35 cents a pound for the wool crop that spring. Before it could be sold, buyers withdrew because of the shaky condition of the market. The traders were forced to consign, and when the final returns came in, wool was worth eight cents per pound. Only a few Indians had held their wool for higher prices and were caught in this catastrophe.

Soon, the Navajos again began to prosper. They were independent, confident of the future, as business on the reservation ran into seven figures. There were periods of drought and flood, but between living in the mountains in the summer and the flats in the winter, the Navajos got along. Then in 1932, John Collier became Commissioner of Indian Affairs, and the Soil Conservation Service became involved. The Navajo economy soon changed as will be discussed later. This is, however, a brief overview of the growth of the trading posts in the Four Corners region prior to the disastrous effects of livestock reduction.

Harry Baldwin and the Hogback Post

A wiry young man, Harry C. Baldwin, came to the San Juan in autumn 1894. His Navajo friends promptly named him Hunter [Naalzhééhii] because he often took his .22-caliber rifle to hunt in the brush along the river and the slopes of the Hogback, where he bagged cottontail and jack-rabbits. For the half-century he lived in this area he kept this name.

Harry remained the winter of 1894–1895 with his uncle by marriage, Henry (Hank) Hull, who ran the trading post on the banks of the San Juan River east of the Hogback. During the previous fall (1893) tragedy struck at another post owned and operated by Hank Hull and a man named Colonel Welch. Hank was in Montrose, Colorado, looking after property interests while Welch manned the store. One day, a Navajo called Fat [Łinishk'aii] shot and killed him, took what he wanted, and fled the scene.

A young lad walking towards the store saw Fat run away and reported the murder. Troops captured Fat, who was tried and sentenced to federal prison at Fort Leavenworth, Kansas, where he remained for several years. Upon release, Fat returned to the Shiprock area, where he raised a second family and gave no one any trouble up to the time he died a number of years later.

After Hank returned from Montrose, he vacated the store, moving the business to the Hogback, where it has remained through several changes of ownership. He took in Doc [William N.] Wallace and began business anew. Doc Wallace was a peculiar fellow, wizened and shrunken with age, with a high, piping voice when I knew him. He came to this country to regain his health and was said to be an accredited pharmacist in his later years. He took an interest in the medical problems of his Navajo friends while at the Hogback and christened himself Navajo Bill. He bedecked himself with Navajo rings on all his fingers, several bracelets on each wrist, and buttons and emblems pinned to the lapels of his coat. Indeed, he was a walking advertisement for the silversmith who had made these items. So these were the traders, Hank and Doc, who introduced twenty-three-year-old Harry Baldwin to the trading-post business.

Harry's new life was a far cry from Phoenicia, New York, where he was born in 1871. This business was also nothing like his previous experience of selling bicycles and prospecting for gold in the Carrizo Mountains. Still, Hank Hull and Doc Wallace were feeling the effects of age and wished to leave the business, so Harry accepted their offer to take over the post. In 1899, he married Ruth Eldredge, the daughter of Mary Eldredge, who established the Navajo Methodist Mission in Farmington and later the mission at Hogback.

While Harry was at this post, government employees built the Hogback canal, perhaps fifteen miles long, and a diversion dam, which became a godsend to the Navajos of this area. These canals supplanted the older ditch dug about three miles southeast of the Shiprock Agency, which had primarily benefited the agency farms. The new ditch irrigated several thousand acres of once-arid land and contributed more to the advancement of the Navajos of the area than any other single improvement. Harry also benefited from the resulting industry. Some paydays he sold an entire carload of oats to feed the Indians' horses used to excavate the ditch. He also handled practically all the hay raised in the vicinity and helped farmers find outlets for their produce. He remained at the Hogback Trading Post for twenty years, before selling out to Joe Tanner.

One time I asked Harry if he had ever had any serious conflict with the Navajos, and he replied that he had, twice in fact. One was with Black Horse, who was a different Navajo than the old fire-eater of the Teec Nos Pos area. Harry said that one day he glanced out the back window and saw Black Horse dealing cards to another Navajo. Superintendent Shelton, at the time, was waging a campaign to break up this vicious habit of gambling because it usually ended up in impoverishment and bad blood among both the Utes and the Navajos. Shelton requested that the traders cooperate in discouraging gambling, and although Harry's store was not on the reservation, it was close enough. He had issued an ultimatum that no gambling was allowed around his store.

Harry walked out back and asked Black Horse to quit playing cards. The Navajo arose in a rush of anger and swung at the trader's chin; Harry dodged, receiving a light blow on the shoulder. He was slender, lightly built, and no match for the 200-pound Black Horse, so he picked up a wagon stake and laid it squarely on the gambler's head. Black Horse fell with a thud. After that, there was no more card playing around the post.

Another incident occurred during the construction of the Hogback Ditch. Navajo workers performed much of the labor. Harry carried a great many of them on his books for supplies. On paydays, a representative of the project brought checks to the store and gave them to the workers, who cashed them with the trader. One evening a long line of Navajos had formed, waiting to receive their government checks and subsequent cash. A one-eyed man called George Peterson received his check, endorsed it by thumbprint, obtained his cash, paid his account, left the line, and pocketed the balance. In a few minutes, he returned, loudly claiming that he had been shortchanged. Another Navajo standing nearby had witnessed the transaction and told Peterson that he had not been shortchanged and had received all that he had coming to him. Peterson had evidently concealed some of his change to reinforce his claim.

Superintendent William Shelton and wife, Shiprock.

This happened on four successive paydays, holding up the line and delaying the payoff. Before the next payday, Harry asked Shelton to send a Navajo policeman to watch the transaction. Tall Man [Hastiin Nez] received the duty, the line duly formed, and he began to watch carefully. When Peterson reached the counter, Nez counted Peterson's money, said it was the correct amount, and handed it to him. Peterson soon came barging back into line with his old complaint. Harry replied that he had not been shortchanged and pointed to Tall Man as a witness. Peterson stuck his face across the counter close to Harry's and called him a liar.

This was more than Harry could stand. He lashed out with his fist and hit the accuser full in the eye, with a corking good blow. Peterson carried a beautiful black eye for several days. Apparently he did not appeal to a higher authority, Tall Man said nothing, and Harry went on cashing checks. Peterson never interfered with Harry again but stayed away from the store, figuring one black eye was enough.

Harry Baldwin, the Hunter, met his maker on December 1, 1950, survived by his wife and daughters. He had lived a long and worthy life. No one could say anything but good things about him as a citizen, a doting father, and a friend to all. The Navajos liked him, which is a mark of well-being and honesty.

Red Rock Trading Post

In the first two decades of the twentieth century, the northern Navajo Reservation witnessed the establishment of a series of trading posts. Thirteen stores sprang up where there were none before. This was a great convenience to the Navajos, especially those living in or near the foothills of the Lukachukai Mountains, because these people had previously been compelled to cross the mountains to Chinle or Round Rock Trading Posts. One of the more successful new stores was at Red Rock, opened in 1907 by Olin C. Walker. Like many other posts, Red Rock had a humble beginning. Here is how it happened, just as Olin Walker told me:

"In January 1907 I had taken a wagon and old Tall Man to locate a place for a store. I had worked two years for the government at Shiprock and gotten acquainted with several Indians, since I had many under my supervision on different kinds of work. I hired Tall Man with his team and wagon to take me into the country that he was familiar with.

"We got to Little Shiprock the first evening and camped on the road. That night I learned how to count in Navajo and the next day how to count money. We reached Mexican Clan's (Naakaii Dine'é) place that day and stayed several days and nights, talking and inquiring about the need for a store in that area. I decided to try it. Close to Mexican Clan's camp was a rock room, about eighteen by thirty feet, with a fireplace in each end. I rented the building from Mexican Clan for six months with the privilege of renewing the lease if I wanted to. We went back to Shiprock, and I got a Mr. Whitcroft from Kansas City, Kansas, to go in partnership with me.

"Mr. Whitcroft and I got a team, a wagon, and a load of goods from Harry and Matt Hubbard at Shiprock. I took my little boy, Claude, along with us. We also brought a few pieces of lumber, a camp bed, frying pan, Dutch oven, and coffee pot. We arrived after dark, fixed supper, unloaded the wagon, and went to bed. Next day, with coffee boxes and lumber, we set up a counter and a few shelves. We had brought a pair of scales along and were opened for business the next morning. The day after that my partner went back for more goods.

"We did not have much trade, nor did we have much to sell, but I kept busy getting things lined up. I had to go three-quarters of a mile to a spring for water and had Indians bring me some wood. Whitcroft returned with a big load of goods, then stayed around two or three days to learn what he could about trading and Indians. He left again to obtain more supplies, taking skins, pelts, rugs, etc., so we could learn what to expect for them. Trade was picking up, and while Whitcroft was gone, the Navajos held a 'sing' three to four miles north in Black Horse's neighborhood.

"By sunrise the next morning, there were about fifty Navajos on horseback at the store. One of them, through a young boy who interpreted, asked me if I had seen Black Horse. I told him 'no' and so the group informed me that Black Horse did not want me there and that I had better see him. I told them that I did not know I had to see him, but they assured me I did and that I would either have to get permission to set up a store from him or get out.

"They talked for quite a while, and I kind of enjoyed it, despite the fact that they said the Navajos would not come there to trade because Black Horse would not allow it unless I went to see him. I told them we came with permission and a license from Washington, Agent Shelton at Shiprock, my friend Mexican Clan, and his family and friends.

"They wanted me to sell goods and buy pelts, rugs, and wool; I told them that I would pay as much as they could get anywhere else and I would treat them fairly. I was not trying to make anyone come here who did not want to come, and the roads to other places were just like they were before we came. I also said that they would all want to come here when they learned who we are and how we deal. As for Black Horse, I had no business with him except to sell him goods, but I would like to see him and if he wanted to see me, they should tell him to come here. This is where I would be.

"One of the Navajos asked me how long I intended to stay there. I replied: 'Until my hair is as white as cotton.' They talked a bit among themselves then began trading. I got fifty or sixty dollars from them, and they nearly bought me out. There was no more trouble.

"When Whitcroft returned with another load of goods, my son, Claude, was getting homesick so I took what pelts and rugs we had back to the San Juan River. Next, I moved my family from Shiprock to Fruitland and began trading for supplies with C. H. Algert Co. In those days, to get back to my post, I had to ford the river; when it was too high to cross below Shiprock, we crossed on the footbridge or in a boat at Fruitland.

"Business went along well, so I stayed at the store most of the time. Whitcroft's wife, who had never seen the post, went back to Kansas City, and he did not like the Indians or trading with them. He had been a streetcar conductor in Kansas City and said he would rather be back there to make a living for his wife and family than stay out here and make a fortune. I borrowed money and bought him out after only about two and one-half months.

Red Rock Trading Post, 1912. Olin C. Walker, standing under the arbor, is with friends and customers. Courtesy of the Houston Walker Family, Farmington, New Mexico.

"I dug a well and found plenty of good water thirty-five feet down. After five months I got a group of the neighborhood Indians together and picked out a place to build a store which is where the Red Rock Trading Post now stands, about one and one-half miles from the rented rock house. I hired Tall Man and Mexican Clan's son (whom we also called Tall Man) to oversee the job. This boy worked for me the entire time I owned Red Rock Trading Post. We moved into the new store in July, then started building another large room to live and cook in. About that time I made a deal with Matt Hubbard to come in with me. We worked together about two years, then I borrowed money and bought him out. I built corrals and started constructing another large room for wool and pelts.

"Black Horse and his wife came over for the first time on their way to Sanostee, where Frank and Hamp Noel were at that time. The party arrived at my place on a stormy night a little before dark. I had no camp hogan yet, so I let them use the unfinished wool room and made a fire in the southwest corner, which blackened the walls and ceiling.[11] I gave them food and a cooking outfit, and they had sheep pelts to sit and lie on, so were fairly comfortable. The next morning they sold some pelts and bought food, but they had a little wool and a rug they would not sell because they were taking it to Sanostee. Black Horse eventually softened and wanted to sell it, but his wife would not because she had pawn at Sanostee and wanted it back.

"They went to Sanostee and returned the next evening to trade a little more and pawn some beads before going home. Black Horse's wife was a fair rug weaver, and they were good customers at the store after that. Black Horse had tamed down considerably from his early years.

"While I was at Shiprock, Black Horse and his friends and relatives came there to get ewes and bucks that Superintendent Shelton had gotten for the Indians. When they saw the animals, they began to help themselves; and Shelton had quite a time stopping them. However, when he got through with them, they knew he was running things; and Black Horse got the bucks on the Superintendent's terms, which meant he was limited to the quantity allowed to other Navajos. Shelton never had any more trouble with Black Horse. The old fellow had been in the habit of doing as he pleased in his part of the country but learned that someone else was in charge and that he had to quit making trouble.

"Soon after I moved to the new store the following incident occurred. I had credited a Navajo for $2.75. He promised to bring me some hay in two or three days as payment. He and three others came late one evening with the hay, so even though I was alone, I went out and purchased it for six dollars. When we came back to the store, I counted out the money and laid it on the counter. I reminded the man of his debt of $2.75, collected it back from the $6.00, and put it in the cash drawer. He said no, he was not going to have it that way, that it was not his hay.

"I told him I had bought the hay from him and that none of the others had sold any. 'I let you have $2.75 in merchandise to be paid for in hay, in two or three days, and that is all I know about it!' He still said that it was not his hay, that he would not take the $3.25 and was going to take the hay back. I told him he would have to pay me the $2.75 before he did. The men had a lot to say about it among themselves. Soon one of them reached over the counter, which was only two boards wide, grabbed my coat, and said 'Come out.' I told him I had done all I was going to do about it and that if he knew what was good for him, he had better turn loose. I never moved and kept my eyes on him. He was the oldest and largest of the group and had killed an Indian in his time. Then he eased his hold, as though he had not grabbed me.

"He then turned around to his friends and said, in a rather low voice, 'He is not afraid.' One of the men came over and picked up the $3.25, and the group went about spending it and even more. Before leaving for home, they all shook hands with me, saying everything was all right. There was never any more trouble with them. One reason I stood my ground and was not afraid was because I had a good .45-caliber six-gun under the counter in front of me.

"Soon after this another incident occurred. Diné Tsosie, Dilwóshí Begay's son-in-law, had lots of sheep. His wife had tuberculosis, and so he employed several medicine men, which cost him many sheep, even though she was not healed. He finally contacted Little Singer to treat her. For a while she seemed to get better, then took a turn for the worse and died. Diné Tsosie blamed Little Singer, saying he gave her whiskey. They buried the woman, in her best clothing and wearing her valuable jewelry, in an acre of open ground surrounded by cedar trees. They did not bury the body deep enough, and so coyotes and other animals tried to dig into the grave.

"Diné Tsosie thought someone was trying to get her out for the valuables, so he decided to find out what was going on. He built four fires, one in each direction, then camped nearby, waiting and watching. After several nights he came to the store and insisted that I go out with him and look the situation over. So I went, took some tools, and found when I got there just what the trouble was; the burial was too shallow. We cut some poles and built a pen about three feet high, four feet wide, and six and one-half feet long around the grave. We packed the pen with earth, covered it with poles, and spiked the whole thing down. This seemed to satisfy him, and there were no more signs of it being bothered.

"When I first went to Red Rock, Mexican Clan had about seventy-five bales of hay, hand-tied with yucca fiber instead of wire, that he had stacked on a strong frame out of the reach of livestock. He wanted me to buy the hay, but I did not know how well it would sell, so I told him to put his price on it and that I would sell it for him. About a week later someone stole two bales. I told the old man about it, and he stuck up two fingers, saying there were only two people in the entire region who would steal it. One man he knew, the other, 'maybe so.'

"We began an investigation and found the man Mexican Clan suspected. The Navajos tried him by their own rules and decided that he should repay it double. I do not know whether Mexican Clan got any money or not, but the two suspects were looked upon as being of no account. All the rest of the Navajos seemed to be above that sort of thing.

"I have noticed that at gatherings, when a head man wanted to speak, all was as quiet as a funeral, and people paid strict attention. Even the little children were quiet, and if not, only had to be spoken to once. I have never seen them spanked to quiet them. I have, however, seen Indians give their children money to go to the store or have stuff to sell and instructed them to buy several articles, even when the children were too small to climb upon their ponies. The trader had to help them up and place the bag containing the goods behind the small customer. The trade articles in the bag had been divided in the Indian manner, so that they would ride evenly on the pony. These children had no slip but filled out the order from memory and seldom made a mistake. Most of them were honest and wanted to do the right thing.

"Some families were not good, but most were all right and could be depended on. The Navajos are an independent race, proud, and somewhat stubborn. If a person drives them at all, they balk, but if they are understood and treated fairly, they will do anything. Let them know you have confidence and are depending upon them, and they will do it if they can. Nowadays, the younger ones are losing the honor of being honest and dependable, and it is primarily because of the white people they have come in contact with who have betrayed their confidence. Even so, they seem to be holding up as well as the whites in that respect."

Olin C. Walker was always a man of his word. After leaving the Red Rock Post, he operated the Two Grey Hills Trading Post but later sold out and retired. He and Mrs. Walker were living in Albuquerque when I visited them in 1949. I enjoyed his reminiscences of life in Navajo land.

Little Singer and the Beautiful Mountain Uprising

Little Singer [Hataałii Yazzie] and his father, Bizhóshí, were not just ordinary Navajos. Both father and son belonged to the old school of those who were unalterably opposed to the white man and benefits of civilization. Their intense devotion to the Holy Beings, intricate religious ceremonies, and deep spirituality sometimes caused their white neighbors to wonder.

Bizhóshí was an esteemed rainmaker. Until his death, he painfully and laboriously mounted his gentle pony—scorning help from his younger associates—to ride long distances into the desert or into the hills to help others. His weather-beaten face, drooping mustache, and serrated teeth, some of which were missing, presented a fearful visage when wreathed in anger. In spite of this appearance, he was a born leader.

Little Singer was a replica of his father. Early in life he became Bizhóshí's pupil, adept in the practice of a medicine man and knowledgeable about the lore of his tribe. He was an unfailing source of those remarkable stories. His knowledge of these things in his early teens supplied the name of Little Singer, a title which remained with him for the rest of his life. While young, his features were smooth, somewhat similar to those of an Eskimo, but in old age he favored his father to a remarkable degree.

Despite the rigid observance of Navajo beliefs and ceremonies, Little Singer's objections to the encroachments of Washington and the Indian

Little Singer, Bizhóshí's son, provided the spark that ignited the Beautiful Mountain Rebellion in 1913.

At the Shiprock Agency Fairgrounds, 1910, Superintendent Shelton stands before his Navajo police force. Only a few of the Navajos are identified. To Shelton's right in front with the badge is Curley Jim. Looking over Curley Jim's right shoulder is Slim Policeman. Directly behind Shelton is Black Whiskers. Left of Shelton is Tľah Begay. Behind him is Hard Belly. To the far left is Louis Cambridge.

Bureau caused trouble only once with these authorities.[12] The issue was polygamy, which he believed in and defended as strongly as he did his worship of the Holy Beings. At the time, Bizhóshí, his sons, and followers lived in Sanostee Valley, near the foot of Beautiful Mountain, thirty-five miles west of the Shiprock Agency and sixty miles down the San Juan River from Farmington.

In 1913, government authorities were trying to curb the widespread practice of polygamy among the Navajos. The Agency received word that Little Singer had three wives and was resistant to change. Acting on this information, Shelton sent a detachment of Navajo police to Sanostee with orders to bring Little Singer and his three wives to Shiprock for questioning and possible trial in a local Indian court. The police returned in three or four days, bringing the women but not Little Singer, who had refused to come. But come he did, several days later.

One day in June, Little Singer and a band of Navajos crossed the river at Shiprock, galloping, whooping, and firing rifles and pistols into the air as they entered the agency grounds. Superintendent William T. Shelton was away on business; there were no armed guards, and only Sephus Jensen, the agency farmer, Mr. Hinds, the clerk, and a policeman called Lame One [Na'nishhod] were there. These men rushed out of the office building to meet the oncoming raiders, but their efforts were futile. One of them grabbed the bridle reins of Old School Boy's [Ólta'í Sání] horse, but the rider whipped him with his quirt and forced him to turn loose. Little Singer beat Mr. Hinds with a riding quirt, while a Navajo named Luce whipped and dragged around Lame One. Any witnesses soon fled for refuge in the buildings.

The three women, one of whom had a baby, were prisoners at the agency. They had been given the peaceful occupation of hoeing in the gardens until Little Singer was captured and brought in. At this time, two of them were in the garden plot hoeing, while the one with the baby, Luce's sister, sat at the front of the jail, which was jokingly called the Department of Justice. During the melee, Luce rode his pony and led a bare-backed horse to his sister, grabbed her and the baby, hastily placed them on the spare pony, and told her to ride home as fast as she could. The other two women mounted horses, the group crossed the bridge, and disappeared in the desert toward Sanostee Valley. Jensen, Hinds, and Lame One could not stop them.[13]

The rebels realized the seriousness of their actions and rode hard to a natural fortification, the top of Beautiful Mountain. This peak is a high volcanic mesa detached from and slightly east of the Lukachukai Mountains.[14] Its crest is surrounded by a high precipitous cliff of lava, providing only one difficult means of ascent on a single-file trail through a crevice in the lava cliff. A few well-armed men could hold off a regiment of foot soldiers. There is no living water, only two small lakes fed by rain and snow, but the grass for livestock is good. The recalcitrants took provisions there in anticipation of defending the site.

Superintendent Shelton returned as soon as notified and took charge of his forces. He fully realized the futility of attacking, but having the dignity of the government to uphold, he notified the Indian office and asked for troops. The government sent General Hugh Scott and a detachment of soldiers in response.[15] Arriving at Beautiful Mountain, Scott quickly sensed the futility of charging the stronghold.

Rumors grew that some of the traders and their families were slated for death. Charley Nelson at Nava, about thirty-five miles south of Shiprock, Frank Noel at Sanostee, and O. C. Walker at Red Rock were among them. However, one old trader, Joe Tanner, volunteered to visit the enemy camp to persuade them to come down and meet with General Scott for a talk. The meeting lasted a long time, the band not immediately

Traders and families gathered at Sanostee for seven days during the Beautiful Mountain conflict. Trader Frank Noel provided the following description. "Front Row: Mary, Floyd, Bessie, Reginald and Wright (Noel), Pratt Nelson, Golden Nelson, James Ayres (sawmill superintendent). Second Row: Jennie, Mom (Mary), Dad (Frank L.), baby Howard, and Clara (Noel), Roswell Nelson, Mrs. Nelson and baby, Julia Nelson, Eliza Robinson (school teacher for the Nelson and Noel families), Mrs. Ayres, Willard Ayres, Alphonso Nelson (Sanostee store clerk). Third Row: Milton and Jennie Steele." Frank L. Noel Collection (P-166), L. Tom Perry Special Collections, Harold B. Lee Library, Brigham Young University, Provo, Utah.

deciding to take Joe's advice to surrender, but only to think about it. He went down the mountain, found his saddle horse, and rode to the Sanostee Trading Post.

Among the Navajos, there was much excitement; more so than with the whites. The Indians were more aware of the prowess of Little Singer and the effectiveness of his medicine. They had heard him boast that his medicine was so strong that it would turn aside bullets fired by the soldiers. There were also threats against any tribesmen who worked against Little Singer. ·

Joe Tanner warned Frank Noel of the possibility of annihilation of him and his family, then sent Indian runners with messages to the Nelson and Walker families warning them of the peril. He advised them to go to the San Juan Valley for protection. Whether either of these families did this is uncertain. Mrs. Noel, however, elected to remain. Later, Joe Tanner said, "That damned Frank [Noel] wouldn't budge; said he knew his

Indians, and I guess he does. They like him and he is good to them. But if he had heard what I [heard], he would not be so sure of his safety. You can't tell what an Indian will do when he is pushed to action."

Noel and Tanner later rode out to a sing the Navajos were holding at the foot of Beautiful Mountain. Chee Dodge, the veteran Navajo leader, and old Bizhóshí were there and expressed concern about the situation.[16] After Tanner had a long talk with them, Bizhóshí and Dodge went up on the mountain and held a conference with the renegades, while Tanner returned home to Shiprock.

Over the years, there have been reports that Joe Tanner did not go to the mountain. His daughter, Loncy Tanner Goodman, in a letter to me confirmed that he did:

> When daddy told Shelton he would go up and persuade them to give up, he didn't go out for show but results. His concern was for the tragedy that could take place; . . . he never made a display for anything he ever did. . . . Frank Noel rode horseback out to the "sing" with dad, . . . for the express purpose of daddy talking with Little Singer's father and Chee Dodge to bring about the surrender of the band. . . . The Indians were nearer and dearer to him than most of his white friends.
>
> Joe Tanner was almost one of them and for good reason: his father lived among them all his life beginning as a young man. They called him Hastiin Shush, Mr. Bear, because he was almost as stout as a bear. When my daddy came along, he wrestled, fought and played with them from the time he was a baby. He grew up, known to all the Indians as Shush-Yaz, Little Bear. He knew their language better than his own and as well as they knew it. There was not a secret, legend, or custom that he did not know. His whole life spent with them was one of trust, confidence and loyalty he had in them and they in him.
>
> When he passed away, by far more Indian friends grieved his passing than white friends. . . . I might add to the episode of the Beautiful Mountain Rebellion: Daddy was not in accord with Mr. Shelton's actions concerning Little Singer's breaking the law. However, when they took the law into their own hands, then daddy agreed that they had broken the law. Dad and Mr. Shelton were always close friends, but daddy was actually in sympathy with the Indians concerning their beliefs and customs, and he many times told Mr. Shelton that they couldn't realize they were breaking the law, as it was a custom they had always lived.

Meanwhile Little Singer and his followers were atop Beautiful Mountain, making plans, singing and supplicating the Holy Beings, and performing the rites they hoped would give them the power to carry on.

There was plenty of excitement in the Red Rock country where Olin C. Walker ran a store. The post was about thirty-five miles northwest of Shiprock. Walker related his experience to me, giving a clear picture of what happened. It seems that a Navajo named Thin Man ['Ánísts'óózí] had held a grudge against Little Singer over some grazing troubles. Thin Man vented his spleen on Little Singer and was the one who reported to Shelton that the medicine man was a polygamist with three wives. Knowing that the superintendent was trying to break up the practice, Thin Man fueled the fire. Also, word later arrived that the arrested wives were being mistreated at the agency, making matters worse. Another story told of how Bizhóshí had led the raid into the agency and assisted in seizing the women. Furthermore, Indian friends reported the renegade gang had decided to fight to the end. This story appeared several days before the surrender. Things looked bad around the Red Rock Trading Post.

Late one evening, Little Singer came by the post, sending word to Walker to come outdoors, to one side; he wanted to talk to him. Walker met him at the spot, but there were no other Navajos around. Little Singer told him that he wanted the trader to hold his pawn and that if anything happened to him, his wives receive it. This pawn consisted of a valuable silver concho belt studded with expensive turquoise; coral, white shell, and silver beads; turquoise-mounted bracelets, rings, etc. He told him that he had heard what had been happening to the women since taken into custody. Walker replied that he did not believe those stories and that the agency authorities could not allow such things while the women were in their charge. There was, however, talk of troops being called out because his party had refused to surrender. The trader ended the interview by telling Little Singer that it was much better for him and his family to surrender on their own accord so that the authorities would not be too severe with him. The Navajo said he would think it over.

Before leaving, Walker reminded him that there were all kinds of reports traveling among the Indians. Some people were in sympathy with Little Singer, and some were not. Most, however, thought it would be best for him to surrender and not risk a battle with the soldiers. A few rumors suggested that Little Singer had threatened that before he was caught he would kill all the traders. He replied that the traders were his friends, adding that it would be foolish even to think of such a thing. The Navajos needed the stores as bases of exchange for food and products. There had been too much talk, which was at the bottom of all the trouble.

Walker did not tell Little Singer that he had heard that his group had sent word that before being arrested, they would kill Thin Man, the informer, and all his group. This created intense fear in that family because the clan was large and many lived in this vicinity.

"The rumors were becoming hotter and hotter by the hour," said Walker. Troops were known to be on their way, and it was feared that the Indians might strike at Red Rock as soon as the soldiers reached Gallup. Knowing of the threats to the traders, Shelton agreed to keep the Red Rock Post informed of the progress of events.

A week before Little Singer surrendered, between fifty and sixty Indians and their families began gathering around the trading post to stay for the night. Walker told them that he did not think there was any great danger, but they still collected there every evening. These Navajos feared that the large piles of cedar and pinyon wood at the back of the store could be used to burn it down. During the night the Indians formed a circle, partly protected by the piles of wood. The younger men bedded along the line of the circle, resting and keeping watch, while the older men, women, and children lay protected within.

During the day, a young Navajo, John Dayish, rode back and forth to the Sanostee post to get news for the Red Rock people. Everyone, including the rebels, wanted to know where the troops were.

One evening at dusk, a lone, bareback rider came galloping to the post. He was one of Little Singer's group, who had deserted from Beautiful Mountain. He reported that the soldiers were approaching, the renegades would be at Red Rock that night, and they planned to kill everyone there. He advised the people to flee, which created more excitement and fear. Adding to the concern, that same day a young thirteen-year-old Navajo boy arrived at the camp with another young fellow and had been frightening the women and children with stories of what was going to happen. At the same time, they helped themselves to foodstuffs.

That night, some Navajos noticed a campfire, not too far away from the post. The fire seemed to be where no dwellings were located. Fear arose, so John Dayish and two others went to the spot and captured the young heckler and his friend, who turned out to be Boyd Peshlakai [Beesh łigaii(silver)], a school boy. (Boyd later became a respected and influential member of the tribe.) The men brought the boys to the post, where they tried to explain that they were coming to the store to get some tobacco. Walker argued that Navajos did not usually get tobacco at midnight, but he let them have some anyways, telling them that under the circumstances they would have to remain at the trading post until the scare was over. Boyd was sensible but did not want to obey. The Indians threw him down, hog-tied him, and told him that when he decided to behave himself they would let him up.

Events quickly progressed, and the tension would soon have to end by either bringing peace or a great calamity to these enemies of the rebels. They waited with great anxiety and in severe tension.

John Dayish brought word from Navajos in Gallup to Little Singer that the troops had arrived and were on their way to Beautiful Mountain. Eighteen hours later a runner from Shiprock verified the report. Everyone went on guard, although the authorities at the agency said that things would now work out satisfactorily. Walker later remarked that through the entire experience he had no fear of anything; however, he thought, "You never know what they [Navajos] have in their minds to do."

The following night all the Indians camped around the Red Rock Post and were filled with dire forebodings of what might happen. One fellow came into the store and informed Walker that his father had gone through a divination rite and had received the same answer several times, that the renegades would be there that night and kill everyone. They would pile wood over the buildings, killing and burning the Walker family. Walker asked, "What would we be doing all this time? We will have no lights inside the building; they will be out in the open in plain sight with no cover. One man in this rock building should be equal to twenty-five or thirty of those attacking from the outside."

The old fellow was still earnestly concerned. His son, Frank, a medicine man, came into the building to perform the divining rite for the benefit of the trader, and each time he got the same answer as his father. The old fellow was more convinced than ever and stressed what he called "the truth of it." The two Navajos insisted the Walker family leave the store and hide in the holes in the red rocks adjacent to the post. The trader declined, saying that the rock buildings were the best place to make a stand. The old man replied that there would be so many raiders that they would break down the doors and burst open the windows, then easily shoot those inside and out.

"We will be okay here," Mr. Walker said. "Besides, I do not think the renegades will show up." The old man remarked that if Walker would not leave, the Navajos would place their women and children in his care and all the men would spread out and provide a guard through the hours of darkness.

The night was misty and disagreeable. Next morning, Frank, the fortune teller, came in bragging about what a sharp watch he had kept. He demonstrated how he had done this and that and what he would have done had the renegades arrived. Walker told him that he was just like a prairie dog—he barked at passersby, but if anyone made a movement toward him he would dart down his hole.

"No, no," said Frank, as he pantomimed his words and showed his hat with dirt and moisture on it. "Sure," said Walker, "You may have heard something and dropped down behind the pile of sand in front of the hole and got your hat dirty." The Indians all laughed but were still worried.

They had learned that the troops had arrived, but they knew nothing of what was happening. Walker tried to reassure them, stating he was certain the matter would be brought to a conclusion without trouble or bloodshed. He tried to impress them that there was no need to worry.

John Dayish went to Sanostee that night to determine the current situation. Next day he returned with news that Joe Tanner had served as a peacemaker, the gang had given up without a fight, and there was no attempted getaway. Peace came again to beautiful Red Rock country.

Frank Noel told of his experiences at Sanostee on the other side of Beautiful Mountain during those anxious days. He listed as the chief reasons for the revolt the government's desire to change old Navajo marriage customs, mistakes by the agency through the native police in seizing the women instead of the men, and the very bad error of using force without the cooperation of the Navajo Nation. Reasons for the easy settlement of the difficulty were that there was no fighting, the common sense and skill of General Scott when working with Indians, the influence of Chee Dodge, and the friendly spirit that existed between the Navajos, white traders, and government employees.

Noel believed that the Shiprock Agency had been badly advised by some men who were supposed to know the Navajos. Trying to change the marriage customs by order instead of cooperation, then calling in troops to arrest the men who raided the agency just escalated the trouble. Sometime before the troops arrived, a few men including Chee Dodge, Joe Tanner, and Frank Noel went to talk to the Bizhóshí clan about the issues. Noel and Joe Tanner made a second visit to Bizhóshí where Joe gave a talk. Some of the Indians believed that he had been sent by Superintendent Shelton, but this was not true.

Noel insisted there was never danger of anyone being killed by the Navajos. To illustrate this, he mentioned how later Scott and his son camped in a tent for three days in the yard of the post, while the Indians stayed in and around a hogan not more than 400 feet away. Some of the Indians had come to Noel before Scott even arrived and asked him to remain until the trouble was over, while several white people advised him to send his family to the river, which he did not do. Bizhóshí came to the store and told Noel not to send his wife and family away because a man needed a wife around and that Little Singer was not angry at him and his family anyways. In my opinion, Noel, with his innate modesty and personal courage, tried hard to minimize the danger.

General Scott, his son, and driver arrived at the Noel Trading Post one afternoon, where the General held meetings with the Indians for three days. The men under General Scott's command camped at Nelson's

General Hugh Scott inscribed the back of this picture: "To my friend Mr. F. Noel, New Mexico, whose coolness amid universal excitement was a refreshment with spirit, during the Be-zo-she Navajo war. H. L. Scott, Brig. Gen. USA, Fort Bliss, Texas, Decr. 6th, 1913." Courtesy of Brigham Young University Special Collections, Provo, Utah. Frank L. Noel Collection.

store at Captain Tom's Wash about twenty miles south of Sanostee. Chee Dodge and other influential Navajos came over the mountain and camped at the post during the meetings, as did twenty or more white people who had been working at the sawmill and other local places. Among them were Mrs. [Roswell] Nelson and family from Nava and the [James] Ayres family from the sawmill. They all stayed for the duration of the conference, playing horseshoes and entertaining themselves as if there were no trouble.

According to Noel, General Scott told the Navajos shortly after he had arrived that he had come a long way, was tired, and knew they were too. He wanted a long rest in order to be fresh in the morning. Mrs. Noel added, "The evening that General Scott and Lieutenant Scott rode into the yard, there were a lot of Indians in the store, and both whites and Indians got excited. The General walked in, shook hands with everyone, then told Frank to feed the Indians. He asked Bizhóshí to come that evening and tell him about Navajos and where they came from.

"After supper they gathered in the front room and began to talk, while the Indians on the outside were looking through the window or running around the house. Our sons were quite excited and loaded their guns to keep watch that night. They made their beds on the floor and slept next to their weapons, but I don't believe they moved all night.

"General Scott was a fine man, congenial and pleasant with us all. He insisted on making his own bed and helping where he could. When he

Robert Martin, Sr., and his wife, Aseneba, at their home six miles east of Shiprock. He worked for Shelton as an interpreter and a general peacemaker. Photo by Richard P. Evans.

talked to the Indians, he sat in the middle of the bull pen with the Navajos all around him. The lieutenant and Frank stood behind the counter prepared for any move the Indians might make, but they made none."

The second day Scott held a meeting at 2:00 p.m. in the store. The General spoke of the government schools and agencies established for the benefit of the tribe and of the friendship that existed between the whites and Navajos. He listed the number of employees necessary to serve the schools and agencies and how it was expensive but necessary to do the work on the reservation. Asking them to think over these things, he agreed to meet with them the next day and again instructed Noel to feed those present.

On the third day Scott spoke at length about the power of the government and the large number of soldiers it could put in the field. He requested that the men he wanted be surrendered.

In a short time they were. Bob Martin and his wife, pioneer residents in the Shiprock area, were present and said that when the Indians surrendered, General Scott handled them "without gloves." He said to Old School Boy, "Why did you do this? Don't you know that you were liable to get yourself shot? What fools you are to buck the United States Government." Old School Boy did not answer and just hung his head. "Come on man, speak up. You are neither deaf nor dumb," shouted the General, but Old School Boy just rested his chin on his chest and began to cry. The other Navajos felt very humble. Even Bizhóshí and Little Singer wept when the General lectured them as only an army officer can. They were a pretty tearful bunch when the General got through with them. The Martins laughed as they recalled the crying renegades.

Scott ordered that six of the original nine spend the next six months under surveillance in Santa Fe. Noel said that after Little Singer and the others received their terms of punishment, he gave them hats, silk handkerchiefs, and tobacco to solace them on the trip that lay ahead. Within three months, however, they returned home, outfitted with new blankets, suits, shirts, and shoes. Thereafter, they stayed out of trouble for the rest of their lives. There is no doubt that the vast majority of the Navajos were relieved when the entire incident was over. They stood to suffer more than the whites in this affair, and they knew it.

The Beautiful Mountain rebellion and its aftermath had little effect upon the marriage of Little Singer and his wives. Most of the white traders thought the situation could have been handled differently, and they all agreed it was too difficult to end a custom that had been practiced for centuries. Education, not force, was the better remedy.

Little Singer lived a long life with two of his wives dying before him. He passed peacefully, without bloodshed; and his body with personal possessions—belt, beads, bracelets, and rings—were placed in a rock cranny. Nature piled other rocks at the foot of a long high mesa, which formed a part of the Rock Fence surrounding Sanostee Valley. This high mesa created one of the lower ramparts of magnificent Beautiful Mountain. Little Singer shared the following chant about the sacred mountains and the land he loved.

Little Singer's Chant
There's a holy place with a god I walk.
To a holy place with a god I walk.
To Sisnaajini [Blanca Peak] with a god I walk.
On a chief of the mountains with a god I walk.
On a chief of the mountains with a god I walk.
In old age, wandering with the god I walk.
On a trail of beauty with a god I walk.
In this holy place with a god I walk.
In a holy place with the god I walk.
On old Tsoodził [Mount Taylor] with a god I walk.
On a chief of the mountains with a god I walk.
In old age, wandering with the god I walk.
On a trail of beauty with the god I walk.

In this holy place with a god I walk.
In the holy place with the god I walk.
On Dook'o'oosłííd [San Francisco Peaks] with a god I walk.
On a chief of the mountains with a god I walk.
In my old age, wandering with a god I walk.
On a trail of beauty with a god I walk.

In a holy place with a god I walk.
In a holy place with a god I walk.
On Dibé Ntsaa [Hesperus Peak, La Plata Mountains] with a god I walk.
On a chief of mountains with a god I walk.
In old age, wandering with a god I walk.
On a trail of beauty I walk.

Prosperity in Reverse

The plight of today's Navajos dates back to the advent of the New Deal of the 1930s, when John Collier became Commissioner of Indian Affairs. He posed as a friend of the American Indian, but long before he left office, his name became a "hiss and a byword," even a symbol of reproach, throughout Navajo land.[17]

Collier was not completely responsible for the troubles the Navajos faced but was as much a victim of circumstances. The Soil Conservation Service was even more responsible. Still, Collier was the target of hatred and scorn by virtue of the position he held. Navajos later claimed that he

Navajo Tribal Council, Window Rock, Arizona. In front are President Jacob C. Morgan (*left*), Commissioner of Indian Affairs John Collier (*Morgan's left*), and E. R. Fryer, Shiprock Agency superintendent (*second from right*). Collier, remembered by the Navajos for his livestock reduction policy, became a controversial figure on the reservation. Photograph by Milton Snow, courtesy of the Navajo Nation Museum, Window Rock, Arizona (NO11-275).

was afraid to come on the reservation and that the only time he did was when he flew in to a Navajo fair at Window Rock, where he was under constant observation before departing in a few hours. I believe that this was the only time he came in personal contact with the Navajo people.

People accused Collier of having sold out to the Soil Conservation officials, who were behind the reduction of Navajo livestock. Not long after Collier took office, he invited all of the traders and government stockmen on the reservation to meet at the Harvey House in Winslow, Arizona, to talk over matters regarding livestock and the Navajos. Here, the traders learned that a general reduction of sheep and horses on reservation lands was necessary because of soil erosion.

The government explained that the annual runoff of eroded soil was finding its way to Lake Meade and the Hoover Dam, which were rapidly filling with silt. The range was becoming depleted by overstocking and drought conditions. The speakers, however, did not explain why there was such a terrific runoff if there was so little moisture.

Officials promised the traders that if they would use their influence in persuading the Navajos to accept a certain percentage of animal reduction, the government would spend two or three million dollars on the reservation. The men discussed the pros and cons of the matter, and since the percentage of the proposed reduction did not seem excessive, the traders agreed to help. Many of them also decided that the promised expenditures would more than offset the proposed stock reduction. So the traders returned home and went to work on the Navajos, who agreed to the program, which called for a moderate reduction.

Commissioner Collier started spending two or three million dollars, with one report claiming he eventually provided closer to five million dollars. The Navajos got rid of the sheep and other stock they were asked to give up, but there was no evidence of either individual or collective recompense for these losses. Instead, the money went to building the Navajo Capital at Window Rock, Arizona, a collection of low, rough-hewn red sandstone buildings, with dirt roofs, scattered among the cedars and over the hills, near the rock formation that gave the capital its name.[18] The construction must have cost a pretty penny. This was done notwithstanding that nearby Fort Defiance was a long-established site, the use of which would have saved millions of dollars.

Window Rock was a pleasing place in some respects. The brilliant red cliffs rising amid the green cedars and pinyons may have had something to do with its selection, but the cheap, unpolished buildings, scattered here, there, and everywhere gave scant proof of the wealth of a prosperous nation. The Navajos were not pleased with this turn of events. They had given up a part of their living which had contributed to their welfare, and they obviously could not eat or wear those scrawny looking buildings. Many of the Navajos lived too far away and so felt that they had been gypped. The traders agreed, believing the millions of dollars should have been spent on the development of much-needed water sources.

The government established a central agency in Window Rock, where the Navajos could tell their troubles. Prior to this, there had been long-established agencies in different sections of the reservation. These provided easy access for most of the people, although there were a few living in remote places. These agencies handled questions and problems in their jurisdiction. Once the government completed construction at Window Rock, the other agencies were abolished, and all business, except that of minor importance, was transacted at the capital.

The bulk of the Navajos objected to traveling long distances to this agency and could get nothing done when they went there. They complained about "buck-passing" and that by the time they ran out of "buck-passers," they were outside and on their way home without having accomplished anything. One of the biggest gripes was the absence of any local authority.

The only thing the district supervisors, who succeeded the agents who had authority, could do is enforce the edicts of those above them.

There are some fine men among these supervisors, but their hands are tied with "red tape" and their jobs are thankless. The Indians demanded the restoration of the agencies, but having no substantial voting powers, they are at the mercy of the statesmen in Washington. A system, once abolished, is hard to restore. "That devilish Washington" is a phrase often repeated by the angry Navajos, who have a just cause when their grievances are fully understood.

Stock reduction did not bring the promised or expected results. The tribesmen were just minus the animals taken off the ranges. They received low prices then being paid for their sheep and goats, which did not offset the loss of the increase. Worst of all was that the first reduction was but an opening wedge for future efforts. Later reductions continued. The Soil Conservationists urged Indian Department officials to remove more and more livestock, talking as if the reservation was going to wash into Lake Meade and Hoover Dam if the majority of the sheep were not removed.

The Navajos protested sometimes with a display of firearms and shooting. The stockmen followed their directives but sympathized with the Indians. Still, orders were orders. During one frantic move, goats were practically confiscated, the owners being allowed only a ridiculously small number. The government shipped the animals away, had them butchered and processed, then sent back to the Navajos as canned goat. What a waste this dole was when freighting is considered—and the fact that the people used practically everything but the goat's bleat.

Workers also made periodic roundups of ponies that were turned into dog food and plant fertilizer. These, too, brought ridiculously low prices, some as low as 50 cents per head. This happened in spite of the fact that Navajos are fond of horseflesh and commonly killed and ate their horses. At this point, the horses were taking the place of the sheep and goat meat that had already been removed in previous stock reductions.

By the time Collier and the Soil Conservation Service had finished their "program," the Navajos were in desperate straits and the land in shambles. In a few short years the New Deal had shattered and destroyed what had taken the Indians and the traders three or four decades to build. Years of effort to bring the tribe from abject poverty to affluence had gone for naught. Poverty and want again stalked the Navajo nation. It seemed as if those in power had lost sight of the human element and worried only about a few occasional trickles of water mixed with a little sediment into the "silvery" Colorado River. Pitifully small herds have taken the place of larger, more prosperous ones.

Today, one sees out on the hills only a little flock watched by a boy or girl, causing the passerby to wonder how even a small family can exist upon such a tiny income. Meanwhile, the land is bereft of its animal wealth. The baas of the sheep, the bleats of the goats, the moos of the cattle, and the whinnies of the horses are seldom heard in the recesses of the huge reservation. The people dream of the days when many domestic animals grazed on their lands.

Oil and Gas on Navajo Land

I clearly remember when the first plane arrived at Shiprock in a field east of the agency. Navajos, young and old, took it in stride, expressing no terms of wonderment or fear but just a reality. Even when Curley Jim, Chief of Navajo Police, went for a ride, he landed with no words of excitement. He remarked that when the plane crossed above the top of Shiprock, he tried to locate the old nest of the winged monsters that lived on the rock long ago.[19] He said there must be large quantities of turquoise from the necklaces of the Hopis and Zunis who were victims of these terrible creatures in the past. He was greatly amused when he leaned over the side of the plane, spit, but it all flew back in his face. Other than these remarks, he had very little to say.

With that same attitude, the Navajos accepted the initial discovery of oil on the northern part of the reservation.[20] However, with the possibilities of wealth for the tribe, discussions and disputes arose as to the distribution of this potentially easy money. The Tribal Council, organized to conduct negotiations on behalf of their people's interests, was soon at loggerheads between the San Juan delegates and the Fort Defiance representatives under the leadership of Chee Dodge. The San Juan Navajos thought the Fort Defiance group assumed too much authority in regulating tribal matters. Since the oil was located in the northern part of the reservation, the Navajos from there argued that the region should have priority in any discussion of leases and the spending of the money.

In the end, good sense prevailed. The Tribal Council became more cohesive as time went on and agreed with government officials that all funds received from the sale of leases and royalties should be placed in the tribal coffers for the benefit of all. Per capita payments to the 50,000 members of the tribe would allow for little improvement. The tribal fund has since helped accomplish much good.[21] It has developed latent springs of water, and windmills have appeared on the horizon in many sections. These developed springs and wells have been a blessing all around.

The scramble for leases by white entrepreneurs provided a flurry of activity. Representatives of all the important oil companies, as well as a few wildcatters, joined in. Some of the companies hired people well acquainted with the Navajos to serve as advance agents to quietly spread the word of the great benefits they would procure from the development of oil on reservation lands. In the past the tribe had vehemently opposed any sort of prospecting in its territory, and a few miners had lost their lives for doing it in the early days. But this quiet propaganda did its work well in the oil era.

During the claims process, when a number of leases were granted, there were some big surprises. One lease, which went a-begging for a paltry $1,000 dollars, became the bonanza of the era: the great Rattlesnake Lease. Oil representatives gave no glowing reports of this dome, interest in it reached a low ebb, and the lease appeared to be the poorest prospect of all in the area. However, the Rattlesnake Lease became the sensation of the entire field, with its production running into the millions of barrels of oil. Some of the other leases for which much greater sums had been paid turned out to be duds but did develop flows of excellent water for families in those areas.

Before oil was discovered, many white men involved with the tribe felt that Uncle Sam had treated the Navajos badly by shoving them into the confines of this reservation then practically deserting them to shift for themselves. Visitors looked over the arid hills and flat, waterless expanse and shook their heads with remarks like "What a worthless stretch of country; what a shame to relegate human beings to such a life." The government had again given the Indians the "short end of the stick." Development has since brought an end to that point of view.

I recall some early impressions about this land that I had in December 1898. As I accompanied the two teams and wagons headed for Sanostee, Wilkins, Dustin, and I crossed the San Juan River at Fruitland, topped the hills, turned northwest, and followed the horse trail to a gap in the Hogback south of the San Juan River. The group next crossed Chaco Wash where it passed through the gap, then left the wash and proceeded to the southwest. Late that evening we reached Barber Spring, where we camped for the night.

We have since named this expedition the Wilkins, Dustin, and Evans safari as we hunted for a location to establish a trading post. What a country we crossed that day. There were no roads because the Navajos had few, if any, wagons at that time. We discussed their plight and how Washington had placed them on a large slice of country that was a useless piece of the earth! This region appeared to be good for only the rabbit drives by mounted, whooping braves, who formed a ring and drove their prey to a designated center. There the rabbits were crowded into a focal point and beaten with clubs. Otherwise, there was nary a dream of future natural wealth unless for scanty grazing of scattered herds of sheep, goats, and horses.

Our safari had unwittingly passed over the Hogback oil dome, later known as the Midwest, and afterwards traversed the Table Mesa dome, over which pounding hoofs and whooping Indians had passed on their hunts. This became the famous Rattlesnake Dome, or lease. The old road, first located by Olin C. Walker, which we traveled from Shiprock to Red Rock, crossed the now equally famous helium-gas lease. But as wayfarers going hither and back, we knew nothing of the oil which lay pent up in the strata beneath our feet. Likewise, we had no knowledge about the vast coal beds that lay nearby. The Great White Father had not done so badly by his Navajo wards after all, even if it had been unwittingly.

As a matter of incidence, much money has been uselessly spent, so far as Indian needs are concerned. The Navajo Bridge across the Colorado River below Lee's Ferry and the subsequent establishment of a feeder highway are the two most prominent examples. There has been, however, much good accomplished by the money derived from oil activities.

A Christmas Eve in Navajo Land

The stars shone brightly that night of December 24, 1942, on the western slope of the Chuska Mountains. This range runs 100 miles north, serving as the boundary between the northern Navajo Reservation and the rest of their territory. From Cottonwood Pass through the canyon toward the trading post at Crystal, the trees on each side of the path were visible in the brilliant starlight. Groves of aspen stood white and stark amid the spruce and pine, resembling ghosts of departed trees, while shedding an eerie beauty. Patches of snow from an earlier storm gleamed in the open spaces, adding pale colors to the images. The quiet along the lonely road in the winding valley was not broken by even a gentle breeze to rustle the evergreens.

But at the Crystal Trading Post, eighteen or twenty miles below the pass, these beauties of nature were lost in the excitement of a Christmas gathering of local Navajos. Plans for it had started the previous fall, when ladies of the Relief Society of the Church of Jesus Christ of Latter-day Saints heard of the Navajos' acute needs. The women sent out a call for

Navajos gathered for a ceremony in the Lukachukai Mountains. This alpine setting with people wrapped in blankets hints of the atmosphere during the Christmas celebration in the Chuska Mountains around this same period of time. Photo by David J. Evans.

unused clothing to assist the people feeling the effects of badly conceived government livestock reduction programs and the events of World War II. The Navajos were now in a pitiful economic state.

Late in the fall, a truck loaded with extra-large pasteboard boxes arrived at the Shiprock Trading Company, where it was unloaded. A letter preceded the clothes, directing that they be divided and delivered at posts on the reservation and distributed to needy Navajos. I conducted an inventory in order to make an equitable distribution and found everything from hosiery to shoes—most of them resoled and in fine condition—to men's, youth, and boy's clothing, women's skirts, waist dresses, coats, all used but in excellent condition.

Howela and Ruth Polacca, friends of Evans, were instrumental in helping Mormon missionaries reach the Navajo people.

Jim Collyer, trader at Crystal, reported that some members planned a Christmas-tree service for and by the Indians and that this would be a splendid time for distribution at his post. On the morning of the twenty-fourth, my son Ralph and I started for Crystal with the back part of the "chuggie" (automobile) crammed with clothes and some Christmas candy and nuts we had added.

We cleared Cottonwood in good time and reveled in the beauty of the aspens, spruce, and pines, as well as the bright red leaves of the frost-bitten oaks. Arriving at Crystal, we found preparations underway. The dozen Indian leaders and Jim had worked hard. Ruth Polacca, Ruth Moore, Mrs. Nez, Rose Roanhorse, and Josephine Salow [Siláo(policeman)] Nez were members of the local Relief Society who took charge of the distribution.

A small building, which had formerly been a schoolhouse when the post was a dude ranch, rested on the hillside above. This became the gathering place with its old school benches, spare chairs, and wooden boxes for the anticipated visitors.

Workers rolled the boxes of clothing into the room, where it was warm and comfortable. A barrel-type stove heated the building, while Guy Moore, the wood chopper, cut a large supply to keep the stove going for hours. Howela Polacca, a Hopi who had earlier left his home on Walpi Mesa to cast his lot with the Navajos, brought a beautiful six-foot spruce cut near his house several miles away. The tree sat at the front of the little school and was already partly decorated.

In the meantime, Jim had stretched a wire from his generator, powering the Christmas tree lights and the lights for the room. When finished, the tree was a sight to behold. Some of the ornaments were modern, but Navajo women and children had made many others. The clothing from the boxes was flung over the backs of the benches with many exclamations of delight from the people: "Oh my, my, how beautiful!" Most of the women could speak English, some of them fairly well, but it was natural for them to turn to their own language.

There were two or three ladies' fur coats, which had been worn a little but were still good looking. The amazing thing to me was the total lack of personal selfishness among this body of women. They knew the needs of their neighbors in the mountains, went into a huddle, and selected items for members of the different families. One of the women would say, "Now this little pair of shoes, this small pair of pants, and this nice warm coat will just fit little Lee Blackhorse. And this warm coat will be right for Red Goat's woman. Her clothes are very thin and ragged and her shawl is almost threadbare." So they went on, all afternoon, until night set in. They had lost sight of self and ministered to the needs of those among them in the true spirit of Christmas. There were a few items after this distribution for others that the women divided. But even then, there was no scramble for this and that, just an equitable division.

The spirit of Christmas had only begun. As the early evening moved toward the appointed hour to observe Christmas Eve, people from the surrounding hills and canyons came trooping into the little hall. As each person entered he or she dropped a parcel at the base of the tree. Howela Polacca had sent word earlier: "Let's all come to the Christmas Eve gathering and show our appreciation to the Relief Society for its welcomed gifts of clothing. But let us also make it a real Christmas of our own. Make presents for each other."

By the time the meeting started, a large number of packages were piled beneath the tree, and the little schoolhouse was filled to overflowing with not even standing room. Silence came when I called, through Howela, who interpreted, the assembly to order. I expressed pleasure at the number there and the good spirit which prevailed. Rhoda Lewis opened with "Silent Night, Holy Night," with the women of the Relief Society and some of the boys who had attended school joining in. Perhaps I have heard this beautiful song produced more musically, perhaps more classically, during previous Christmas festivities, but owing to the people, the spirit present, and the beautiful surroundings, it had never sounded better.

People

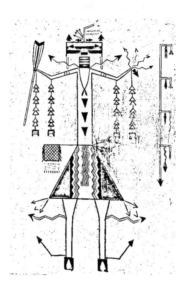

Navajos I Have Known

People were important to Will Evans. He often wrote in personal corre-spondence of the necessity of talking to interesting and significant char-acters who represented, in his mind, an era, lifestyle, event, position, or quality. As a result of these interviews and encounters, the reader is intro-duced to a variety of individuals who provide a slice of Navajo personality that spanned a hundred-year period. For the descendants of these indi-viduals, what is recorded here is even more of a treasure.

Each of the following biographical sketches gives insight into impor-tant human qualities, as well as historic times and incidents. Take, for example, the great faith of Ugly Man, who called rain from the heavens, or Many Goats, who through ceremony and prayer, located a boy lost in the mountains. What about the polygamous couple who, rather than face separation, chose death together in a lonely hogan or Dan Pete, with his infectious laugh and gift for storytelling that taught of special events dur-ing the period of Creation. His explanations of why things exist in their present form provide understanding of Navajo customs and culture. Then there were the kindness and service shown by Slim Policeman, who felt that his efforts had gone unnoticed and unrewarded. His disagreements with some of the more powerful leaders caused him anguish.

Indeed, if there is a single theme that courses through many of these biographical sketches, it is that of conflict. Whether looking at Costia-no and Blackhorse, whose sub-rosa resentment of the white community occasionally flared into open agitation, or the trying period of the Long Walk or the accusations and struggles with witchcraft, there appears to be little that was idyllic about these times. Bizhóshí and his sons engaged in armed confrontation with Evans on a number of occasions and seemed to represent the problems that many Navajos felt in adjusting to a changing lifestyle. Even Sandoval, who served as a policeman for the Shiprock Agency, had his run-ins with the white community.

Each of these personalities, however, Evans treats with respect. Even with those whom he seemed to have the greatest reason to resent he puts into a context that helps the reader understand underlying motives. No one is treated shabbily, although some were obviously not his favorites. If he appears somewhat prejudiced at times, that too was a part of life and a hallmark of his times.

Evans, by collecting these biographical sketches, has provided the reader with a wonderful opportunity to listen to a trader's thoughts on people and events of a bygone era. Not without his own problems, he gives his evaluation, which helps us understand the history of the Four Corners region. Not as an anthropologist or historian, but as a conduit for the people, he records the stories of humans living under difficult circumstances. And not as an outsider, but as a participant-observer, he tries to present their point of view. He was a man of his times, who preserved what he saw and heard.

Costiano

When establishing white communities close to Indian populations, there always arose an individual who stood out above the rest. He was the one who dealt with the white settlers in matters of interracial harmony, which was not always friendly. But whether the negotiations were peaceful or conflicting, one of the Navajos would arise to a position of prominence and be remembered long afterwards for his part in these relations.

The pioneering and settlement of San Juan County, New Mexico, provides a good example of this. Ask any old-timer to think back to those early days, and one name above all others will come to mind. His answer: "Costiano."

Costiano was, in many ways, a remarkable man. His name derives from the Spanish "Costellano," meaning a native of Castile, Spain, and was probably given to him by the Mexicans of this area. The whites picked up the Spanish name and changed the spelling but not its sound. In Navajo his name was The Talker [Adiits'a'í], which describes one of his accomplishments. He had a fair knowledge of English and Spanish, a little of Ute and Paiute, and understood more than a little of two Pueblo dialects.

Costiano in an early street scene taken in front of the Farmington blacksmith shop. Captions written on the photo identify the following (*left to right*): Jake, Lee, Brown—man with bike and man to his left are unidentified —Costiano, Dr. Wallace, and H. Perce.

He was born around the time gold was discovered in California, about 1848–49, so was a lad of about fifteen on the Long Walk to Fort Sumner and nineteen when he returned to the San Juan. He left no spoken history of any outstanding events at Fort Sumner; but some Navajo elders told me that for a young man, he was a great hunter at the Fort, tracked antelope long distances, and killed them with bow and arrow. Navajo hunters occasionally slipped away from their guards and went on several days' march to the east looking for buffalo in hostile Comanche country. The boy, Costiano, was also a good fighter when under the protection of his older Navajo companions.

He was a member of the Red Goat Clan. Like so many of his tribe, he was of mixed Pueblo and Navajo blood. His story begins at Acoma, the Sky City of the Pueblo people, whom the Spaniards had a lot of difficulty subduing. One Acoma family was more than unwilling to go along with the Catholic priests, but one padre was determined to break their will and convert them. There were two daughters in this family so their father told them to go to Navajo country and join those people so the girls could worship in the old way as they wanted.

They made ropes of yucca fiber and buckskin, and one night the family let the sisters down through a crevice in the mesa. The two girls secretly and with some hardship made their way north to the Navajos. One of them joined the people of the Zuni Clan [Náasht'ézhí dine'é] and faded into history. The other sister went to a family of the Red Running into the Water Clan [Táchii'nii] and told her story.

She said that she was willing to do anything the Navajo family wished. She would help with the work and try to be a faithful daughter, and so they took her in and raised her to womanhood. She eventually married and procured a large herd of sheep, among which there were many red goats. Costiano came from this marriage.

In the Navajo kinship system, the line of descent is traced through the mother and not the father, which is sometimes confusing to white people. Thus a child belongs to his or her mother's clan and is thereafter known by that clan name.

Costiano was small of stature, physically resembling Pueblo people. But the Navajo blood flowing in his veins made him restless and dominant over his associates. His sense of pride prompted him to slap his chest in the presence of white people and exclaim, "Me Costiano. Me big chief." He was too, judging by the way he ruled over the San Juan group of Navajos. They were naturally wary of him, and his word was law. His main power derived from his being a medicine man. Because he was skilled in his work as a singer, he was called to many parts of the reservation and was widely known.

There are many medicine men among the Navajos, some of them of great power and skill. A person of Costiano's mentality would never be satisfied by anything of little consequence, and so he became a master in the use of the Night Chant [Yé'ii Bicheii].

With the exception of the Mountain Chant, there is no other ceremony which approaches the Night Chant in importance and solemnity. Its sandpaintings illustrate some of the most important events in the religious beliefs of the Navajo. The sacred nature of these designs are linked to the story of how the Navajos received them. Tradition tells how Holy Young Man was caught up by lightning and carried onto a cloud where he was taught certain songs and sandpaintings, which the Holy Beings allowed him to bring back to the earth for the Navajos. The gods gave him blessings and promises if he was faithful to the instructions he received.

And so the Yé'ii Bicheii ceremony is considered so important and sacred that from earliest times, only a few people were initiated and could

Curley Jim, also known as Jim Curley, was named for his hair.

practice it. These were men of standing and power.

Costiano, because of his knowledge and dominating personality, assumed a position of leadership that no one dared dispute. Some of his followers included Mormon Charley, Jose Antonio, Hastiin Bik'is, old Tótsohnii, Shaky Head, who was big enough to pick little Costiano up and spank him if he dared, and others. The younger fellows of this time who survived are now gray-haired men. One of them, Curley Jim, was a relative and served as Chief of Police at Shiprock Agency.

Costiano got along fairly well with his white neighbors across the San Juan River, but a man of his temperament could not fail to run into an occasional problem. One time he tried to drive out the white settlers in the lower Waterflow valley, east of the Hogback, and also in the Meadows north of the valley. He fought long and earnestly for this strip of country but failed. He held no grudge, for he mixed freely with the whites, who welcomed him into their homes whenever he felt the urge to visit.

During the later years of his life, he lived across the river from Fruitland in the summertime and in the Westwater area during the winter. He was personally known by almost every white man from the Hogback to Farmington and Aztec. One night he appeared at a dance in the Fruitland settlement having had too much to drink. Many of the people were frightened when he walked into the dance hall, but the leaders took him out and told him to stay away until he was sober. This was perhaps his only offense against the peace of the settlement and one which the people overlooked because of his many friendly actions.

When I was a boy, I was invited into a hogan where Costiano was making the sandpaintings of the Night Chant. I sat watching his work, the large hogan packed with Navajos, who followed his every move as he directed his assistants. Costiano was perhaps the smallest man present in that group, but his personality, dignity, and knowledge were undeniable. If one of his assistants made a mistake, Costiano snapped a sharp word at

Two Grey Hills Trading Post, 1910, which Evans helped build. The photo is actually a postcard mailed to him.

him, and the correction was made, while the guilty party sat embarrassed and shamefaced but smiling.

Another experience I had with Costiano occurred while I was working at the Two Grey Hills Trading Post, which I helped build as a young stonemason and carpenter. This was a second trading post established at Little Water a year before Sanostee was built.[1] The dreadful winter of 1898, which I spent at Sanostee in three feet of snow, cut deeply into Costiano's sheep and cattle, along with the rest of the animals of his people.

On this occasion, I was traveling north of Two Grey Hills, heading for Fruitland to visit my parents and brothers and sisters. My pony belonged to Henry Noel, one of the partners at the Two Grey Hills Post. I approached the San Juan River at a ford where the river passed through a large gap in the Hogback before I crossed the river and headed east towards Fruitland about eight or nine miles away.

At the river, I drove my pony into the water at the same place we had crossed several months before when I was heading south to Two Grey Hills. The river was in flood; and when the pony went into the water, both of us went under for a moment. My horse came up swimming strongly, and I hung onto him with all my strength, remaining in the saddle. Costiano and his companions, standing in front of the old Hull and Baldwin store east of the Hogback, recognized me before I went into the river.

When they saw me go under, they came running to the north bank, where Costiano stood shouting and pointing the way to get out of the water. By that time my pony had gained his footing, but we were heading for quicksand; because of Costiano's shouts and pointing, we made it to safety.

I very much appreciated this act of friendship, and I give my old-time Navajo friend the credit for either saving my life or at least helping me avoid serious difficulty. He knew the river as no white man possibly could. He had crossed it a few hours before I did, carefully exploring his way through the high water caused by rain in the mountains. I benefited from his knowledge and experience.

Costiano passed away when he was about fifty years of age, around 1902 or 1903. He died near the old, now gone and nearly forgotten, Westwater Trading Post, six or seven miles north of Waterflow.[2] Crossing the wash, the road wound its way across the grassy flats called The Meadows, came in sight of the river valley just after entering a pass through rock-covered hills, went down the old Coal Bank hill just west of the present Zia Bar, then made its way southeastward into the Fruitland community. At this time there was no Shiprock Agency, thus there was no road westward along the river. This northern route brought the pioneers into the area where Costiano was so well known. The store operators supplied his two widows, who were with him, with a new blanket, shirt, pair of Levis, stockings, and shoes. His family had silver dollars stuffed into his pockets before burying him in the rocky, rugged hills in an unmarked grave.

The traditional beliefs of his people appealed to him strongly, and the passing of the old way of life of quiet isolation was a keen regret. But he was far too intelligent to ignore the changes he could plainly see taking place. Many of his descendants have since attended the government schools and are quick to take advantage of modern conditions. They are beginning to feel like one educated Navajo told the Tribal Council some time ago: "You old fellows don't know anything. The white man, through education, is producing the marvelous things of today. He makes trains, automobiles, airplanes, and all the wonderful machines now in use. He even makes most of the things you eat and wear, and you can't even make a small pin. We want education and educated men to look after our future and affairs." To this, Costiano would have only grimaced.

Black Horse

Black Horse was another Navajo who left a deep impression on me. He was the virtual chief of the northeastern part of the reservation, his influence

Black Horse (*left*), an important Navajo leader, as he appeared in 1905. His influence ranged from Round Rock, Arizona, to Shiprock. He was especially prominent in his attempt to prevent schools on the reservation. To his left, in a blanket, is Taiyoonihi (Squeezer). Photo by Simeon Schwemberger, used with permission of the Franciscan Fathers and the Sharlot Hall Museum, Prescott, Arizona.

being felt across the Lukachukai Mountains as well as in the Teec Nos Pos area. Black Horse belonged to the Sand-hogan Clan [Séí bee hooghanii] and lived in his camp in the Cove District near Red Rock, New Mexico. In the 1880s and through the early part of the twentieth century, Black Horse ruled his people with a firm hand. In 1900, I was still a clerk at Sanostee. I was alone at the store most of the time, so had laid down some strict rules to include no loitering after closing time.

Late one afternoon a tall, raw-boned, gray-haired Navajo rode up, accompanied by a bodyguard of four men. They dismounted in front of the hogan we had erected some distance from the store for people who traveled a long way and wished to stay overnight. The tall elder left his horse to be cared for by his companions and strode into the store. After buying feed and groceries, which he passed on to his assistants, he said he was Black Horse and wished to sleep in the store that night. I had previously heard something of the old fellow's history, but not as much as I learned later. I replied in Navajo that the hogan had been built for his use and that I could not possibly let him sleep in the store.

He insisted, saying that all the traders allowed him to stay in their stores. Our discussion ended with the angry Black Horse consigned to the common hogan. The night was not a comfortable one for me, an inexperienced youthful trader. However, the morning broke bright and pleasant as Black Horse and his companions proceeded on their way to the Navajo agency at Fort Defiance, Arizona. The next time he came through, the owner was at the store and allowed Black Horse to sleep in front of the counter on the bull pen floor but his ever-present cronies stayed in the visitor's hogan.

I had many other opportunities to study this important character in Navajo history. Black Horse was a very tall man, perhaps six feet five inches. Raw-boned, with not an ounce of surplus flesh on his massive frame, he presented an imposing figure. Character marked his stern face. He always wore his pearl-handled .44-caliber pistol strapped to his side, the holster hanging from his belt filled with a bright row of cartridges. This was more for ornament than utility. He also carried the old-time "war bag" on his left side held by a narrow leather strap over his right shoulder. Silver buttons lined the strap, each button having an inset of excellent turquoise.

He wore the typical old-time unbleached white muslin pants, slit from the knee down with the ends of his loin cloth hanging above the front and back of his belt. Knitted blue wool stockings held in place with garter straps of woven red and white wool covered his legs. These socks had no heels or toes; a band under his instep held them in place inside red buckskin Navajo moccasins with soles of rawhide. His shirt, draped over the waist of his trousers, was patterned calico and secured by a belt of large hand-designed silver conchos, laced with intricate patterns and studded with pieces of turquoise.

His hair was tied in a bob at the back of his head and secured by a woven string of hand-spun, colored woolen yarn. A piece of turquoise dangled from an end of the string, a fetish or guardian for some unseen danger. Around his head was a folded, colored cloth band tied in a knot on the left side, above the ear. This knot carried an ancient arrowhead, also a protective fetish. Above this band Black Horse wore an immense western-style black hat. His head was very large, requiring the largest hat available.

Black Horse's stern princely bearing was never mean unless angered by what he thought an injustice. He was a pure-blooded Navajo of the Black Mountain type, who were far different from the short and stocky people on the borders of the reservation who had more Pueblo blood. Black Mountain Navajo men were tall and rangy, the women large, full-breasted, and not inclined to be pudgy. This segment of the tribe could be easily identified.

To my regret I have little information about the events of Black Horse's life. He and his contemporaries have all died and told few of the things that happened in those early days. He left several sons, big stalwart fellows, whom I knew well, but they were loath to discuss their late father's activities due to a belief which forbids discussion about the dead.[3] Now [1949], two sons are still living, but they are younger and know little of his doings.

I have heard one story from the Navajos of a heated discussion Black Horse had with a pompous and tactless Indian agent from Fort Defiance, Arizona.[4] The event is said to have occurred at Round Rock, Arizona, in the early 1890s. The agent called Black Horse there to explain why he had not brought his children to the community school at Fort Defiance. Black Horse said that they were scantily clothed and had no shoes. The winter weather was very severe, and he felt it was foolish to make the long trip by wagon and horseback. The children would be in danger of perishing when traveling through that mountain country. The agent insisted that the children be brought to Fort Defiance, but Black Horse refused.

Words led to more words; tempers heated and finally Black Horse reached out, grabbed a handful of whiskers on the agent's face, jerked them out of his chin, and strode angrily from the room. He and his escort mounted their horses and headed home through the biting, cold weather and across the snow-covered mountains.

The Agent returned to Fort Defiance without the Black Horse children and minus a small handful of whiskers. I was told that these hairs were given due honors in a victory ceremony, which Black Horse's young men celebrated following the confrontation. They were sure that Black Horse had the better of the argument, and I am inclined to think they were right.

Bizhóshí

Bizhóshí was a symbol of Navajo life from the past. He clung with stubborn loyalty to the old customs and legendary lore of his people and resisted the gradual encroachment of the white man. His name, Bizhóshí, meant The Gambler; but he was also called Lightning, and I called him "Missing Link." The one outstanding thing to me about the old fellow was his Mongolian appearance. He was not from that race although his rugged features, drooping mustache, and baggy eyes resembled those of Asians.

His ancestors lived in a small world which lay within the boundaries of the La Plata, Mount Taylor, San Francisco, and Navajo mountains. The rock outcropping known as the Hogback was the backbone of this world. The Navajos of his day did not venture far beyond their region, with only an occasional trip to the Jemez and White mountains.

The Navajos believe the creation of this world began atop Huerfano Mesa, making San Juan County, New Mexico, the cradle of humanity. It was there the Holy Beings created the sun, moon, and stars, then placed them in the sky. Plant life originated when the gods buried seeds from the mesa top and a fog watered them. This is also where First Man and First Woman were created. Bizhóshí firmly believed and taught these things.

He also believed that Anglo ways were good for the white man but never for the Indian. Native logic guided him in a code of rules and customs where unseen powers seemed to have no effect upon the white man but were very potent in Navajo life. The things the white man could do with impunity brought blindness, disaster, and death to his tribesmen. For example, he taught that eating fish was harmful. He believed that blindness struck anyone who looked at one's mother-in-law. He cautioned his people that eating pork, birds, or their eggs was dangerous and that weaving sacred symbols into a rug caused blindness and death to the weaver. There was no doubt that songs performed by certain chanters caused the wind to blow or the rain to fall; and when a person met a bear on a mountain trail, a certain song or fetish turned the animal away.

Bizhóshí, a strong defender of the old way of life, as he appeared around 1930. The Navajo rug on his shoulders is for effect in this studio portrait. Photo by William Pennington.

I remarked to him that the bear would normally turn aside because of a natural fear of man, and that the wind and rain resulted from natural forces and phenomena. He shot back at me, "That may be true for the white man, but we are governed by other forces we dare not resist. We cannot take the attitude you do because we are different. You do not occupy the same place in the scheme of things. We wonder why you ignore so many of the prohibitions which are so important and which bring evils to us if we flout them."

This was Bizhóshí, the tough, wiry little old man who became ferocious when aroused. Born two decades before the American Civil War, he entered this world at a time when the tribes of Arizona and New Mexico had just begun to emerge from primitive living conditions. No doubt the old veteran had a share in the harrowing deeds of the Long Walk years when Kit Carson captured many of the Navajos and sent them to Fort Sumner on the Pecos.

The first time I really got to know Bizhóshí was in the spring after that lonely Christmas I spent during the Big Snow. When Ed Dustin and Joe Wilkins returned with supplies, we set about with renewed activity to build a more permanent Sanostee Trading Post. The construction attracted a large crowd of Navajos, the Bizhóshí clan being well represented and headed by the old man himself.

Bizhóshí told Wilkins he must stop his building at once because the Navajos did not want a store in that area. Wilkins pulled his trading permit out of his coat pocket and showed it. Bizhóshí roared that the "Wáashindoon paper" meant nothing to him and that we must stop building. Wilkins and I paid no attention to him and kept working. Ed Dustin sat on a nearby fence with a rifle across his knees. The situation became tense. Men on horseback wheeled their horses and wildly shouted to each other, while those on foot gestured and shouted at us and to each other.

Bizhóshí came alongside me and hissed a challenge in his native tongue, which I understood but had some difficulty in speaking. I can still visualize that fierce old fellow's bristling gray mustache and his outthrust jagged teeth as he grated out his words with all the venom he could muster: "If you don't stop this work, I will slit your throat like I would a sheep!" He emphasized his threat by jerking the edge of his hand across his throat. To say that I was scared is putting it mildly, but Joe quietly eased my anxiety when he said, "Let's go ahead; they won't do anything." We continued working. The shouting persisted for some time; but finally the small mob disappeared, and we had no more opposition.

We discussed Bizhóshí and his group's actions during our evening meal and concluded that perhaps some of our distant competitors had egged the old man on, seeing a reduction in their own trade. We learned later that most of the Navajos in that area wanted a post. Their nearest source of supplies was across the Lukachukai Mountains, a long tiresome trip in the best of weather and nearly impossible in the winter.

We finally agreed that even those who objected were not against having a store near their homes, so we moved forward with our post.

In his final years the old man had considerable trouble mounting and dismounting his horse when going to a sing. Still, old age did not diminish his power as a medicine man, and many older Navajos respected him for it. He was too deeply set in his culture to change. "You white men have your own laws and religion. I have mine. I do not ask you to accept mine. We have our own ways, and we do not thank you for trying to change them. We have the right to choose our way, as you do yours." He was right; his argument was constitutionally sound, but his influence made it hard for those who wanted to Americanize the Navajos in one generation.

In the early days of trading and especially in new territory with strange faces, it was hard to "keep books" on the customers. "Keeping books" meant primarily accepting and handling pawn. It was common practice for traders to receive items such as bracelets, rings, coral and shell beads, turquoise beads, silver bridles, concho belts, etc., as security for merchandise advanced, until the owners were able to redeem them. It was the general custom to advance about one-half the value of the pawned item to assure its redemption. Only the retail prices of the goods advanced were charged against the pawn with no interest added. Thus, state and federal governments were not able to charge pawnbroker fees against the traders.

At that time, the practice of using numbered brass tags for pawn had not yet come into play. We recorded names, dates, and amounts of the transaction on large metal-rimmed paper tags tied to the articles hocked. It was somewhat ill-mannered and embarrassing to ask a Navajo his name.[5] Usually he answered, "I don't know. Ask someone else." I was able to get some of the names of members of different families, but these were strange to me at first, and it was difficult to coordinate the names with the faces. To overcome this I gave people English names, sometimes based on personal appearance or an oddity of character.

I had given a name to Bizhóshí quite a while before I learned his real one. He was not hard to dub, and it did not take a stroke of the flat side of a King's sword to make it stick. When he was aroused, he was ferocious; but when relaxed he was an extraordinary little pixie-grown-to-manhood.

He wore a thin, grisly mustache, which did not hide the fact that he looked as though every other tooth in his mouth had been knocked out to make room for the others. He had an overhanging bottom lip, which seemed to lower when he became angry. His small, beady eyes underslung with pouches, wrinkled skin, and general appearance gave him an eerie look. He reminded me of pictures I had seen of primitive men, and I

Little Singer participated in the Beautiful Mountain conflict and later spent time at the federal prison in Ft. Leavenworth, Kansas.

began calling him "Missing Link." And so thenceforth he went down in Sanostee Trading Post history by that unusual name.

This designation did not end there. Missing Link had four sons, whom we called "Big Link" (eldest), "Middle Link," and "Little Link." Sandwiched somewhere in between was Little Singer (Hataałii Yazzie), a prototype of his father.

I "tangled" with two of the "Links" one summer evening. Life was going on serenely at the post, with no trouble and business good. I had established and rigidly enforced the rule that sundown was closing time, all year round. As the sun slipped behind the Lukachukai Mountains, a number of Navajos stood around in the store, finishing their trading, smoking free tobacco, and chatting. I called to the crowd, "Let's go. The sun is down." Reaching for the keys, I jumped over the counter into the bull pen. There was a gate into this area, but we kept it locked. The Navajos filed out through the door—all but one, Middle Link. He elected to stay. I put my arm around his waist and said, "Come on 'Son-in-law,' let's go."

He was a big husky fellow and started to grapple with me. Big Link stepped back into the store and tripped me while the rest of the Navajos remained outside and kept hands off. There I was, down, tussling with two of the huskiest Navajos in the valley, but Lady Luck was with me. I grabbed Middle Link by the throat and squeezed. Seeing the opportunity, I gave Big Link a belly-warming sort of drop kick, driving him back on his haunches and temporarily out of the fracas. Middle Link's clutch relaxed because of my grip on his throat, so I shook him off. Scrambling to my feet, I jumped over the counter after the loaded rifle hidden under it. The two Links undoubtedly sensed what was on my mind because when I straightened up, the bull pen was empty. As I reached the store

Bizhóshí and Little Singer sitting on wool bags outside the Sanostee Trading Post. Frank L. Noel Collection (P-166), L. Tom Perry Special Collections, Brigham Young University, Provo, Utah.

door to lock it, the Navajos mounted their horses and rode away. The brief episode over, the evening shadows lengthened, and night fell quietly.

With some trepidation I slept outdoors, my usual practice, because of the summer heat. Nothing happened. The Links did not return for about two weeks. When they did, a big grin and a hearty handshake demonstrated there were no hard feelings. From that time on, the entire Link family gave us no trouble and was always friendly in their greetings. However, the day after the excitement, I was told by Dan Pete, a Navajo worker at the store, that the Links had held a council the previous night with their friends to discuss whether they should kill or drive me off the reservation. The group decided that the Links were to blame and that I had not broken the peace or dignity of the community. They dropped the matter.

The end of the Link dynasty was tragic. The old patriarch, Missing Link, died many years ago. Not long after his death Big Link died in Sanostee Valley when the dirt roof of his hogan caved in on him while he slept. Both Middle Link and Little Link died during the flu epidemic of 1918, along with hundreds of their people. Little Singer passed on a few years ago, the image, in his old age, of his truculent father. The family has dwindled on the male side to a middle-aged son of Big Link and a younger son of Middle Link, called by the unromantic name of Johnny Cow.

Ugly Man

Ugly Man [Hastiin Chxó'í], a great chanter and rainmaker, was a person I shall never forget. One day at Two Grey Hills, this aging Navajo limped into the store and up to the counter. The gentleman helped himself to the free tobacco located in a small lard-pail cover nailed to the top of the counter by many small nails and tacks driven through it. The points stuck up through the bottom of the lid so that not all of the tobacco could be taken at once. Each morning the contents of a small cloth bag of Dukes Mixture or Bull Durham was poured into this container. Most Navajos carried their own cigarette "papers," made from the innermost husk of a carefully selected ear of corn. The husks were cut and carried like a deck of cards in a vest or shirt pocket.

Ugly Man had difficulty rolling his cigarette. His hands were gnarled, fingers bent, arms misshapen, with poor control of all of them. His scarred face was wrinkled, and he had a hole in one cheek. He finally finished rolling his cigarette, and I gave him a light. A thin line of smoke came through the hole in his cheek, eddied around his head, then drifted toward the ceiling. He paid no attention, continuing to smoke and puff. "Well," I said to myself, "here's another story."

Obviously, this man's life had been hard. He was born on the Tohatchi Flats before the Mexican War when his tribe was small, but by now he was about sixty-two years old. He spent his boyhood in extremely primitive living conditions and often remarked that in his younger days it was either feast or famine. The pointed sticks his people used for arrows were not much insurance against hunger; even the ancient Anasazi Basketmakers had better weapons. If he had been fortunate to bring down a deer or antelope, the family and neighbors held a continuous feast until the meat was consumed. Then rabbits or prairie dogs sufficed for future meals until a skilled hunter brought down another buck. When he was a boy, his clothing was either hand-woven or made from animal skins. I often wondered why these people did not pick up ancient arrowheads, which were so plentiful in their land. Perhaps they could have fared better hunting and in battle had they used these razor-sharp points.

Ugly Man was in Kit Carson's great Navajo roundup and went with his people to the Pecos River, New Mexico, between 1864 and 1868. While there, he made a lone raid away from Fort Sumner and returned with several souvenirs: his first scalp—a lock of Mexican hair—as well as the dead man's clothing and long butcher knife in a rawhide sheath. He was esteemed for having great courage by taking the dead man's belongings. Navajos are averse to being near the deceased and wearing their clothing. To do this was a blatant temptation of fate. The raid also netted him a good horse and some fresh beef, a rare commodity. He showed the harvested scalp lock to a select few but adorned his medicine bag with it until the day he died, when it, with other precious items, were consigned to a secret place.

Several years after the return from the Pecos River country, an event occurred which brought renown to the future rainmaker. Ugly Man's father was a well-known medicine man who understood the Fire Dance ritual, known as the Mountain Chant. Late in November the father was conducting a Fire Dance on the mountain northwest of where the Tohatchi Indian School now stands. Ugly Man and a friend left their hogan on Tohatchi Flat and walked up the canyon toward the ceremony. As they passed a clump of scrub oak, a bear rose up on its hind legs and with little warning attacked Ugly Man, who was in the lead. The youth drew his butcher knife from its sheath and defended himself the best he could, while his companion ran quickly to the Fire Dance and told of the attack.

A rescue party raced down the trail and, to their surprise, found the bear lying dead. Ugly Man also appeared dead, but members of the rescue party discovered he was alive though unconscious and terribly mangled. He had stabbed the bear in a vital spot, but it had survived long enough to bite and maul him. The men made a litter of oak poles and blankets to carry the young man to a hogan near the Fire Dance. Crude but careful nursing and the prayers of the singer brought the sorely wounded boy back to life.

But what bad shape he was in! His arms were twisted and bent, one leg healed crookedly, and his features became a crude caricature of the once handsome, bronze face. The bear had bitten him about the head, and the razor sharp fangs had pierced the boy's cheek. This wound healed around the edges, but the open tear never closed.

From this frightfully crippled condition he was given the name of Ugly Man. But his scary appearance did not keep him from fame and fortune. By killing the bear he became well-known, and his appearance reminded others of his valor. Their faith in his powers increased, and as time passed, he became the most famous singer in that part of the reservation.

Rainmaking was his special gift, but in years of severe drought his people became impatient with him. "Wait, wait," he would say, "the time is not yet. I must sing to the God of the Waters a little longer. I

shall make the medicine of the Waterway ceremony, and soon you will
see the thunderclouds rise above our mountains. And when Black Wind,
God of the Storm, shoots his arrows of lightning, thunder will roll along
the hills and valleys, and soon rain will fall. The parched corn and dry
soil will quench their thirst." Ugly Man was a student of nature and its
moods. When the time was ripe and the gods appeared willing, he began
his rain chant and one more success was added to his list of achieve-
ments.

One time he was called to a certain place to sing for rain. The people asked him if he really could bring them the sorely needed moisture.
"Well, if I don't," he said, "you can kill me." This seemed fair enough. He
unrolled his medicine kit and took out his charms and medicine rattle,
then selected a young girl to be blindfolded in a very peculiar manner.
He took a piece of the flank of a freshly butchered goat, tied this over her
eyes, and told her to go forward, feeling her way. When she came to a
certain plant, which she would recognize by the texture of its foliage, she
was to pluck some of it and bring it back to camp.

Ugly Man began his chant about the time she started, and his song
guided her back to the camp. The rainmaker took a portion of the plant
from the girl, chopped it with a hand-chipped spear point, placed it in
water, drank a portion of it, and sprinkled the rest to the four directions.
Next, he blew small quantities of sacred yellow corn pollen in the same directions, speaking a prayer as the pollen flecks floated toward the ground.
He then settled down, with eyes closed, medicine rattle in right hand,
beating the rhythm of the chant for rain. After hours of singing he announced a shower would come in two days; sure enough, it rained.

Ugly Man performed other rituals and miracles. He could make the
yucca plant sprout, grow, and bloom in a short time, and feathers dance
on the edge of a board in the Fire Dance. These acts of magic are almost
extinct now, but in his day the rainmaker was the foremost exponent of
the art. Here is a chant for rain.

Navajo Rain Chant

Far as man can see
Comes the rain,
Comes the rain with me.

From the Rain Mountain
Rain Mountain far away
Comes the rain,
Comes the rain with me.

Amid the lightning,
Amid the lightning zigzag
Amid the lightning flashing,
Comes the rain,
Comes the rain with me.

Amid the swallows
Amid the swallows blue
Chirping glad together
Comes the rain,
Comes the rain with me.

Through the pollen
Through the pollen blest,
All in pollen hidden
Comes the rain,
Comes the rain with me.

Far as man can see
Comes the rain,
Comes the rain with me.

Ugly Man was a kind fellow, but his speech was odd because of his facial disfigurement. Those who knew him delighted in imitating his peculiar speech, but everyone holds his memory in awe. Other powerful singers were Bizhóshí, who had many followers and led by the undisputed force of his personality. Long after his physical decline, he laboriously packed his leather medicine bag with sacred items, mounted his favorite pony, and rode long distances to heal a patient. There was also Many Goats [Tł'ízí Łání] of the Toadlena district, Smelly Water [Hastiin Tó Niłchxon] of Sanostee, and Tall Singer [Hataałii Nez] of Teec Nos Pos, all of whom were outstanding figures of their time. I think of Ugly Man and these other chanters as men of great faith. The Navajos still rely daily upon medicine men, but modern singers seem to not have the great faith of their elders, although they carry on the traditional practices. Their contemporaries cling to the belief that they still retain ancient powers.

Of course, there were other prominent figures who were not medicine men. Manuelito, called by some the last war chief of the Navajo, was very powerful in his area, until his last years, which were marred by too much alcohol. Black Horse was highly esteemed in the northern area, retaining his dignity and power until his death. Today [1937], there seems to be no outstanding personality with the power to lead his people.

Perhaps the future will produce one who will govern his people with wisdom and prudence. The reservation is made up of a number of areas separated by geographic obstacles and educational limitations. Sectionalism is rampant, particularly between the northern and southern peoples. It will take a keen mind and level head to guide the future of the Navajo through the crises which loom in the future.

Fat One and Son of Fat One

Neesk'áhí, The Fat One, was a medicine man and warrior of note, having killed Utes, Mexicans, Comanches, and at least one white person. He was a tall, fleshy, powerful man and a remarkable example of physical fitness. In later years, as he increased in girth, he obtained the name "The Fat One." He was well known in the Fort Defiance area and was the leader of the band of Navajos who tried to hide between the rocky walls at the head of Canyon de Chelly when Kit Carson rounded up the Navajos and forced them to Fort Sumner, New Mexico.

For twenty years after his return from the Pecos country, Fat One presided as head man of his community and practiced as a medicine man. He not only understood the Shootingway, which he inherited from his father, but also the Enemyway, the Evilway, and the Chiricahua Windway.[6] This gave him a wide range of activities. In 1888 he died, revered by his nation.

His son, Neesk'áhí Biye', then a youth of about eighteen, had learned medicine lore ever since early boyhood and, despite his youth, was ready to carry on his father's practice. When I knew him, he was a peaceable man of about sixty, a gentleman in his humble way, and had never shed blood, though he came from a long line of warriors.

His gift as a medicine man was not confined to that of merely administering to the needs of the sick. He combined a fair knowledge of the medicinal properties of natural herbs with that of the manipulation of certain fetishes; he was at once physician, high priest, and historian. A medicine man of his caliber was thoroughly trained in traditional lore. He learned the story of creation, the work of the gods before the advent of man, the bringing forth of animals, the medicine songs, and the art of sandpainting.

Like other medicine men, Fat One's Son had to first establish his reputation by performing an outstanding feat of healing before calls for his

Fat Medicine Man, or Fat One (Neesk'áhí) and his youngest son, Frank Allen, in 1920.

assistance increased. He did this by bringing back to health a young woman who had been poisoned by witchcraft.

At that time Navajos believed implicitly in witches, who might be a medicine man gone wrong. A favorite method of bewitching a person is to project a poison dart, through supernatural means, over a distance. Anyone unfortunate enough to be disliked by a witch is liable to become the victim of a long sickness and painfully prolonged or short but dreadful death unless some medicine man counteracts the powerful spell.

Not long ago, a medicine man returned from federal prison at Leavenworth after serving time for a revolting crime. The Navajos of his area were glad to see him go, not so much because of his crime, but because he had acquired a reputation as a dart-thrower and witch, of whom they were supremely afraid.

Fat One's Son had to treat a young Navajo woman who was sick and near death. She remained very ill even though her people had tried every medicine man around, using all their resources to no avail. No chanter seemed to have the right "medicine." When one man's songs failed, they tried another, but there was no relief. Her family had heard of young Fat One's Son and sent for him as a last resort.

Upon arriving, he diagnosed the problem as some witch having shot a poisoned dart, perhaps from some other part of the reservation. Fat One's Son lost no time in putting his sacred objects from his medicine bundle to work, some of which he had obtained from his father. Before the Fat One died, he taught his son how to break the spell of this kind of witchcraft. For twenty-four hours the son sang these songs, drew a sandpainting, placed standing feathers, scattered corn pollen to the four corners of the earth, and administered sacred cornmeal.

The song which Fat One's Son sang was a peace song, a chant of the mountains. The ordinary medicine song is not only an appeal to the gods but also contains a note of defiance to the powers of the destroyer. This peace song was of a different nature, pleading for peace on behalf of the suffering girl. He sang and worked, stopping at intervals to eat. The notes of the chant drowned out the moans of the sufferer. The rough pole-and-dirt medicine lodge became a temple of faith, and before his mind's eye were the Holy Beings from the past. His faith buoyed his spirit, and he asked that an eagle be killed and brought to him. Early the next evening, the peace song ended, and it was time for the manipulation of his fetishes.

He called for the slain eagle and opened its intestines with the sharp edge of a large obsidian arrow point. Taking out the gall sack, he poured the contents into a gourd drinking cup, mixed it with a little water, sprinkled pollen and a pinch of sacred corn meal, and gave the bitter potion to the patient to drink.

Results came soon. The woman vomited violently, spewing a large quantity of black slimy stuff, which Fat One's Son identified as the poison the witch had injected into the woman's body. She immediately felt better, and by morning was able to get around. She was now a living example of the power of the Fat One's Son, whose fame spread over the northwestern part of the reservation. Whenever a case of sickness baffled a local medicine man, the people sent for him. He had remarkable success, losing only a few of his patients. Desire for further success grew into using different songs.

As he aged and his fame became secure, his influence increased among the people. His word and advice was peaceful and well accepted. His wife and daughters were expert weavers, who specialized in producing copies of various sandpaintings which he created. To other Navajos, copying these sacred designs carried serious risks, as the actual paintings in sand must be erased before the sun sets to avoid dire consequences. If the sacred symbols were made permanent, as in a blanket, the weaver could become blind and suffer an early and painful death. These women were taking terrible chances, and other Navajos looked with awe upon them and feared for their welfare.

One day Fat One's Son went to the trader and said, "During the period of many sleeps my women have made Yé'ii Bicheii and sandpainting blankets to sell to you. My wife's health is not good. She is failing. I fear the efforts of the sacred designs, and I will hold a sing for her benefit. Will you help me?"

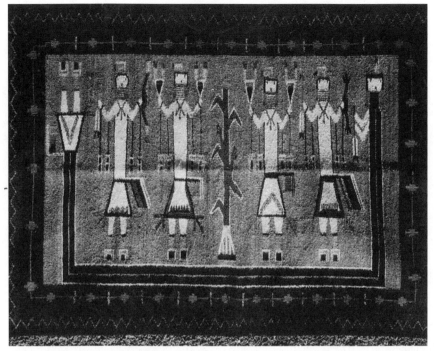

This Yé'ii rug shows Holy Beings associated with the Yé'ii Bicheii ceremony held in the winter. These figures are sacred to the Navajos and elicited a sharp controversy when traders encouraged their depiction on rugs.

The trader said he would and gave a liberal supply of coffee, sugar, flour, and baking powder to the old man. The food helped him feed the company which is always present at a sing.

Fat One's Son did not use his peace song this time. Instead, he sent for a famous medicine man from across the mountains, and for three days they sang, used their sacred objects, and created sandpaintings. Relatives provided a continuous feast for visitors. They consumed a fat horse, several goats, and two or three sheep, along with the flour, coffee, and sugar donated by the trader. At the end of three days, Fat One's Son said, "It is finished. The medicine has worked. My women will be protected. The medicine tells me more. Many times we will sleep before the heavens will pour refreshing rains upon the earth. In our sandpaintings we have used an earthen bowl in the center, filled with water, to represent the fountainhead of all waters which the Holy Beings have given us. The sand picture of the various forms of plant life taking root at this central fountain is symbolic of the dependence of all life upon the great source of water. I have noticed, my children, that the water placed in the little earthen bowl quickly dries up and disappears. This is the sign of a long spell of dry weather. If the water had remained in the bowl, rains would shortly come and refresh the earth."

The old man's prophecy proved true. One of the driest years followed, and many of the springs disappeared. But the sing proved beneficial to Fat One's Son's wife. She continued to weave sandpainting blankets; and she, her daughters, and daughters-in-law were preserved from evil by his powerful medicine. When he dies, there will be no more medicine blankets from the looms of his women; their protection and shield will be gone.

Now [1928], the years rest lightly on him. He is still vigorously practicing his medicine, his fame undimmed, and his dignity impresses those who know him. He is one of the very few of the last great historians of his tribe. Because of this, he has given me the legends and traditions of the elders in detail. His people will be indebted to Fat One's Son for this valuable contribution.

Faith, an Episode

During the summer of 1923, a mysterious rumor spread among the Navajos on the northeastern part of the reservation. They believed a flood was about to occur and that the people should flee to the mountains for safety.[7] For days many of the People trekked from the lowlands to the summits and slopes of the Lukachukai Mountains. Day and night this steady stream of men, women, and children, with their sheep, goats, horses, cattle, teams, wagons, and ever-present dogs, crossed the bridge over the San Juan River at Shiprock.

In a few days the lowlands were deserted. By common consent the people declared a holiday spent feasting, dancing, and horse racing on the mountainside. They also held a ceremony to pray for their deliverance from the impending doom. At one campsite on the mountain was Shawl [Dáábalí] and his family from Sanostee Valley. Some white people had named him "Chinaman" because of his facial characteristics which suggested a connection.

One day some people held a ceremony in a canyon some distance from the Chinaman's camp. He sent his six-year-old son along with his older brother to round up enough horses to travel to the ceremony. The boys walked a long distance from camp before seeing a herd of horses across a clearing in the forest; however, they belonged to another family. By this time the smaller boy was getting tired. Older brother decided to go alone and find the horses, so told the boy to go back. He instructed him to keep to the trail they had followed which would lead him directly to camp.

Hastiin Dáábalí, sometimes called "Chinaman," lived in the Shiprock area and survived the flu epidemic of 1918. Photo by William Pennington.

After they parted, it began to rain; and in the storm that followed, the younger boy became confused, roaming in the opposite direction. His brother found the horses and returned early in the evening only to discover that his little brother was missing. A party of Navajos hunted until dark but could find no trace of the lad. For the next two days, parties scoured the canyons and hillsides, searching everywhere, but found nothing, not even a footprint.

The Walker family, children of Jesse Hunter Walker and Loretta Hunt, at a family reunion at Will Walker's store, Kirtland, 1929. *Left to right:* Frank, Elzie, Ella, Will, John, Loretta Hunt Walker, Sarah Walker Evans. Photo by Richard P. Evans.

Now, the Navajos were aroused, and since supplies were getting low, they sent word to the Walker family, traders at Sanostee, telling them of the predicament. The Navajos respected the Walker brothers, John L. and the older W. J. called "Will" [brother of Sarah Walker Evans]. John was known over a large portion of the northeastern part of the reservation as the Man Who Moves Slowly [Hastiin Házhó'ógo Nahanání]. He was quiet and unassuming, with never a harsh word of criticism for anyone.

John immediately saddled his horse, loaded a pack animal with supplies, and traveled to the mountains to join the hunt, leaving Will to man the post. For two more days the search continued without success. The Navajos became discouraged and were about to give up; but John urged them on, reminding them that no clothing or bones had been found and that the boy might still be alive. He promised to send for more supplies if necessary, insisting the search continue.

During the hunt, medicine men worked day and night singing and praying. The songs were prayers of hope and beseeched the Holy Beings to assist in the search. The hunters would search for a few hours, come in and feast for a time, help in the sing, then return to look for the lost boy. By this time the old one-eyed medicine man, Many Goats [Tł'ízí Łáni], had come from Toadlena. The Navajos had great faith in his powers, and although the situation seemed desperate, the feasting and singing had given them determination to press on.

While the sessions of prayer and ceremony continued, the Navajos did not permit John to witness the actual ritual, but they anxiously sought his advice and followed it. On the fifth night, the concentration of the prayer became intense. People packed the medicine lodge, and the devotion of the medicine men reached a new height. The songs and prayers of the previous four days and nights finally concluded about midnight. There was silence for a time, and then the one-eyed one spoke, "In the morning we shall have word of the boy. I want you to have your horses saddled and ready to leave at the first sign of day. If you will go to the place I indicate, you will find him. A Holy Being has shown it to me in a vision. That is all. I have spoken." A low hum of voices followed the awed silence as all departed to get a little rest before daylight.

In the morning, just as the search party prepared to mount their horses, a voice called from a nearby elevation. It was an uncle of the lost boy declaring he had found fresh tracks. With a shout the party started off in the direction of the voice and the place designated by the old medicine man. On the far side of a clearing there stood a fallen pine tree. The party halted some distance away, and the leader blew a medicine man's whistle. The boy's head appeared above the log. The leader dismounted, told the party to remain in place, advanced a few steps, and again blew the medicine whistle. The boy stood up, the upper part of his body showing above the log. The man started talking to him and slowly advanced, talking to him until he reached the log.

The little fellow seemed rather dazed and somewhat wild but allowed the leader of the party to take him, ending the six-day hunt. The lad was in good physical condition. The Navajos at first believed the bears had fed and cared for him, but later told the story the boy had shared. He said that an old woman, one who had been dead for several years, came and looked after him and fed him.

When the party reached camp, they placed the boy in a mud bath and, after washing and clothing him, made corn meal gruel. They allowed him to suck a little of the gruel off his mother's finger, feeding him by degrees until he was able to take stronger nourishment. Today [1938], he is a healthy twenty-one-year-old man.

Tragedies in Navajo Land

Another young man I remember very well was Theodore; I think Mrs. [Mary] Eldridge gave him that name.[8] He was quiet, unassuming, never raised his voice, and had a smile for everyone he met. His features and build revealed Pueblo descent somewhere along the line. His youthful appearance belied his age.

Theodore had a small farm on a flat near the foothills of the mountains below Toadlena, west of Bennett Peak, right on the trail from Two Grey Hills to Sanostee. In front of his well-made, two-room log house were two beautiful maple trees growing in the yard. I often stopped and visited with him while I traveled this trail, resting from the saddle at his halfway place between the two posts. He had access to a fairly good stream of water coming from the foothills, where he raised fine crops of Indian corn, squash, and melons. He owned another hogan on the mountainside above Toadlena, where he spent part of his summer.

Theodore also had two wives and, by doing so, ran afoul of Uncle Sam's regulations. His first wife was nearly his age, but his second one was young. One day a Navajo policeman from the Shiprock Agency rode to Theodore's place on the mountain. The officer told him that he had been sent to bring him and the younger wife, Theodore's favorite, to appear before the agent at Shiprock. "All right," replied Theodore, "you go back, and I'll saddle our horses and start right away." He kept only part of that promise. The two saddled up and rode down the trail which led off the mountain. Each carried a quilt and woolen blanket tied in a roll to the back of the saddle, while Theodore carried his rifle in a scabbard.

Somewhere along the trail they came to a vacant hogan, tied the horses to a hitching pole, went inside, and made a bed of quilts and blankets on the floor. Theodore unsaddled the horses, shot each one in the head, and carefully laid the saddles alongside the animals where they lay. His young wife lay down on one side of the bed where Theodore shot her. Then he lay down beside her and shot himself. This was a fearsome thing to do; but love remained to the end, and he had cheated the white man's law. Death had not separated him from his beloved young wife, as they sat astride their spirit horses, wending their way northward to the home of their ancestors' spirits.

Another love tragedy occurred north of the Sanostee post, just below one of the sandstone ledges which gives the valley its name. I knew the people involved but was not at Sanostee when it happened. My brothers-in-law, John and Will Walker, were running the store; and their mother, Loretta, was spending time with them, having left her home in Kirtland for a visit.

A young Navajo, called Chatterer [Ha'dilch'alí] because of his incessant talk, desired the hand of Hastiin Washburn's [a Navajo] daughter. Chatterer was already married but wanted this young woman as another wife. I knew the Washburn family well and remember Mrs. Washburn's hearty laugh. Occasionally she would come into the store and bawl me out, scowling heavily and pretending that I had done something wrong. Then she would burst into a hearty laugh, pointing her finger as if to say "See what a donkey I made out of you!"

The Washburns' daughter was very good-looking, as was the rest of the family, but I do not know if she had any romantic feelings for Chatterer. Her mother resented his attention toward her daughter, disliked his hanging around, and detested his incessant gabbing. He came frequently to the house, trying to get the girl to elope with him, but Mrs. Washburn always drove him away and told him not to return.

One day Chatterer buckled on his pearl-handled .44-caliber pistol and rode to the Washburn home. He again pled for the girl to go with him and again her mother ordered him to get out. Instead of leaving, he pulled the gun and shot Mrs. Washburn. Her daughter dashed out the door past Chatterer and ran across the field; he stepped outside and shot at her. She fell and lay still. Thinking he had killed her, he ran to a deep ditch, dropped into it, and followed it for a short distance, where he shot and killed himself. Here was the score: his wife and two or three children were at home, fatherless; Mrs. Washburn was dead; but her daughter was only superficially wounded. A short stay at Shiprock Hospital put her back on her feet.

The grieving Washburns left Mrs. Washburn where she fell, according to Navajo custom, boarded the doors and windows of the hogan, and deserted it, never to return. The house still stands, and Mrs. Washburn lies undisturbed inside her home.

Sandoval

"Old Man Sandoval!"—that is what his son, Hans Aspaas, called him.[9] It is uncertain where Sandoval received this Spanish name, but when his friends referred to him by it, it always came out sounding like "Sen-da-wahl." In Navajo, he was called Tall Grass (Tłóh Nineezígíí). He once told me that he was of Hopi and Navajo blood. In stature he was short and stocky. Neither he nor any of his immediate family is big, husky, and raw-boned, which is the old Navajo appearance.

Sandoval was born about ten years before the Long Walk and incarceration of the Navajos at Fort Sumner in 1864. As a boy he used his bow and arrow to bring home small game to add to the family's food supply. Rabbits were a necessity for food because antelope and deer were steadily disappearing due to continual hunting pressure. His family was fortunate to occasionally bag an animal of this size. After

Sandoval, of Hopi-Navajo descent, was an excellent farmer, silversmith, policeman, and judge at the Shiprock Agency. Courtesy of Museum of Northern Arizona Photo Archives, Earle R. Forrest Images (MS 43, Neg. #497).

hunters brought in large game, all hands set about jerking meat when the weather was favorable for drying. During winter months, the people took advantage of natural refrigeration. Wanton waste of any part of their scanty meat supply was strictly prohibited.

At this time there were not the countless sheep and goats that there were in later years. Hunting small animals became not just a diversion but a stark necessity. Even so, there were unavoidable periods of want and distress. Older people now look back on these hard times with feelings of thankfulness for the sheep and other animals which eventually came to them in abundance. Youngsters who hear these stories of famine and deprivation accept them with the callousness of youth who have not survived the trials.

In the spring, Navajos planted small patches of corn where the ground was flooded by the diversion of water from small streams or in sandy areas where rainwater was retained after flowing down from the hills. By breaking the top crust, soil moisture was carefully preserved, preventing rapid evaporation by holding water around the roots of each plant. Plows were unknown in Sandoval's youth; Navajo farmers planted squash, corn, and other vegetables in moist holes dug with a pointed stick.

This was part of the primitive life Sandoval had before he went on the trek with his mother and siblings to Fort Sumner. They all went on foot, with only the doubtful luxury of one horse to carry the few crude possessions they owned. The scorching stretches of trail blistered and burned them, and they had little means of carrying water, adding to their suffering. Throats dried and lips cracked. The route of march took them across the Continental Divide, on the eastern side of which they encountered extensive lava beds that cut their moccasins and feet to ribbons. Family members spread out on either side of the trail to hunt for game, but earlier marchers had depleted the animals, while the troops that escorted them had limited rations to dole out.

Sandoval provided a vivid description of the trek. When the marchers reached a point on the trail where they could see the Pecos Valley and the camps at the fort ahead, the young man felt as though he could not take another step. They pressed wearily on, some of them taxed physically and emotionally to the point of death. The prospect of internment saddened and depressed others.

The following four years were trying. Common ailments were rampant; contagion spread and took its grisly toll. Abject poverty set in, while government officials attempted to feed and clothe eight thousand prisoners from distant bases of supply with wagon trains that were too slow. The captives chafed miserably under these restraints.

In 1868 the tribal headmen signed a treaty that freed the people to make their way back to their beloved homeland as best they could. Sandoval had somehow grown to be a husky lad of fourteen. When the people returned, they found the supply of game more to their liking; the four-year respite from heavy hunting had brought a large increase. Sandoval and his family headed for their old homeland on the plains and ravines just south of the Mesa Verde plateaus. As they crossed the San Juan River, he spotted, stalked, and killed an antelope on the future site of the Shiprock Agency. Large game at this point was indispensable for food and clothing, since there were not yet traders in this area.

Life settled down again to the old way. Early in 1870, pioneer wagons began crossing Navajo land. Small towns sprang up in the San Juan Basin; cattle drovers and sheepherders arrived; and the Navajos began to acquire a few animals. They learned how to care for them; Sandoval was among those who caught on quickly. The art of weaving became prominent now that wool was available. Sandoval encouraged his daughters to become skilled weavers and good homemakers. As the ever-venturesome whites pushed across the borders of Navajo land, products of Indian art and skill became commercialized, allowing the Navajos to take advantage of goods becoming available in increasing variety.

The old years of grinding, abject want began to fade. The products of the loom became known far and wide. Lambs and wool in their proper season were sold or traded for food, clothing, and building materials to make existence more pleasant. A Navajo family could return home with a feeling of safety for the future, as the flocks and herds added a reassurance the old days never promised.

During this period of change, Sandoval reached young adulthood, his voice being frequently heard in the councils of his people. He was considerably younger than Bizhóshí, Black Horse, Costiano, and other forceful leaders, yet they always gave his views consideration. If he had become a singer, he might have gone far, but he left that profession to others of the tribe. The chase, however, intrigued him, and he was often found on the game trails of the hills and plains.

He did not resist the encroachments of the white race as bitterly as others. He plainly saw that with growth of inter-racial commerce the old days of feast then famine—with more famine than feast—would dwindle into the forgotten past. More than once he told me that the coming of the white man was no calamity; no times of oppressive hunger had come since the Anglos' arrival even though all the game had been killed off.

Old Man Sandoval was a shrewd dealer, but a kindly leader of his clan. He managed to establish rapport with the whites, although there were times when settlers of the San Juan had to deal with his strong character. In those days there was no Shiprock Agency, and no agent to arbitrate differences between the two races. The reservation headquarters was at Fort Defiance, Arizona, and travel by horse or wagon was three or more days away.

He had the reputation of knowing much, possibly more than other Navajos, of the lore and legends of the tribe. He could relate stories handed down by his ancestors and give a good description of the beliefs of the cliff dwellers. Through his Hopi lineage he was undoubtedly a partial heir of that interesting race of people. However, as a young man, Sandoval seemed to have little belief in the old gods and sacred possessions of his people. Sometime in his later years, Bishop James B. Ashcroft, an old friend, baptized him into the Christian faith as a "Mormon." Many of his sons continued to practice the traditional Navajo religion, but one of them told me that Sandoval said that if they decided these teachings and ceremonies were not for them, they should join the Christian faith at once. I have known this family for a good number of years, and they are fine people. Sandoval's wife and children have been honorable in their dealings and deserve kind words.

The winter of 1898–1899 was the most severe in the memory of the pioneers of northwestern New Mexico. Ice on the San Juan River was twelve to fifteen inches thick, and the river was completely frozen over. Wagon drivers, who usually had to struggle up the steep grades of Harper and La Plata hills, took advantage of the thick ice and hauled their heavy loads of coal over the ice, entering the river at the old Woolery place and getting back on the road at the Troy King ranch. This was the first winter highway on the river that is recorded.

The February following that great snow, Sandoval was involved in an incident with my father, Thomas Evans, and my brother, John. They had started on a trip to Bluff City, driving a team and wagon. They entered the reservation at the Hogback and reached the future site of Shiprock Agency early the first evening. A grove of cottonwoods and a few deserted hogans stood there at the time. John led the horses to the river for water, but because the ice was still very thick, only a small opening of water showed here and there. Somehow one of the horses got away and plunged into the river. After a fearful struggle, the animal reached the opposite bank.

Next morning Sandoval and another Navajo appeared at the camp. He admitted having the horse but protested that he could not return it because of the dangerous condition of the ice, even though he and his companion had just crossed it. Sandoval was plainly stalling. A nice fat horse was a great temptation in a land of winter-starved ponies, and the white travelers realized that they had no way of recovering the horse except at great risk from the ice and a struggle with the Navajos. Giving up, John rode the other horse back to Jewett Valley east of the Hogback, where he obtained another one. They returned, bringing the wagon back to Fruitland.

On the way home they visited with a great missionary to the early Navajos, Mary Eldredge whose mission buildings still stand east of Hogback Ridge. She was doing a splendid work there and earned the love and respect of the Navajos. John and Thomas told Mrs. Eldredge how they had lost their horse. Her only comment was "That old rascal; I know him" and immediately sent a young runner to retrieve the animal. In due time the runner returned, bringing Sandoval and two or three other Navajos. The proper owner received his horse back after the payment of a small fee for "expenses." Sandoval explained the delay of two or three days in returning the animal because it had strayed and was difficult to find.

In 1903, the government began the Shiprock Agency on the San Juan River. Sandoval's efforts during this early period bore fruit. He had worked long and hard for the establishment of a school and agency at Shiprock and, in doing so, met much opposition from the traditionalists. One diehard opponent earned a lifelong title because he opposed the education of Navajos in white men's schools; his name became "No School" [Dooda'Ólta']; I never did learn what his real name was.

Since Sandoval developed a certain spirit of cooperation with the government authorities, the agent eventually appointed him to serve on the Navajo police force. He fearlessly assisted in bringing some of the worst offenders of the tribe to justice. Sandoval was the one in charge of the police who arrested Little Singer's wives, creating the incident which flared into the Beautiful Mountain Uprising. Later, he became chief of Navajo police, not only gaining the confidence of his superiors by his courage and strict attention to duty, but also because of his great influence among his people as an outstanding leader.

Once Anglo entrepreneurs discovered oil a few miles southwest of Shiprock and the tribe formed a council, the latter began to handle business and the issue of oil leases. A division among the people arose, becoming particularly intense between the delegates from the San Juan and the Fort Defiance area. The younger council men from the San Juan, who were former students or "school boys," felt that the older statesmen from Fort Defiance, under the leadership of Chee Dodge, seemed more concerned about their own area than that of the tribe. Those from San Juan believed that since the oil came from their region, the others should not dictate what ought to be done with it. Whatever the merits of that position, Sandoval saw fit to cast his lot with the Fort Defiance delegates because of his long friendship with Chee Dodge. This cost him a loss of prestige with his people; in fact, he almost became a pariah among them. With the passage of time, this animosity spent itself, and his people again accepted him as a leader.

Several of Sandoval's sons and daughters and a number of grandchildren, even to the third and fourth generation, have completed schooling. To the extent that these younger ones are aware of his work, they appreciate the old man's efforts.

One of his sons, Hans Aspaas, was a product of the Indian School at Carlisle, Pennsylvania. He was a member of the football team that included the illustrious Jim Thorpe. Hans was a dependable worker, a genial friend, and worked for the Indian Irrigation Project at Shiprock. He cut his finger on rusty wire, the resulting infection quickly turning into blood poisoning. Without the antibiotics which we so casually use today, Hans's life ebbed away in agony. Had he lived, he would have had an excellent chance of becoming a leader of his people.

Sandoval Begay was Sandoval's eldest son. He worked as a laborer during the summer for a number of years at Mesa Verde National Park. Many Navajos worked there, repairing older buildings, erecting other structures, and doing general maintenance work. Each evening they performed native dances for the benefit of tourists. They danced excerpts from the Nightway and became immensely popular at the nightly campfire talks. The dancers always passed the hat for contributions after each performance. The team of dancers divided the proceeds equally, providing a tidy sum for each man at the end of the season.

Sandoval's son, Hans Sandoval Aspaas, attended Ft. Lewis College in Colorado, the Carlisle Institute in Pennsylvania, and later worked at the Shiprock Agency. He died from blood poisoning after scratching his hand on a rusty wire. Courtesy of Museum of Northern Arizona Photo Archives, Earle R. Forrest Images (MS 43, Neg. #502).

Sandoval Begay worked as a foreman during the daytime and was an active participant in the dancing at night. His wife and children remained home during the summer, so before departing for Mesa Verde, he would come to the trading post and ask us to let his wife have anything she needed while he was away. His honesty knew no equal, so we always agreed to take care of her. Every fall he paid his account and always had plenty left over to see the family through the winter.

One autumn day Sandoval's son came to the trading post and requested the amount of his wife's bill for the summer. She was never a foolish shopper, asking only for essentials. We checked the books; her account came to seventy dollars for clothing and groceries over a three-month period. We told him the amount, but he did not inquire into her purchases; he trusted us and we trusted him. From under his jacket he pulled a bandanna handkerchief stuffed with coins. His only request was that he open it in private. That granted, he untied the corners of the handkerchief and rolled out an assortment of small change—dimes, nickels, quarters, pennies. He had more than enough to pay his bill, with a considerable roll left over when he retied the corners of the bundle.

Old Man Sandoval lived beyond the allotted three score and ten years before he died. He was buried in his beloved hills, in a grave hidden away from others. According to the old Navajo way, his saddle was "killed" by mutilation so that its spirit would be ready for use on his spirit horse, which had been killed nearby. Sandoval rode on to whatever awaited him in his next life.

Slim Policeman

Slim Policeman [Siláo Ałts'ózí] was directly connected with the captivity at Fort Sumner and the Long Walk, but he remembers nothing about it except what he has been told by his parents. He has since become widely known on the northern Navajo Reservation as a member of the police force, appointed by Superintendent William T. Shelton, founder of the Shiprock Agency.

At the beginning of the Navajo captivity at Fort Sumner, Slim Policeman's father and mother were a young married couple. His father was already a medicine man of growing fame and ability and was known as Tall Water's Edge People [Tábąąhá Nez], the name indicating his clan and also his stature. The family belonged to the Bitter Water [Tó dích'íi'nii] Clan.[10] The name of this clan originated during the wanderings of a large family, some of whose members camped near a small lake. The water tasted bitter, and so that branch of the family became known as People of the Bitter Water. Another part of the family moved near the same lake. When they tasted the water, they pronounced it salty and became the Salt Water [Tó dík'ǫzhí] Clan. Another group came in and scooped all the water out of the hole thinking that it would return as sweet water. Because of this they were named Tó Káán [Scooped Water]. Yet another group came in, scooped out the water, and smeared themselves with the mud, receiving the clan name of the Mud People [Hashtł'ishnii]. A final party camped on a grassy spot near the spring and their descendants are called the Meadow people [Haltsooí Dine'é]. Thus, five clans became established, all belonging to the same family group. After they separated, each formulated rules concerning their social status with the others. Members from these clans do not intermarry and, according to tribal customs, are required to marry into unrelated clans.

Slim Policeman's parents told him he was around a year old when his parents and the other Navajos left on the long march back to their

Slim Policeman was a year old when the Navajos returned from four years' internment at Fort Sumner on the Pecos River. He later served in the Shiprock Agency police force.

homeland. He was a very sick child and was not expected to survive the arduous journey. As the tiresome trip extended from days into weeks and months, the health of the boy deteriorated even more. The military furnished the parents with a wagon to carry the ailing infant; but the jolting was too severe, so his parents took turns carrying him in their arms, walking behind the vehicle.

By the time they reached Fort Defiance, the youngster was exhausted. Following two or three days' rest, the parents started traveling again. At the noon camp on the first day, the baby seemed to be in the last stages of life. The father and mother discussed the problem, deciding if they should wrap the child in a bag and leave him, as is the custom when an individual is near death. If they took him and he passed away, the father, in preparing the body for burial, would become unclean and four precious days would have to be spent in a cleansing ceremony.

They decided to leave the infant since they believed he was going to die anyway and they had quite a distance to go before reaching the San Juan country. Perhaps it would be best to leave the baby to expire and hurry on to the home country which they were so anxious to see once more. It has long been a Navajo custom to carry a dying person outdoors when death seems imminent. Before resuming their journey, however, the parents wrapped the little one in some old bags. The mother kissed him tenderly and laid him on a pile of ferns under a tree. They both kneeled beside him, the father offering a simple prayer before starting off. They could hear the feeble cries of the child, their only offspring, as they slowly moved down the trail. The mother could not stand it, asking that the weary team be stopped. Tearfully she ran back, took the infant in her arms, and resumed taking turns with her husband carrying their baby until they camped for the evening.

There was another party just ahead of them, and they saw its smoke. Encouraged, they traveled farther and camped with the others. These Navajos had killed some game and invited the struggling couple to a feast that night. The grandfather of the child was in this group and berated the young couple for attempting to leave the child where it would become the prey of wild animals. He told them that the infant still had a chance of becoming a man, perhaps a useful one at that. He then took charge of the baby, holding a ceremony of songs and prayers throughout the night.

Since the grandfather was a medicine man, he sent the father out to gather some cactus apples and remove their thorns. He squeezed the juice of the fruit into a small clay pot which he placed on the ground in the center of a group of medicine men. They sang a long four-part chant over the clay pot. When the singing ceased, amid intense silence, the grandfather dipped his finger into the cactus juice several times and encouraged the ailing infant to suck it off. This unique way of administering the medicine took effect. Shortly the dysentery which had been bothering the child began to ease its grip, and in a day or two, the child began recovering.

The delighted parents gave a wayside thanksgiving ceremony, the father in his role as budding medicine man, taking the lead. They then continued happily on their wearisome journey. Thus the child, which had been left by the roadside to die, finally recovered and became known as Tall Edge of the Water People's Son and later as Slim Policeman.

Although the Navajos never heralded Slim Policeman as a great man, he worked quietly and efficiently for the good of his people. He has an unassuming character, which, over the past thirty or forty years, has led and guided their destiny. He did not always work in harmony with the leaders of his day because he felt that they were not always on the side of peace and good will. He was contemporary with such men as Black Horse, Bizhóshí, Ugly Man, Yellow Horse, Costiano, and a few others in the tribal limelight. Of course, Black Horse and Bizhóshí were generally against white men. They never became reconciled to the dominance of "Wááshindoon." Ugly Man, Yellow Horse, and Costiano were more conciliatory. Slim Policeman was somewhat younger than these men and did not have the influence they did. He gained it later.

Since he grew to manhood, Slim Policeman has lived near Shiprock. He knows every foot of the territory surrounding it and has roamed it by walking, on horseback, and in a wagon. He looks upon this pile of stone that rears its pinnacles into the sky with feelings both of awe and safety. Awe because of the legendary stories connected with it and a sense of security because the rock seems to stand guard over the destinies of the Navajos.

He told me one time of an exciting experience he had, which occurred quite awhile before the establishment of the school at Shiprock. Three white men wanted to start a trading post at Beclabito [Bitł ááhbi-to']. A crowd of Navajos were there, including Black Horse and his followers. They objected very strenuously to the establishment of a post, laying most of the blame for the coming of the white men on Slim Policeman. They censured him very strongly for being a friend to these foreigners, taunting him and asking him how much money he had received. Black Horse became extremely angry and threatened to kill him and the white men if they did not leave.

For some time Slim Policeman said nothing. The Indians kept circling, waving guns, sticks, or anything they could find to threaten him. Finally he got angry and said, "All right, go ahead. Kill us if you want. All you men look for is trouble and if you are not careful you'll get plenty of it. Why don't you go ahead and kill us? Then you will have more trouble than you can take care of. We are not afraid to die. Go ahead."

This seemed to have a sobering effect upon the mob; soon they scattered and were gone. The white men left too and never came back, thinking they did not want to start a store at that point; they had had enough. Later, however, they decided they would like to open one at the mouth of Red Wash, where it empties into the San Juan River. When they talked to Slim Policeman about it, he told them he would help. They held a meeting with the Navajos, who decided they did not want a post there either; the men abandoned the idea.

Slim Policeman has also been an advocate of schools for Navajo children. While still a comparatively young man, he became interested in them for young Navajos who lived along the San Juan River. At that time the only schools available were the ones at Fort Defiance, Arizona, and Fort Lewis, situated just a few miles south of Hesperus, Colorado. Fort Lewis had originally been built as a U.S. Army post and was in direct line of wagon and pony-rider communication with Fort Defiance.[11] The old road ran through the Meadows, north of Fruitland, into the Jewett Valley, the old ford of the San Juan River being near the Taylor ranch in the valley. It then followed up the eastern foot of the Hogback, across country to the Two Grey Hills section, over Cottonwood Pass, down the canyon to the present site of Crystal, past Red Lake, and on to Fort Defiance.

After the pacification of the Indians, Fort Lewis was abandoned by the War Department and turned over to the Indian office, which established a school there. The children did not like the location, and many ran away, some of the deserters suffering much on the trek home in the dead of winter. The altitude and extreme winters caused a heavy death toll, principally from pneumonia. For that reason the Navajos loathed sending their children there. Slim Policeman had often accompanied representatives from Fort Lewis when they were gathering children for the school; he was also one of the first to recognize the necessity of providing education nearer home, where the winters were not as rigorous.

One day the Indians of the Shiprock area held a meeting. Slim Policeman spoke, saying, "Why have we not shown more interest in those things as time has gone on? Our children are running away from Fort Lewis. Some of them get lost; some of them lose a hand or foot from freezing. We should take more individual interest and get together and work for a school in our home country. Two of us can go to Fort Lewis to talk to the superintendent. We will ask him to write a letter to Washington, requesting a school in the Shiprock country, where our children will not run away and suffer from the cold weather as they do now. Let's do something."

The group delegated him and Yellow Horse to go to Fort Lewis and talk with Superintendent Willam M. Peterson.[12] They had a long talk with him; in fact, they had several meetings and told him of the difficulties, how they would like to have a school on the river where the climate was milder, and why the children would not suffer so much. They insisted that the children would be more content and less apt to run away. Mr. Peterson listened, treated them very kindly, promised he would write to the Indian Office in Washington, and asked them to come back in thirty days for an answer.

Slim Policeman and Yellow Horse returned on horseback to Fort Lewis a month later. There they received a favorable answer and promise to build a school on the San Juan River at Shiprock. However, owing to much red tape, they had to wait two years before a realization of their dream occurred. At the end of that time, Superintendent William T. Shelton came to the river and picked out the site of the present school. It was another two years before the builders had a structure that allowed students to attend.

Once the organization of the new school was complete, Superintendent Shelton called Slim Policeman into his office and had a long talk with him. He told him that he had realized for some time the good work his Navajo friend had done for the establishment of the school and his people. Shelton said he wanted to continue these good efforts by asking him to become a member of the Navajo police force. Slim Policeman accepted the invitation and soon received his name. He served for eight years, retiring when he felt that he had fulfilled his duty and that the job should go to a younger man.

Years later, in speaking of his efforts towards the betterment of the Indians, he displayed a note of disappointment. He said, "I feel that I have done all I could towards helping my people, but no one says anything about it. I am hurt because of this neglect, that I have not received due credit for my work. People ignore these things, and my heart is sore and hurts because of it." Perhaps some day he will receive credit for what he has done.

Slim Policeman was never a well-known person like his father but did do a little singing for a number of years. At one time he owned considerable flocks and herds and was independently wealthy according to Navajo standards. But drought and the government's reduction of livestock brought him almost to the point of penury. He has had three wives and sired many children. The last wife was a young woman whom he had taken as a child with a promise to the dying mother that he would raise and take good care of her. When she was about eighteen years old, they were married and one child, a boy, resulted from this union.

This December-May marriage, however, did not last. Disregarding the home ties, the younger woman eloped with a fellow nearer her own age. This has since become a source of regret to Slim Policeman. He feels that he was poorly paid for his care and nurture of the young woman. Now the old fellow lives practically alone, except for the occasional visit of his young son, who is attending school at Shiprock. He raises a little crop on his farm allotment and sings once in a while to earn a few dollars; he manages to eke out a scant existence. He is always in attendance at ceremonies, whether he takes an active part or not, and is devout in his allegiance to traditional beliefs and the old school of Navajo thought.

His life nearly spans the years of warfare in the 1860s to the present time of peace and expansion. He has been a peacemaker, not because he was born and reared in times of peace, but because he wasn't. But he had the good judgment to realize that opposition to superior numbers is futile, that the best course is one of cooperation and of taking advantage of the advent of the white man.

When asked what he thought of conditions now compared to the olden times, he said, "There is no use talking about it. Our younger people may not know, but I know we are better off even though we have lost some of our old liberty. None of us would care to go back to the primitive conditions which existed when I was a boy. There is really no argument, no other way to look at it. I have worked long and hard to better the condition of my people. I have done all I could to help them realize the advantages of schools and what the white people, through the government, have tried to teach us. I ask no reward but that my people will give me credit for doing these things. I am sorry that they have forgotten them, and my heart is sad because of it."

In closing, I want to relate an episode in which I told a fib to Slim Policeman and never corrected it. Perhaps his descendants who read this can tell him the truth. While I helped record information for the Navajo Census of 1930, I made this mistake. One morning it happened that the first home I visited was that of Slim Policeman. After I filled the family list with the information I wanted, we sat around talking about other things. I had learned from reading the newspapers of an impending eclipse of the sun that morning. Knowing the belief of the Navajos that Owl sometimes foretold things, I looked at Slim Policeman and told him that an owl told me something the night before. He stared at me and asked, "What did the owl tell you?" I pointed to the sky where the sun would be around 10:00 a.m., made a loop of my thumb and forefinger, designating that spot, and answered, "The owl told me that when the sun reached that spot this morning, a great black something would gradually cover the sun. Then it would gradually leave."

I had just barely made the announcement when the eclipse began. Slim Policeman looked at me in astonishment. He hung his head in thought, muttering words of wonderment, and shook his head. What a wonderful thing it was that the owl should tell me of a thing that actually happened.[13] I did not let on that I was only joking, nor have I told him since. I hope this will serve as an apology for my perfidy.

A Dedicated Medicine Man

I contracted to build a school for the children in the Tohatchi area and hired many Navajos to work with me. I knew the Navajos to be hard workers and almost immune to the hot sun and backbreaking labor. The erection of the stone base for this school would be no small job, the foundation being nine feet high at the eastern end and two feet at the western end. Built on a low spur of hills which splayed out from the Chuska Mountains, the building's stone foundation and walls were joined with plain mud mortar. Cement just cost too much.

We made adobes on the bank of Tohatchi Wash near a low bench of rich soil, just below the school grounds. It was easy to turn the water from the wash onto this soil to soak it in preparation for making large heavy adobe bricks, 6 x 12 x 4 inches. We used primitive methods, not even having a homemade horse-driven mill, found in settlements along the river. So we dug a pit about ten or twelve feet in diameter, created an earthen dike to hold the water around the edges, shoveled soil back into the pit, and let the mud soak all night. Next morning the saturated earth was ready for mixing. My Navajo helpers rolled up their trousers, stepped into the pit with bare feet, and tramped through the mud, kneading it to make it ready for forming.

We moved the molding table close to the pit where a worker shoveled mud onto the table. The wooden molds formed two adobes. I did the shaping, slapping the doughy mud into "loaves," which were placed in the mold. Then two workers removed it from the table to the drying yard, where the bricks were pushed out onto the ground to dry and cure. The men were also required to quickly sand the molds on the return trip to the table.

The trick to dumping adobes out of the mold is to avoid disturbing the fragile ones already drying in the yard. The bricks had to be turned so they would dry uniformly and not develop cracks; so we turned thousands of adobes, and while not at all difficult, it is backbreaking work since one has to remain bent over for a long time.

Every afternoon we dug earth and shoveled it into the pit in sufficient quantity for the next day's run. I calculated how many adobes we could make in a day and knew how much earth was required to soak overnight. Sometimes we had more than two thousand of these large bricks in the drying yard.

A good adobe molder was supposed to be able to fill a form with a couple of armfuls of mud then rake off the surplus with both thumbs quickly enough to keep the two bearers busy. We found plenty to do during the day's work. Not only did we mold and move the bricks, but there was the digging and filling of our mud pit, trampling and mixing the mud, turning the drying adobes, and stacking the dried ones to make room in the yard.

The workers seemed to enjoy trampling and mixing the mud. They often relieved their efforts by singing songs that provided a rhythm. It was music to my ears. The plaintive tone, the melodies sung in a minor key, have never ceased to charm me. One of the songs which appealed to me is called the Zilth Neyani [Dził łíʼíní], or Prayer to the Mountains. The words "beauty" and "beautiful" are repeated many times in this song-prayer and in other Navajo chants. I found the simple repetition irresistible. It goes as follows:

Reared within the Mountains!
Lord of the Mountains!
Young Man!
Chieftain!
I have made your sacrifice.
I have prepared a smoke for you.
My feet restore for me.
My legs restore for me.
My body restore for me.
My mind restore for me.
My voice restore for me.
Restore all for me in beauty.
Make beautiful all that is behind me.
Make beautiful all that is before me.
Make beautiful my words.
It is done in beauty.
It is done in beauty.
It is done in beauty.
It is done in beauty.

Those were busy days, with a lot of hard work. My helpers and I lived life to the fullest in the sun all day long and the great open spaces of Navajo land.

While I labored at Tohatchi, I learned something of the ways of medicine men. A short distance from the school, in a crudely built stone hut surrounded by a few peach trees lived Fast Running Horses [Biłíį Néiltihígíí]. He and his wife had a son about six or seven years old. One warm afternoon the lad was playing among the rocks, having a good time near the hogan. After a while he came crying into his home, complaining of a severe pain in his stomach. He cried himself to sleep but awoke a short time later, still complaining of great pain and asking for a medicine man.

The boy's father had already sent for a famed singer, Tall Man [Hastiin Nez]. Like other Navajos of that time, Fast Running Horses became alarmed at the first sign of illness. He felt that some unknown but dread evil might have caused the boy's illness. He depended heavily upon the singers to discover the evil influence and break it.

Tall Man arrived several hours later with his medicine bag, a large deerskin pouch which held a number of smaller bags containing several herbs he had collected and dried from the mountain. Finding that the boy was in great pain, the singer mixed one of the herbs with water and gave it to him to drink.

It was a very bitter plant used in a cleansing rite in which both males and females sit in a close circle inside the walls of a hogan. A bright fire burns in a central pit and all present are stripped to the waist. A small mound of sand is placed before each person; a hole is made in the sand in a conical cup shape. The singer gives each person a portion of the bitter herb mixed in water to drink. Each man and woman joins in a song led by the singer, but they soon lose interest in the chant as they vomit profusely into the heaps of sand. The belief is that by sitting in front of a warm fire and sweating, plus drinking the bitter herb, the body is cleansed inside and out, but the atmosphere is almost unbearable.

Soon after Fast Running Horses's little boy drank his potion, he vomited freely and often, but nothing came up but what he had eaten before the attack of pain. Tall Man said he was sure no one had shot a poisoned dart at the boy. So he began an all-night chant, stopping occasionally to arrange his eagle feathers in the sand floor before him and to roll a cigarette. He was laboring to have something come to his mind to aid him in finding the source of the lad's trouble.

Nothing came. At daybreak the boy still suffered. In reply to the singer's questions, the lad said he was running over the rocks, tripped, and fell on a jagged stone which had hurt his stomach. The singer replied that he did not believe this was really the cause of the trouble and began to question the mother, asking if something had happened to her even before the birth of the child, which might have had a bewitching effect. She could not think of anything at first, then recalled that while she was still carrying the child, she was riding along a trail one day when her horse shied and almost threw her off. Looking about she discovered the cause; a large green lizard had darted across the path and startled her sleepy mount.

That was it! The mother felt certain the lizard was the cause of the boy's illness! Tall Man now knew what to do. Mister Bull [Hastiin Dóola], who was a neighbor, had been assisting the singer. Mister Bull was sent out to a certain place to dig some roots about the thickness of a man's thumb and about three times as long. I knew at once what the roots were: Canaigre or Sour Dock [*Rumex hymenosepalus*]; I had known of it since I first came to the San Juan as a boy.

Bull came in with four of the roots. The singer selected the largest and began peeling off the dark covering. Believing that no white man's steel should touch this object, he used a serrated obsidian knife to shape the root into the form of a lizard. Then he powdered the sticky effigy with some of the abundant green shale he found on a hillside, and the object began to look something like a green lizard. In its head he placed two pieces of turquoise for eyes and a row of red beads for a mouth. Along its belly he put a row of white shell. The lizard was now re-created and ready for the ceremony.

The singer sat cross-legged facing east. He placed the carved root in front of him and sprinkled it with sacred corn pollen after surrounding it with four eagle feathers. He placed one feather to the north, the others in the remaining cardinal directions. Then Mister Bull and Tall Man sang a chant, asking for relief of the boy's suffering.

Next, the singer spoke prayers, which the boy's mother repeated word for word. Under the direction of the singer, Mister Bull took the lizard into the hills, where he broke it in two and buried it under the rocks. They repeated the ritual four times. While completing the fourth lizard, the little boy fell asleep, but when he awakened hours later, he was free of pain. Tall Man's prayer was answered. Breaking the lizard effigies in two had broken the spell and its influence, which had been dormant for a number of years. The lizard would never trouble the family again. This is how Tall Man explained the situation to me, and I respect his belief. I tried much later to find one of the broken images but failed. It is just as well that I did not. What right had I to pry into the sanctity of his belief?

Dan Pete

Among the many Navajo friends who first come to mind is Dan Pete, who worked with me during the early years at Sanostee. He was a jolly little fellow, singing as he chopped firewood, carried domestic water from the wash, sacked wool, baled pelts, and carded blankets.[14] Always ready to joke or tell a tall tale, he followed either with a hearty laugh. Pete laughed much and talked more. He also enjoyed smoking and was happy to keep his own tobacco in his pouch and use the free tobacco doled out in the lard-pail lid on the counters while working at the store.

Dan Pete was an apprentice medicine man. He attended all the sings and ceremonies in the district and was usually a leader in the group of singers at these occasions. He possessed a good knowledge of his people's myths and traditions, though his reputation as a practicing medicine man was purely local, simply because he was overshadowed by such stalwarts as Bizhóshí, Ugly Man [Hastiin Chxó'í], Many Goats [Tł'ízí Łáni], Be Dugal Chun [Mustache Smeller], and others. But as a sandpainting artist, he was expert. There were very few sandpaintings within his home area that did not bear his deft touch. From his experience in sandpainting, he learned the stories and personalities he depicted, giving added fervor to his work.

Dan Pete freighted supplies to Shiprock from Gallup for Evans. To dress up for this photo, taken in 1940, he borrowed "something to make me look better." He is wearing beads, a silver concho belt, and a bowguard or k'eet'oh lent to him from the Shiprock Trading Company. He died in 1945.

It was a treat to watch Pete deftly trace the lines of colored sand comprising these religious pictures. He rarely made an error; but when he did, he quickly corrected it, muttered a wisecrack, then ended with an infectious laugh. He maintained a ceaseless chatter as he worked, punctuated occasionally by a hearty guffaw.

Pete dressed as a traditional Navajo of his time. His hair was tied in a bun, his trousers were made of unbleached muslin with slit legs, he wore a loose shirt of printed calico, and a homemade vest, which he rarely removed. In its many pockets he carried matches and other valuables. He also wore the traditional Navajo "war bag," a stiff leather pouch about four by six inches with a wide flap over the front panel that sported a large silver concho. The shoulder strap, decorated with handmade silver-domed buttons, was worn over his left shoulder, holding the bag about waist high.

This pouch contained a cloth sack of Bull Durham smoking tobacco, a number of corn-shuck cigarette wrappers, and sometimes a pack of commercial cigarette papers. There was also a pair of tweezers made of a strip of tomato can, bent into the proper shape for Pete to pull his scanty facial hair. He and his friends spent many an idle hour sitting or reclining, swapping stories, and plucking their sparse beards with these tin tweezers. If they had no tweezers, they used natural ones: the thumbnail and the nail of the third finger. They were effective, feeling for a whisker, locating it, gripping and then pulling it.

Contrary to popular belief, Navajo men are not beardless. While their facial hairs are not generally heavy, they are obliged to keep them under control by plucking. Whiskers on the chin can be pulled with little pain, but hairs on the upper lip are another thing. I have watched Pete many times, crooning some sort of squaw dance song, come to a sudden stop and grimace with pain when his tweezers pulled a hair on his upper lip, then resume singing as his fingertips searched for another whisker.

Pete would go along "shaving," while some acquaintance told a story, grunting at the end of a phrase as if to say, "Interesting, very interesting, go ahead with your story, I'm with you." He kept himself well groomed in this manner without using a mirror, although he carried a small round one in his vest pocket.

My friends also spent much time in seeking out and destroying lice. Men, women, and children took turns in "reading" heads for vermin. Lice and bedbugs were quite prevalent in those early days and were a source of great torment to the people. I watched one woman squat in the shade of the store with a little girl beside her. She was searching the girl's head carefully, parting her hair a lock at a time. When she found a louse, she picked it out and cracked it between her teeth, while the little girl watched several bugs in the upturned lid of a baking powder can. The Navajos took readily to combs with their fine metal teeth [that] we sold in the store.

One day I watched Hastiin Tapaha "reading his shirt," which he did in an unusual way while he sat in a clump of tall greasewood. He removed his shirt, turned it inside out, and bit each seam as he moved it from one end to the other. His teeth were even and flattened from years of eating gritty cornbread, ground from flour prepared with a stone mano and metate. This technique with his firm, flat teeth must have been very effective in smashing the bugs that lived in the folds of his shirt. Pete had another way of destroying lice. He crushed them between his thumbnails, and the stains of these "executions" remained on his nails for days at a time. Fortunately, the government conducted an extermination program for vermin many years ago so that now the Navajos and their homes are clean and remarkably free of body vermin.

One morning, business was at a low ebb. I had filled a few empty shelves and used the old-fashioned turkey-feather duster here and there, but the work was pretty well done. Pete had his morning chores finished and was sitting cross-legged on the bull pen floor, smoking a cigarette rolled from Duke's Mixture tobacco set out for patrons. He was alternating his attention between his cigarette and the sand box spittoon, while crooning some Navajo melody. I listened to him for some time, pleased with his excellent, high counter-tenor voice and his plaintive melody in a minor key. Finally I interrupted him, saying, "Pete, why are you singing and what is the song about?" He smiled, showing a perfect set of white teeth.

"Yesterday (Sunday)," he said, "I went up on top of the mountain. I was very pleased with everything there. The lakes and little ponds are full of water, the springs are running fast, and there is good grass for the sheep and cattle. Many berries and acorns will fatten Grandfather Bear this fall so he will not bother our flocks. We will have a good summer. My song was one of thanksgiving to the Great Ones of long ago, for their good ways toward us. It is a blessing to them for what they have done."

I replied, "I am glad you express yourself that way. I am happy to know just how your people feel about those things. You remember that some time ago you told me that you would tell me the story of how the Shiprock moved. It is a quiet morning; nobody is around to bother us; why not tell it to me now?" Pete took a long pull on his cigarette and squinted through the smoke as it rose in front of his face. "All right, I will tell it."

"You know, my friend, that the People call Shiprock the 'Rock with Wings On (or By) It [Tse'bit'a'í].' Long ago, the old men tell us, this rock stood in the land of the Utes near Sleeping Ute Mountain. It was so high that jealousy arose between it and Ute Peak, especially when clouds settled low on each of them with just their tips showing above. They quarreled about which one reached higher into the sky.

"Sometimes Child of the Wind (usually referring to a whirlwind) would swirl along the foot of one of the rivals and whisper, 'You are the highest!' Begochidi (one of the capricious gods) whispered to the other, 'Not so, you are the higher!'[15] These two seemed to take delight in stirring one mountain against the other.

"Year after year this went on as the snow of winter followed the warmth of summer. They never reached an agreement. One day, a great leader named Nah O Kanh Gahilgiih [Nihookáá' Yígałígíí] was visiting Talking God [Hashch'eelti'i], another of the great ones, on the north bank of the San Juan River. Talking God is the god of the Mountain Chant and is sometimes called Dawn Boy.

"The river was in a great flood. The water reached all the way to the hills which line the San Juan Valley. Nah O Kanh wished very much to cross the river and return to his people but could not get across. Talking God said, 'I'll tell you how to get across. Climb on Shiprock, and we will make it fly you over the water.'

"Nah O Kanh looked up at that high rock and shook his head in doubt, but he had to cross the river, so he climbed up the pinnacle. Then something happened. There was a great rumbling and roaring. The ground shook. The great rock twisted itself loose from its resting place and flew into the air. Its two great wings and tail, that are still there for everybody to see, churned the air into a mighty wind that bent the tree tops to the ground. Great gusts swept over the cottonwoods and bent them like a hard wind blows the grass on the flats.

"The rock flew higher and higher and Nah O Kanh squeezed himself into a small crevice to get away from the strong wind. High above the place where it now rests, it flew like a great eagle searching for prey. Four times it circled and then descended, swiftly at first and then more slowly as it neared the ground; finally it settled gently with its wings outstretched where it still stands.

"My friend," said Pete, after a pause for a few puffs on his cigarette, "that is the end of the story. Some day I will tell you another about that great rock which says it was a boat a long time ago. And I will also tell you why Navajos do not eat fish and also how there came to be Utes." This was the first of many stories I heard from Pete and a number of other Navajo friends.

Pete's other story about Shiprock explains how it once stood in a land far across the Wide Water (ocean). The people who lived there also

This aerial view of the Shiprock formation shows the three major dikes fanning out from the main volcanic plug. These dikes are what Dan Pete described as the wings and tail that allowed the formation to fly to its present location. Photo by David J. Evans.

recognized the rock as a landmark, just as others do today, and held it in great veneration. For a long time the People were at peace with their neighbors and prosperous and happy. But evil times fell upon them, and they were beset by enemies and threatened by extinction. In desperation they climbed into the cracks and crevices of the rock and began to call upon it for protection, but having no idea how that protection would come.

Then the rock began to move, continuing when it reached the shores of the Wide Water. It came across the water until it arrived at its far shore. It did not finally stop until it reached Navajo country where it came to rest. The People climbed down from the rock then spread throughout the land.

In 1911, just ten years after Pete told me the story of the flying rock, the San Juan River had a great flood, which extended literally from hill to hill. But Shiprock did not move. Evidently Nah O Kanh had no further business on the north side of the river.

One day, a short time after Pete had related his story of how Shiprock flew, I walked out of the store into the warm sunshine to get a breath of fresh air. I found him seated in the shade around the corner, "reading his shirt" and conducting slaughter with his thumbnails. He was deeply absorbed in his task, and each time his nails caught a hapless louse, his face puckered to suggest that his work was serious and strenuous and his enemy difficult to exterminate.

As I watched him, I could not help smiling. Suddenly he became aware of my presence, looked up, and chortled that infectious laugh. "My friend, you white people do not seem to have to do this. Maybe they do not like you as much as they do us."

I replied, "Well, Pete, we do all we can to keep ourselves clean. We bathe and keep our clothing washed all the time, so we do not have these pests to pass on to each other. We get them only when they crawl off you fellows in the summertime. Someone may lean on the counter, and a pest will drop off his shirt or blanket, then it crawls across and gets on my sleeve as I lean on the opposite side of the counter. But the cootie usually lets me know he is on my neck or shoulder right away, and washing in boiling water usually takes care of him. Cleanliness is the secret of louse-less-ness."

"Yes," said Pete, "that's true; but we have little water and little chance to keep clean." He added, "My friend, I have been wondering if lice have smaller lice on them. It seems as though one thing lives upon another. After all, we are only lice upon the body of Mother Earth [Nahasdzáán]. Would it not be a terrible thing if old Mother Earth had a big pair of thumb-nails to crush us poor humans between!" Pete laughed uproariously and thought that a great joke. Then I reminded him of his promise to tell me the story of the Utes' origin. He replied that he would, but first he would tell me the story of Mother Earth and her husband, the Sky [Yá'aash].

Earth and Sky are pictured in sandpaintings as two very corpulent figures with heads, arms, and legs. They stand side by side with the right wrist of one crossing the left wrist of the other. This denotes the relationship of the two in a spirit of friendship and interdependence. The large rounded body of Mother Earth has a white background and in her navel small colored rings in the four sacred colors representing the fountains of waters.

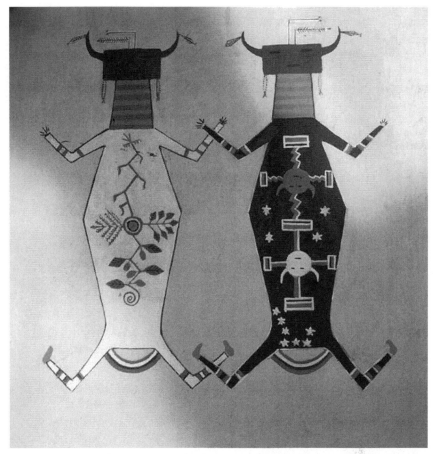

Will Evans painted this mural of Mother Earth (Nahasdzáán) and Father Sky (Yá'aash), under Fat Man's supervision. Approximately sixty other depictions of various sandpaintings by Evans remain in the L. Tom Perry Special Collections, Harold B. Lee Library, Brigham Young University, Provo, Utah. Photo by Richard P. Evans.

Radiating from these rings to the cardinal points of the compass are four sacred plants. In one direction the corn plant spreads its broad leaves, its roots close to the fountains. In another direction, the roots and stalks of the bean plant; in another the roots and tendrils of the squash plant follow their course; and finally, there is the native mountain tobacco plant smoked in ceremonials.

Father Sky is drawn in a background of black. In his body is shown the Sun, Moon, Big Dipper, North Star, and others. The rainbow spans the space between his feet and is also shown between the feet of Earth. Earth and Sky are as man and wife. In the past, during the passage of many seasons, their relations were cordial; only occasionally would a minor spat arise, just as among people, but these were not serious, being quickly settled.

Then a real crisis arose. Pete did not know the nature of it, but said that Earth became very angry and told Sky she would have no more to do with him. He begged and pleaded and tried to make peace, but Earth turned a deaf ear to his words so firmly that he shrugged his shoulders and in their language said, "All right, if that's the way you wish it, we shall see what we shall see."

After a while, Mother Earth noticed that Father Sky was sending no rain to her, which was unpleasant but not yet serious. But as the plants began to suffer and the trees dried, their leaves dropped. Herbs and brush drooped to the ground, and the grass turned yellow and seemed to be dying. Now Mother Earth became alarmed and realized that she must do something and quickly. She began to make advances toward the Sky and finally got him to listen. She poured out her soul to him, explaining how she was sorry and would be more sensible in the future; she had learned her lesson. Then Father Sky spoke: "All right; I will take your hand again, and we shall be good to each other."

After this reconciliation gentle rains fell upon the earth, vegetation restored to life, and nature was happy. The pair have been firm friends ever since. Sometimes Father Sky forgets to rain upon the earth, but this is by mistake; sooner or later he gets around to it, and she smiles up at him as only Mother Earth can.

Pete's story of the origin of the Utes is a simple one but gives insight into the attitude of the Navajos towards them. Though they live within bordering reservations, they have been enemies for a good many years and have not intermarried very much. There are many stories of the early days when well-armed Utes raided the Navajos, who had mostly primitive bows and arrows. They were no match against Ute rifles.

The Southern Utes seem to be rapidly dwindling. They number only in the hundreds, where the Navajos have grown into many thousand. Pete said that the Ute language was not extensive when compared to the Navajo, which seems to grow to cover each new situation.

He began, "Long ago there lived a man with a wife and daughter.[16] The girl developed into a beautiful but lonesome young woman. The parents worried about her because there were no young men in that part of the country, and her mother was particularly anxious for her to marry a worthy young man and have a home of her own.

"One day her father told her mother he was going away for awhile. If any worthy young man should come to visit them, she was to let him take his daughter. Later the father returned, but the girl was still single. Soon the father became ill; but before he died, he asked his wife and daughter not to bury him in the rocks as was customary. Instead, he wanted his body placed in the branches of a large tree which stood at a distance from their home.

"He then pretended to die, so the women placed his body in the tree. A few days later, a man came to the home and immediately set to work helping the women. He chopped firewood, carried water, and hoed corn. It was not long before he asked the widow for her daughter, and she replied, 'Yes, you seem to be all right. I have always wanted her to have a good man. You seem to be just that.' So they were married. One day the bride was combing her husband's hair with a grass brush so she could tie it up into a hair bun, when she discovered a wart on the back of his neck, exactly like her deceased father's.

"She told her mother of her discovery, and both became suspicious. The mother asked permission to comb his hair. Then both women knew he was the girl's father, who had feigned death and disguised himself so that he could return to marry his beautiful daughter. The women were furious, driving him away with curses, sticks, and stones. Later, his child was born to the young girl.

"Neither mother nor grandmother wanted the child because of the circumstances of birth, but they also did not wish to destroy him, so they carried the baby away from the home and placed him in a badger's hole. Owl came along, found him, and took the child home to his wife. After discussing the situation, they decided not to eat the boy but raise him. They hunted diligently for the proper food and fed him until he was twelve or thirteen years old.

"The youth, Boy Raised by Owls, learned to make a bow and arrow and to hunt, bringing food to his owl foster parents. But once he grew to manhood, he tired of living with them and struck out on his own. He wanted to associate with others like himself and to go into the world to learn.

"As he passed Huerfano Peak (Dził-Hanáádlí, "Place of Creation," or, in Spanish, Huérfano, "the Orphan," because this mesa stands alone on the prairie), he found some ironwood brush. Cutting some of its boughs, he made a bow and several arrows, then fashioned some stout shafts, which he carried with him.

"Not long afterwards he reached Big Sheep [Dibé Ntsaa (Mount Hesperus, Colorado)], where he met Big God [Yé'iitsoh]. This big oaf knew nothing of hunting and subsisted on nuts and berries. Boy Raised by Owls tried to teach him to hunt but had no success; the fellow simply could not learn. So in disgust Boy Raised by Owls left Big God to his nuts and berries and went westward towards Furry Mountain [Dził Dítł'ooii (Blue or Abajo Mountain, Utah)]. He found no people there, but in camp that night, some of the ironwood staves he carried turned into human beings."

I asked Pete who these people were, and he replied that they were Utes, adding, "That is why Navajos believe that Utes are crooked in their dealings. They came from those ironwood sticks, which are never really straight and so [are] unreliable. Boy Raised by Owls was no longer alone. He stayed there some time with the ironwood people before returning to the place he was raised."

As I heard these stories, I remembered that the Navajos were reluctant to tell them to people not of their race. But I had gained Pete's respect and friendship and had little trouble in having him teach me. He was a natural, avid storyteller. I also learned that the recounting of these stories was indulged in only during the summer months, between the last frosts of spring and the first frosts of autumn.[17] Otherwise, it was taboo during the winter to discuss these things. When I tried to get an explanation of this practice from different medicine men, the only answer I got was "Our fathers told us so." It being summertime, I made use of this opportunity.

Pete said he would tell me the story of how deer, once tame, became wild. He said that it was rather odd to tell deer stories while there were no deer on the reservation or near it. Of course, in the old days there were plenty of them on the mountains and antelope in the valleys. But with the advent of the drought years, these animals had either drifted to better grazing areas or had been exterminated by the ever-growing tribe.

An occasional small group of these fleet animals attempted to cross the reservation from some mountain range to the south toward the lofty hills of Colorado, but they rarely left the confines of Navajo land. Some crafty hunters would bring an end to the migration. I saw mute evidence of this one summer when riding along a trail in the Lukachukai Mountains. Reaching the camp of Benito, one of our customers, I found that he had stretched a rope between two pine trees. On this rope were hanging the skins of three grown deer, a buck and two does, as well as a fawn. He said he found the deer browsing in the forest, heading north, and that the fawn was unborn when he shot the mother.

This same Benito was in the habit of bringing wild turkeys to the store each Christmas. There were a few wild turkeys on the mountain during the early days at Sanostee Trading Post. Today they are extinct in the Lukachukai Mountains and have been for several years.

Pete's story of how the deer became wild is as follows. "In the old days, when the Boy Raised by Owls was living, as a youth, the following incident occurred. When he became twelve years old he made a bow and arrows. From then on he provided meat for his foster owl family. He had good luck for some time, but one day he could find no deer and went home without the usual supply of meat.

"He was sad and hungry, as were his foster parents. They hooted among themselves and decided that the young man must try his luck again the next day. So he did. But after hunting far and wide, he still had not killed anything and was tired and sad. About the middle of the day"—and Pete made a circle of his thumb and forefinger, lifted it towards the heavens, indicating the position of the sun at that hour of the day—"the boy saw a crow. He had heard from the owls that the crow had a lot of knowledge and could tell many things besides just cawing.

"'They tell me,' Boy said to the crow, 'that you fly everywhere, that you go all over the country and see everything.' Crow said not a word, but when Boy asked the question four times, the bird answered, 'Caw, Caw. Yes, I know where the deer are. I will take you there.'[18]

"Crow flew from tree to tree, waiting for Boy to catch up. Finally they reached the home of Monster Slayer, firstborn of the Twins and child of the Sun. Monster Slayer was the one who killed the great winged creatures who once nested on top of Shiprock. He also rid the Navajos of other terrible man-eating creatures.

"Crow took Boy some distance from the house to a large stone corral filled with deer. Monster Slayer had gathered all of them in that section of the country and placed them there. Crow told Boy that these animals were tame and that if he opened the gate of the corral, they would pay no attention to it, stand around, remain quiet, or lie on the ground. He also said that if the boy wanted the deer to leave the corral and scatter, he must get the gall from a dead buzzard and touch their noses with it. 'Then,' he said, 'you will see what happens.' Boy hunted around the forest and at last found what he wanted. Returning to the corral, he saw Crow sitting on top of the fence, with the gate of the corral mysteriously fastened. There were, however, four stone skinning knives, one of black, blue, white, and yellow, hanging nearby. Crow told Boy to strike the gate with each of the knives in turn. When he did this, the gate flew open, and he walked in.

"As he touched the noses of the deer with the buzzard's gall, they became very wild, snorting and stomping. Then away they went, out of the corral, running in every direction. Boy returned home on the trail he had taken with Crow. Thereafter, wild game was plentiful. 'That,' said Pete, 'is the story of how game became wild.'

"In days past, deer were the same as sheep, and antelope were like goats, except that they were wild. The Navajos were very sorry to lose the venison and antelope meat they once had. To get it now, they have to go into the white man's country, where I know we are not welcomed. Of course, we have mutton and goat meat, and we like it very much. But our ancestors lived on the wild meat, and we still have a lingering desire for it."

"Speaking of meat," I asked, "why is it that Navajos do not eat fish, fowl, or eggs?"

"Well," he answered, "there are long stories behind these things, and perhaps sometime I will tell you. This much I will say now. There have been stories told of the Navajos killing Cliff Dwellers and casting their bodies into the San Juan River and that we believe these bodies turned into fish. This is not so, my friend. I have never heard my people tell such a story.

"I think," continued Pete, "that it is because of the time when a great fish swallowed Chee-Kent-De-Ghunnie, a character from the past, when he waded too far into a lake. In fact, the story says he was swallowed by four fish in succession, as he cut his way out of each of them. There was one fish that was white, another blue, another yellow, and one that was black.

"The reason for not eating fowl or any winged creature is because of the story of the great winged monsters that once lived on Shiprock and created such havoc among the Navajos. This is why eggs, coming from feathered creatures, fall under the taboo."

Several years after I had heard the story of why deer became wild, I met Pete in Shiprock on the first day of the nine-day Yé'ii Bicheii ceremonial at the annual all-Indian fair. He was glad to see me and I him as we shook hands warmly. His laugh was as infectious as ever, and his somewhat toothless grin comical but pleasing. The years had dealt kindly with him, except that the white man's sweets had been harsh on his incisors.

"Pete," I said, "Have you been doing any singing and sandpainting lately?"

"Yes, I have," he answered. "I have just returned from Toadlena, where we performed a ceremonial which took us several days to complete. I am sure you know Mister Pinto Horses [Hastiin Łįįłkizhí]?"

I knew him because this was during the pre-trucking days, when teams and wagons hauled freight to trading posts, mostly by Indian outfits. Pinto Horses hauled a large portion of the supplies from the river to the post at Toadlena. He was patient and reliable, making his trips regularly, rain or shine, wind or snow, until . . .

"What happened to Pinto Horses?" I asked.

"Well," Pete answered, "he was in bad shape. He couldn't eat or sleep and was in a very nervous condition. In fact, he was almost scared to death. He thought he was going to die right away. He called in Many Goats [Tł'ízí Łani], the chief medicine man in that region, who sent for me to assist in the sandpaintings.

"When I arrived at the hogan, the people were almost ready to begin the ceremony. Many Goats had spent most of the previous night singing in preparation for the event. The sick man looked very bad and was quite worried.

"What was the matter with our friend, Pinto Horses?" I asked.

"Well, as you know, he was a longtime freighter for the trader at Toadlena. Several days ago he was making a return trip to the post and was on the last lap of the journey when darkness overtook him. He had left the canyon above Tocito, and was climbing the heavy grade to Toadlena. As he passed a large grove of pinon trees, an owl hooted. Soon another answered and then another. He told me that it sounded as if there were several of them in the clump of trees. They hooted back and forth, talking in owl language that seemed to carry a message."

"In those days Navajos seldom traveled after dark. However, this night the moon was shining, and Pinto Horses had decided to keep going until he reached home. It was a strange night. The eerie shadows under the trees, the pale moonlight, the hooting of the owls, and the surrounding emptiness had a magical effect upon the lonely traveler.

"But what bothered Pinto Horses was what he thought the owls were saying. It seemed as if they hooted, 'Pinto Horses, come, come, come.'[19] As he traveled on, it seemed as if the invitation became more eager, and at the same time he became confused and frightened."

"Don't you think he became sleepy and that the sudden hoots of the owls startled him so he thought they were saying things to him?"

"Perhaps," Pete answered, "but, he said that he knew they were talking to him. He thought they were carrying a message to him from his ancestors. We believe that owls carry messages to us. We have been told this by our fathers for generations, so Pinto Horses became very alarmed. He was frightened to the point of illness, being sickened in his mind. He drove home as fast as the team could take him while still pulling a heavy load. However, he had four horses and immediately, on reaching his hogan, he sent his son on horseback to bring the medicine man, old Many Goats, to start a sing. Many Goats saddled his pony and soon arrived, then sent for me.

"I reached there fairly early the next morning with my supply of colored sands for the sandpaintings. We requested a supply of clean sand and prepared for the first painting. The sand, spread out on the floor of the medicine hogan provided a smooth surface for the laying of the colored pictures. In the meantime Many Goats resumed the singing, aided by the Navajos who had gathered to watch and give assistance. They offered prayers to the Holy Beings for the preservation of Pinto Horses's life.

"We sang the songs of the Shootingway ceremony, made the proper sandpainting, and completed it in a half-day. In the afternoon we had more singing. During the main ceremony, we sang lengthy songs of prayer, after which we placed Pinto Horses naked, except for a loin cloth, in a sitting position in the center of the painting. After the songs and prayers, he got off the picture, which we destroyed with the flat piece of wood used to pound tightly the yarn when weaving blankets.

"This batten scraped the colored sands into a heap in the center and they were then deposited on a blanket or robe and dumped outside some distance from the hogan. This is always done because sandpaintings must not be left after sundown. Otherwise they would lose their healing powers, and the Holy Beings would be very displeased. The singing continued long into the night with a few intermissions for rest and refreshments.

"Next morning Pinto Horses was still feeling bad, showing little, if any, improvement. So that day we used the Evilway songs and sandpainting. The same routine during the evening and night brought only a little improvement. We continued the ceremony and songs during the third day and night. The morning of the fourth day Pinto Horses was a little better.

"The men decided to appeal to the Song People. The most important of these four Holy Beings was one of the greatest medicine men in the past when the world was young. He had learned sandpaintings and the songs which go with them under miraculous circumstances and taught them to other medicine men. On the fifth morning Pinto Horses was much better. He figured that through the intervention of the Song People, the day of his passing had been postponed. I left there two days ago, and here I am, ready to take part in the great Yé'ii Bicheii ceremony."

"Pete, why do Navajos believe that owls can tell them things?"

"That story," he answered, "goes back to long ago when Monster Slayer slew the great winged, man-eating creatures which nested upon Shiprock.[20] After he killed the parents, he spared the lives of the two young ones he had found in the nest. One of them was transformed into an eagle, from which this bird's family sprang. The other became an owl. As he tossed the bird into the air, he said, "You are now an owl. You will fly through the woods; and at night, as you rest on the branches of the trees crying Hoo-hoo, Hoo-hoo, you will tell the Navajos of things to come and give warnings to them. As he flew away, the owl said, "Yes, and I will tell them plenty, too. Hoo-Hoo, Hoo-Hoo!"

"All right, Pete, but why are Navajos afraid to go abroad at night?"

"There are several reasons. Among them is the loss of sunlight. The light of the stars was usually insufficient to light one's way. This faint light, and also the infrequent moonlight, was often obscured by clouds and storms. Also, the sun might not return in the morning, although it has done so for many ages. Long ago the singers of the chant to the Sun expressed that fear when they sang: 'Perhaps the Sun will not come back in the morning,' they said, even though they predicted that it would.

"Then there are the skinwalkers who prowl at night. Meeting these creatures is something that no Navajo cares to do. These human wolves take delight in digging into the graves of our dead, particularly those that contain babies or young children. The home fires are more pleasant than prowling around after Sun Bearer has gone to rest at the end of his daily trail."

After I left Pete, I saw him a few times during the fair and Yé'ii Bi-cheii dance, but that was the last time. A few short years later, he died. As I think of my good friend of many years ago, I know he was a devout believer in his gods and the lore of his people. He was a happy, kind, good-hearted fellow who was my friend.

Culture

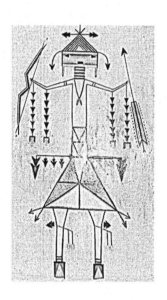

Daily Life and Customs of the Navajo People

Culture and customs hold a fascination for someone living outside of that society. Evans readily admits to this fact by expressing his love of and interest in various aspects of Navajo culture. There is no missing his all-encompassing passion for sandpaintings and products of the loom. This appeal served as a springboard for his inquiry into the how and why of many daily activities and cultural practices. The answers he received give an interesting glimpse into Navajo thought.

One strength of the following section is in Evans's descriptive power based on observation. While he does not use an analytical approach in an anthropological sense, he was a keen recorder of what he saw. His description of the conditions under which he viewed his first sandpainting is one that has been reproduced on a number of occasions. In it, he captures his feelings, a turning point that he recognized in his own life. Another time, one can sense the warmth of the woman who invited him into her hogan during a rainstorm, then fed and cared for him until he was able to leave. Gratitude resulted. Also evident is his reflective excitement—two words not usually juxtaposed—when he attended a "Fire Dance" (Mountainway Ceremony) and watched the performers with fascination. The feeling and sensing of these events is as compelling as the actual description.

As with the other sections of this book, the cultural aspects he discusses are neither tightly woven together nor analyzed. The general flow of what the reader encounters lies in two categories. The first could be characterized as the life cycle of the Navajo. Topics range from birth to *death and include parenting, grooming, marriage, hospitality, and burial practices. The second is more of the public side, with views of herding, weaving, sandpainting, trading, and entertainment. While a lot of these topics have now been thoroughly detailed and analyzed by specialists in the field of Navajo studies, Evans still provides interesting commentary and differing insight. His discussion of the "spirit road" found in woven rugs is a good example.*

At one point, the author comments on how the culture is changing. He compares the knowledge of the elders with that of the youth, who are now the elders of today, and sees the diminution of traditional Navajo beliefs and practices. His zeal in collecting information was reinforced by what he saw as a loss of the irreplaceable. In the same light, he compares white society to that of the Navajo and often finds the latter more acceptable. Take, for instance, his experience as a lone rider in the desert when he came upon a band of young Navajo men who had been drinking. Discussing the incident, he wonders what would have happened if the situation had been reversed and it was a lone Navajo with a group of inebriated whites. He next tells of a poor elder whom the court system took unfair advantage of for a minor infraction. Evans's support for a culture that fosters respect and kindness is obvious.

Evans begins this section using a common technique in western literature—the country man versus the city slicker. With apparent glee, he becomes the seasoned veteran of the desert with a group of novices. Playing off of the tension between East and West, the dignified and the down-to-earth, and even the Navajo compared with the white man, he lets a middle-aged woman from "civilization" know with whom he identifies. In a very real sense, this is not a show. Although he was never able to attain a total insider status with the Navajos, he still ventured where most white men have not been able to go. He has gone with the Navajos' permission, which says a lot for both the man and the People.

People often ask how long I have lived in Navajo country. I joke that when I first arrived, Shiprock was just a small mound and has since grown to its present size. Since 1893, my first year in this region, I have pursued my hobby of studying the Navajos, their religion, traditions, habits, and customs. It soon becomes evident that the land and environment have had a lot to do with the secular and religious life of these people.

A few years ago a well-groomed party of travelers from the eastern part of the United States stopped at my post in Shiprock to refresh themselves with cold drinks and purchase a few souvenirs, having just crossed the "desert" from Gallup. There were several Navajo men and women

The second Evans-built Shiprock Trading Company, as it appeared in 1925. Trees in the background mark the site of the agency.

busily engaged in trading, but it fell to me to wait on the tourist party. A middle-aged woman gazed at my customers for some time. Turning to me she said, "How do these people get along in this dreary land? We saw nothing but wilderness between here and Gallup. How in the world do you people stand it out here? It seems so terribly boring."

"Why, lady," I answered, "we love it out here. It is a veritable wonderland." She shook her head in disbelief, looking at me as if I had suddenly gone insane. But it is true; the country embraced within the borders of the Navajo Reservation is a wonderland. There are valleys and tablelands, canyons and mountaintops, rocky and brilliant pinnacles, as well as flat grazing lands. Some of the wonders include Canyon de Chelly, that red sandstone thousand-foot-deep gorge; Monument Valley with its inspiring spires and fantastic formations; Chaco Canyon, with its magnificent ruins, the largest in North America; Hopi land with its mesa dwellers; and the Shiprock pinnacle, with its legendary lore sacred to the Navajo.

The People recognize the beauty of this land, offering prayers of thanksgiving to the trees, mountains, and spirits of the region. Nature has been their teacher. They have learned to respect the powers of nature and see in them either help or trouble. In thundering and lightning, amid the black clouds, they do not see the natural workings of the elements, but a powerful demonstration of the might of a god who pulls his great bow and lets fly a lightning arrow. In the days after a terrifying storm, if a sheepherder or traveler finds an arrowhead or spear point, it is not regarded as the product of a departed race, but rather an object from the sky, hurled as part of the lightning by the storm god. Arrowheads are thus valued as charms and fetishes used extensively in the rituals.

Evans's depiction of the Storm God with his lightning bolt arrows. This and other paintings decorated the walls of the Totah Theater and the Farmington Hotel for many years. The theater is currently undergoing renovation. Photo by Richard P. Evans.

Daily Life in a Hogan

Navajo hogans also reflect closeness to nature and use of the land. They are made from local materials and may be constructed entirely of cottonwood or juniper logs or partly of stone and logs. If made of cottonwood, a circular trench is dug in which vertical posts are set closely together to form a wall about four feet high. Earth is firmly tamped into the trench around the posts to hold them securely. Logs, which form a dome-shaped

A family in front of their stone hogan. Evans believed that the Navajos borrowed design elements of this structure from the Pueblo Indians. Photo by William Pennington.

roof, are laid on top of this wall. The hole at the center of the roof permits smoke from a fire pit or stovepipe to escape, while admitting light and air. In winter a supply of wood feeds the central fire, keeping the hogan warm at night without requiring a lot of fuel.

Stone-and-log hogans have the same general form. Where wood is scarce or has to be hauled some distance, stone is used to bring walls up to the usual level, after which logs are formed into a domed roof. I believe that Navajos copied this roof design from ancient kivas in pueblos; the art of construction was probably brought to the Navajos by Pueblo captives. Where rock walls are used, mortar binds them together, which also serves as chinking when posts form a foundation for the roof.

Older Navajo hogans were tepee-shaped.[1] Two rather long poles set upright in the ground formed a doorway and also a support for two parallel ridge poles, one end of which sat atop the uprights. Their opposite ends rested on the ground at a slope, depending upon their length. Poles or saplings covered the basic framework. Both types of dwelling used juniper or cottonwood bark and brush as filler material between the logs and as a binder to hold the mud plastered on the exterior surface. The older type of hogan began to fall into disuse in the 1920s. There was much less space and headroom in them compared to the dome-shaped dwellings.

The entrance of a Navajo hogan faces east. When the door is pushed open or a blanket which covers the opening is drawn aside, the rising sun's rays pervade the interior, cleansing and rededicating it with life-giving power. An early riser can take a few steps into the open and greet the early streaks of dawn.

Some travelers have said that Navajos sing a visiting song when they go calling, and that when a visitor approaches a hogan, it is impolite to go out to see who is coming. This might be true in a few sections of the reservation, but I have been unable to find any practice of it locally. To the contrary, when Navajos hear the approach of a visitor, a member of the family goes outside to see who is coming. When Navajos travel either alone or in groups, they often sing as they ride along the trail. This is a prayer for safety, especially when alone.

Life in a hogan lacks privacy since there are no inner partitions. Simplicity of life and in furnishings are its principal features. These homes are comfortable in winter and summer. Heating and cooking are done in an open fire pit, though Navajos now try to obtain even a secondhand kitchen range.

Old-timers used to sleep on the earthen floor, using sheepskins for mats and robes and quilts or blankets for a covering. Now bedsteads and mattresses are widely used. Before retiring, a long sheepskin, wooly side up, is placed on the floor, over which a blanket is laid. A woolen robe or comforter, or both, serve as a cover. Most Navajos pull off their shoes or moccasins when retiring. If a number of people are sleeping in a hogan, they lie with their feet to the center and heads next to the walls. Every morning, the bedding is placed on a pole rack in the sun to air and dry. Navajos are very careful about this, and so outside any hogan one may see sheepskins, blankets, and quilts hanging in the sun.

A few of the more well-to-do Indians erect stone or log square-roomed buildings. These, for the most part, have almost flat roofs covered with soil. Some have pitched roofs with gable ends; others have hip roofs. Either a stove or fireplace is used for heating and cooking. Some Navajos build a white-man style frame house but eventually discard it for a hogan and use the cottage for storage of harnesses, saddles, and other gear. Bedsteads with sheepskins covering the springs or on top of cheap mattresses may be found in these newer homes. Most Navajos still live in traditional hogans and sleep on a sheepskin on the floor.

In the past, Navajos seldom built hogans near their water supply, which may be as much as ten miles away. Livestock was driven to it, while wagons hauled water for domestic use. The reason for this was that often the best feed for stock was some distance from the water. It was easier to watch the animals when they grazed near the place of residence. One or two family members and their dogs herded the livestock to water once a day; the rest of the time was allotted to grazing.

During the first half of the twentieth century, the federal government created many wells, which enriched the parched Navajo desert. Here, a mother and child water their sheep before starting a day of herding. Photo by Richard P. Evans.

There is an erroneous idea that sheep, goats, and other animals are permitted inside a hogan. Cats are always allowed inside, but never dogs. Sheep and goats are brought in only when it is necessary to warm a kid or lamb back to life. Once they have grown large, they are forbidden to enter. A dog must always stay outside and, if found within, is driven out with a tongue-lashing.

Navajos are early risers, getting up before daybreak or earlier. In the old days this was entirely true; today it is only relatively so. They went to bed earlier in the past, after the fire, their only source of artificial light, died down. In those days there were very few who went abroad from the hogan at night, except in times of ceremonies. When they did, they traveled in groups. Some of the people believed that night excursions would bring them in contact with departed spirits or skinwalkers. Navajos retired to their hogans by nightfall and spent the evening telling traditional stories or passing along gossip. Kerosene and gasoline lanterns have since provided artificial light, and so they go to bed and get up later.

In the early days, as long as a Navajo had food, he was duty-bound to share it with his extended family. Hungry relatives called upon their more fortunate brother or cousin, which often reduced his household to poor circumstances. If there was illness in the family, the poverty problem compounded. Having medicine men attend the sick for long periods and feeding the crowds who attended the ceremony further reduced assets.

Navajo Hospitality

Navajos are very friendly and hospitable if they know you and you can speak a few words in their language. I have traveled to other parts of the reservation which were strange to me and have spoken to the Navajos there in English; I was either casually or coldly received. But when I spoke a little of their language, especially to their children, their attitude changed, and I was welcomed as a guest. I told them what part of the reservation I was from and soon was treated as one of them.

I well remember one striking act of friendliness I experienced in the early 1900s. One afternoon while doing contract work for the government at Tohatchi, I started out on horseback to Gallup. Since it was a warm summer day, I rode off without a coat, although I could see thunderheads rising from the horizon. Just before I reached the foot of the low mountains, ten miles north of Gallup, rain came pelting down in great drops. I approached a few clustered hogans just off the trail and headed for shelter in the nearest one. After dismounting, I tied my horse to a post, threw the stirrup leathers over the saddle to keep the seat dry, and dashed into the hogan.

I startled a woman, boy, and girl, huddled together attempting to stay dry beneath a leaky roof. Their fright melted when I said "much rain" in Navajo, and the woman smiled. Seeing that I was coatless, she told her little girl to give me the woolen blanket covering her, then took the girl in her arms and covered herself and the children with her own blanket. The roof was quite leaky, but I managed to keep fairly dry. The storm soon passed, and the sun came out, drying my saddle and clothing. I gave the little girl a coin, she smiled sweetly, and I mounted my horse and was on my way. But I will never forget that act of kindness.

I had a similar incident a little while later. One Sunday morning at Tohatchi, I was starving for newspapers and the voices of friends, so I saddled my pony and struck out on the trail to Gallup. I saw clouds building ahead, threatening rain. I had no waterproof gear but pressed on. As I rode past the Twin Lakes area and towards some low sagebrush hills, violent thunder and lightning struck to my left and right.

Then, while I was still in the flats approaching the foothills, the storm broke over me. Thunder rolled and lightning snaked across the sky, while rain slanted in sheets. In minutes I was drenched. Seeking shelter, I saw a small corn patch to my left and beyond it a domed hogan with smoke blowing out of the roof into the rain and wind. I turned off the trail towards it, tied my horse to a convenient rail, and left him to his fate.

Navajo madonna with her baby wrapped in a Pendleton blanket. Photo by William Pennington.

I softly knocked on the door, and a woman's voice answered in Navajo, "Come in." I pushed gently on the door and adjusted my eyes to the dim, round interior. Seated before the central fire pit was a woman of perhaps thirty years, holding a baby of several months. There was no one else. "Much rain outside," I said, in Navajo. "I was riding to Gallup, but the rain was too much."

"Yes," she answered. What fear she may have felt at this intrusion into her home by a strange white man was apparently dispelled when I spoke to her in her native tongue.

"Much rain. Take off your coat and let it dry before the fire. Sit on this sheepskin with your back to the warmth and get dry, then turn around and dry the front of your shirt and legs," she invited.

She laid the baby on a folded blanket and brought the sheepskin to me. I followed her instructions and was soon comfortably dry. "I am going to eat so I can feed my baby. It is nearly the middle of the day. Will you have something?" she asked.

I had eaten nothing before leaving Tohatchi and was starving. "Yes," I replied, "I am very hungry."

Taking the lid off a large blackened vessel which stood at one edge of the fire, she spooned a stew mixed with vegetables into an enameled bowl. Once filled, she handed it to me with a metal spoon.

"You eat," she commanded. Then she served herself and began to eat. She offered me coffee, which I declined; I saw a package of the old, strong Arbuckles Coffee on a rough table and knew the source of her brew. She poured a cup for herself.

My meal consisted of mutton stew to which she had added potatoes, wild onion bulbs, and the powdered leaves of some herb, which made it delicious. I have eaten a lot of mutton stew before and since, but never has it tasted so good.

I spoke to her: "The father of your child, where is he?"

"In Fort Defiance," she replied, "He returns tonight, if the rain will let him."

We spoke of different things, her manner confident, her speech ready; she had no fear of this white man who made every effort to speak her language clearly and correctly. I was at times unsure of myself, but she seemed to understand.

In about an hour the rain ceased, and the sun came out. She had picked up her child and was nursing it, the edge of her velvet blouse lifted unashamedly to give the baby milk.

I arose to leave, thanking her for the shelter and food. I offered to pay, but she would not accept my coins so I laid several on the rough table, opened the door, and stepped out into the mud to mount my horse and head to Gallup. Running water was everywhere; and when fording the deeper washes, I had to lift my stirrups to keep my feet dry.

I arrived in Gallup, purchased a number of newspapers and magazines, visited for a few hours with friends, then in the late afternoon, started for Tohatchi. Dusk fell as I rode back onto the flats and past the hogan where I had found shelter from the storm. I have never forgotten that act of hospitality and have driven past that site many times in later years. As I do, I drift into reveries of the early days and of the shelter and kindness I received in that humble hogan.

Such hospitality is not always possible. Sometimes Navajo housewives are caught short when mealtime arrives. She may be out of sugar or coffee or salt. Then again, she may be out of shortening, which to the white woman would be a calamity. I know of one woman in Monument Valley who solved the problem nicely. She had several guests, including me and a friend, John Stewart MacClary, from Pueblo, Colorado. She had a large pot of boiled horsemeat and was making a foot-high stack of bread, cooked to a golden brown. As she went to make more, the guests attacked the food.

By now she had run out of salt and fat, with not even a spot of horse grease. What could she do to keep the dozen or so pieces of dough from sticking to the fry pan? The smiling and hospitable wife knelt before the campfire with her pots and pans within easy reach. Just to one side was a small but ample pile of very fine wood ash. She pinched off a portion of the dough, patted it in her hands, flattened it, then flapped it from hand to hand, back and forth, until it reached the desired thinness. She carefully dipped the edge of the fry pan into the pile of fine ash, shook it to scatter the ashes over the bottom, then placed the dough inside. Shortly after one flip, it was done. The bread did not stick to the pan and tasted good. The ash flavor was not disagreeable, and I was told it aided digestion.

When greeting each other, Navajos do not really shake hands, but lightly touch palms in a quiet and reserved manner.[2] At a trading post, a Navajo may enter when there are already a number of his or her friends present. He or she will silently stand near the door for some time, perhaps several minutes, without a word to anyone. Then the newcomer will walk over to an acquaintance, speak in a low tone, and hold hands for several seconds. There is no pump-handling up and down, merely a light pressure. A white man soon learns to avoid a loud, conspicuous, backslapping greeting.

Trading with the Navajos

Traders estimate that at one time, 80 to 90 percent of the groceries Navajos purchased were flour, sugar, coffee, and shortening. Their diet used to be comprised entirely of bread, meat, and coffee; but in later years, they bought ever-increasing amounts of potatoes and onions, mutton or beef, and more tallow than lard. If their sheep were poor late in winter or during periods of drought, then they purchased large quantities of lard or shortening.

Navajos have distinct trading habits. If they are taking merchandise instead of cash for their products, they want to know after each purchase how much is still due them, not how much has been spent. When giving change, one must be very careful to extend the proper amount, for once the money is placed on the counter, it is immediately covered by the customer's hand. If the amount should happen to be less than the correct change, a cry of woe comes forth immediately. In many cases, if the amount is more than that which is due, nothing is said. The customer appears to believe that he is that much ahead and feels no need to return it. Navajos expect the strictest honesty from the white man, but many of them think nothing of defrauding him and consider it smart to do so. The most serious feature of wrongdoing was in being discovered.

When a Navajo woman purchases a length of cloth, she does not want it cut off the bolt with a pair of shears, but torn. If the trader attempts to cut the fabric, she exclaims, "Just tear it!" The tradition reflected in this practice comes from the ceremonies where a spear point or arrowhead cuts the material used during the ritual. A steel knife is never used. They prefer the cloth for clothing to be torn, rather than cut by a white man's knife or shears.

A husband often usurps the rights of his wife when trading at the post. More often than not he will make purchases accruing from the sale of her blanket, in which he has had no part. This is sometimes because of sheer proprietary feelings on his part, but other times it is because he thinks she is not capable of keeping track of the amounts due after each purchase.

Navajos also measure wealth in commodities, such as sheep, cattle, horses, silver jewelry, and turquoise. These last two, in particular, are an Indian's "bank account." In times of stress these treasures are readily pawned with the local trader as security for supplies. If they are not redeemed by a certain date, they become "dead pawn" and can be sold for the amount they were originally held for. A majority of the traders are loath to sell pawn once "dead," which they are allowed to do, because the credit of the owner is lowered by that much. Sometimes these articles are kept in a pawn case for two or three years and occasionally longer, for the simple reason that the owners may redeem their treasure and pawn it again. The trader does not object to this practice because it gives him a regular turnover each time the article is paid out.

A Navajo values turquoise much more than he does a diamond, which to him is just a clear piece of rock and means nothing. If one showed an

Judge Clah (Tł'ah, "Left-Handed") and his two wives from Teec Nos Pos, Arizona, 1930s. Disputes in transactions were often solved through traditional Navajo law. Photo by William Pennington.

Indian a fine diamond ring and told him what it cost, he would probably think the white man a crazy fool for paying hundreds of dollars for a clear rock. On the other hand, turquoise has a religious significance to the Navajos that comes from their legends of how the Holy Beings wore this stone. So, too, did the great traditional medicine men. We know that the ancient cliff dwellers as well as modern puebloans used the stone which "robbed the sky to get its blue color." The descendants of these people gave the stone to the Navajos and make use of it today.

A Navajo mother will often give her baby a piece of turquoise the first time the child laughs. This is accompanied with a feast, in which small quantities of food are placed in the hand of the baby, and then are passed on to the members of the family or others present. This custom assures that the child will develop a spirit of generosity and willingness to share with others.

Navajo Blankets

Navajo women are known for their beautiful handwoven rugs and blankets. The words "blanket" and "rug" are used interchangeably, because the same item has been used by the Indians as a body covering and by the whites on a floor. While watching a woman at the loom, there appears to be nothing complicated in weaving a blanket. But skill, patience, and long years of training are necessary before she becomes a good weaver. Unlike the Hopis, Navajo women are weavers rather than the men. Hopi men weave only ceremonial robes, belts, and garters, while Navajo women weave blankets in commercial quantities. The art of weaving among the Navajos is not hereditary. They acquired the ability during more recent centuries from the Pueblos.[3]

Many people do not realize that the actual weaving of a blanket is only about one-third of the entire operation. The other two-thirds consists of preparing the materials, such as carding, spinning, and dyeing the wool. A woman cannot weave a good blanket unless she is a good spinner, and she must learn to shade and combine the colors she is using.

The weaver practices placing the yarn so it is even and tight, and she must learn to keep the product the same width throughout, the edges of the fabric being evenly finished in spite of her crude loom. At times, a good weaver turns out a poor product because she hurried through the spinning process or did not get the warp sufficiently tight or straight. This sometimes occurs when her larder is approaching empty. As a rule though, she tries to maintain the standards she has set.

Raw wool from a sheep's back is the material from which the rugs come. Often the weaver shears the sheep without anyone else to help her, before she washes, dyes, cards, spins, and weaves the wool. In addition to a blanket's intrinsic value, charm of color, and artistic design, the fact that it comes "from the back of the sheep to the user" is one of the deepseated reasons why so many people appreciate these woolen creations.

Navajo weaver at work while grandmother tends children. Oral accounts of older women tell of the endless hours spent weaving to support their families. Based on an hourly wage, they received a pittance for their time.

Because the weaver completes such a beautiful article from the first process to the last lends enchantment to the finished product.

Most Navajo women know each sheep in the flock, even if there are a hundred. This is because the women care for them from lambing time to maturity. Sheep seem to be individual in their looks and actions, although to the uninitiated they all seem alike. The belief that Navajo women sometimes suckle an orphan lamb until milk can be found for it is not true. It is best to dispel this fiction by remembering that Navajo women take very good care of their sheep in practical ways. A common procedure to help orphan lambs is to rub the rump of the orphan against the rump of another lamb which has a living mother. She smells it, recognizes the odor of her own lamb, and allows the new family member to suckle.

Navajo women seldom have pictures of patterns or designs when weaving but form a mental image of what they wish to create. Ordinarily she decides before starting just what the pattern is going to be. Occasionally she may be given a specific design by the trader for a special order.

Usually when weaving a blanket with a solid border, the woman runs a thread of a different color through the border, near one of its corners. It has been said that this is in order to provide a "road" to release any evil spirits which have found themselves trapped within the solid border. Therefore, this thread is called the Devil's Road [ch'įįdii 'atiin]. I have never subscribed to this idea. I do not think Navajos believe in such an evil spirit. In their traditions and legends, of course, there are evil actions of certain Holy Beings, but not in the sense of old Satan. In reality the word "ch'įįdii" means "dead body." When the weaver leaves a road or trail through her blanket's border, she has no thought of an evil spirit.

The idea is more like this, as nearly as I can explain it in English. An old-time weaver, one of the best in the Northern Navajo Agency, and Navajo John, a veteran medicine man, put it this way. "The weaver has put something of herself into making her rug. By weaving, she has placed a great deal of her energy into the task. Her thoughts and something of her very soul have been continually with her as she works. So that these attributes shall continue to return to her, she leaves an opening, thus never losing them." They added that this information was handed down from the elders.

The weave, texture, and design of many Navajo blankets identify them as coming from different localities. A trader can easily trace one, no matter where it may be found, to a weaver from the various districts of the reservation. Distinctive patterns such as ceremonial designs from Shiprock, the outline patterns from Teec Nos Pos, and the black, white, and grays from Two Grey Hills and Toadlena are easily recognized by an experienced trader.

One family, which formerly lived in the Shiprock area, always wove a peculiar pattern of their own; sometimes it varied a little, but it was always recognizable. There were four weavers in this family, the mother and three daughters. Their blankets were unusually popular, and I bought quite a few of them over the years. Then they abruptly stopped coming to Shiprock. Perhaps, I thought, they moved closer to some other post or became scattered as a family. Then a few years later an old woman brought me a couple of blankets, and I immediately recognized their design. I looked closer and saw that this woman was the mother of that family. She told me that all four daughters had passed away and that she was too old to do much weaving. That is why I had not seen her designs for so long.

This does not mean that designs evolve from a certain weaver and are absolutely the same. Rather, there are basic designs which certain weavers always use. Changing the design results from a realignment of basic figures.

Many people are not aware that Navajos also make pottery. It is rather scarce, of coarse quality, and has scanty decoration. Generally, it is red and used mainly as a common container, although some of it is black and used for cooking. Black clay pots are also formed for the body of drums used during ceremonials. Their bases are egg-shaped and do not stand

The loom inside this hogan has a framework of juniper or pine; the log
on the floor is tied to the side posts to give weight and keep the loom
tight. The rope looped over the top beam and secondary pole perform the same function. The weaver does not sit on a chair because
the weaving progresses upward; the loom is loosened and adjusted
downward to working height then retightened. The willow rod above
head level is tied to every other strand of the warp, which enables
the warp threads to be alternated as weaving progresses, locking the
yarn into place. The wide spreader bar, generally made of juniper
wood or mountain mahogany, separates the warp strands so that the
weaving yarn can be placed and beaten down with a long-toothed,
long-handled comb made of a similar wood. The woman's multiple
skirts of calico or sateen and a velveteen blouse with air holes in the
armpits for ventilation is typical. Photo by William Pennington, Durango, Colorado, ca. 1930.

Navajo silversmith sits on a sheepskin with his tools. Finished silver conchos are on one side of the anvil and silver blanks on the other side. Photo by William Pennington.

upright without support because they are made to set down in the ashes of a fire.

Silversmithing

Navajo silversmiths have established a reputation for producing ornaments and articles of utility. This reputation is well deserved when one sees what they have made with very crude means of production. Although the work of his white brother with his modern tools may excel in smoothness of finish and intricacy of design, the native article bears the stamp of originality.

A typical Navajo silversmith shop may look like this. A shade is built with a framework of a few poles. Against the sides and over the top are laid cottonwood boughs with the leaves still clinging to the branches. They are layered sufficiently thick to form a windbreak and to keep out the scorching rays of the sun. The leaves dry quickly and rustle with the motion of a gentle breeze, permitting just enough ventilation between the branches to diminish the hot desert air. In a corner sits a crude forge, not taller than six or eight inches above the smooth dirt floor. This is moderately small and built of rocks which are laid together with a mixture of sand and clay mortar.

Connected to the forge is an equally interesting homemade bellows. The top and bottom are constructed of pieces of boxes procured at the local trading post. The sides are flexible tanned goatskins, a good substitute for buckskin. The nozzle is shaped to fan the fire to a proper heat that melts the silver, formerly Mexican dollars, but which now comes in one-ounce squares. These are placed in a small melting pot made of native clay and baked sufficiently hard to withstand extreme temperatures. When the metal is melted, it is poured into a groove which has been carved into a piece of sandstone. Once removed, the cooled silver is hammered into the desired shape.

The silversmith sits near the forge, squatting tailor-fashion, upon the wooly side of a sheepskin. Nearby, on a sheepskin laid skin up, are the few tools he uses. A hammer, a file or two, and a few steel dies or stamps with which to engrave or stamp constitute the equipment of his workshop. The stamps are the work of the smith himself, for each one prides himself upon his originality of designs. The stamps are made from waste pieces of steel obtained from the agency smithy. The anvil upon which he hammers may be a piece of railroad iron or a small anvil given to him by a trader who wants his work.

Once the small ingot has been hammered into the desired shape, it is finished by filing and sandpapering. Next the dies and stamps decorate the work. The delicate task of inlaying hand-polished pieces of turquoise is done by placing a thin bead of melted silver on top of the ring or bracelet. The amount of metal must fit the size of the stone before it is welded to the object by heat and a fusing agent like borax. Wide bracelets may carry as many as three to five dozen small pieces of turquoise in beautifully intricate designs.

As the years pass, native silversmiths are becoming more proficient in their work. A silversmith toils hour after hour, melting and hammering, filing and sandpapering, polishing and engraving, bringing his handiwork to a point of beauty.

Cleanliness, Clothes, and Manners

Navajos often use sweat houses to ensure personal cleanliness and good health. Sweat houses are made of poles leaned in to the center at the top and covered with brush and earth.[4] These structures are usually about

Sweat lodges are heated with hot rocks (right corner of the clearing) placed inside. After sitting in the lodge, participants may roll in the sand, wash with water,
or bathe in a river before repeating the process four times.

three feet high and five feet in diameter at the floor level. The lodge has
a small opening, just large enough for one man, doubled up, to squeeze
through. The structure is often located near a stream or pool of water. A
number of rather large rocks which have been made almost red-hot in an
outside wood fire are placed in the sweat house and left there until the interior is like an oven. Sometimes cold water is poured over the hot rocks
to produce steam. Three to five men strip off their clothing before crowd-
ing into the tiny structure, and the sweating begins. Having withstood
the heat as long as possible, an occupant will rush out completely naked,
plunge into the stream or pool, and do a thorough job of bathing. In the
summer, the water is usually warm, while a winter plunge, which seldom
is indulged in, is a real ordeal. I have observed that Navajos are cleaner
than many other people I have met. Where water is easily obtained, they
wash their hands and face often.

Most women appear at the trading post in neat, well-washed garments
and shoes, which they have saved for trips. At home, they will often go
barefoot. Many women wear several skirts at a time, especially during the
winter, but only one blouse. When a new skirt is donned the inner one is
discarded. It takes from eight to ten yards of cloth to make a skirt for a
young girl or a small woman. The average Navajo woman wears from ten
to twelve yards, while some wear fifteen. The gathered and tiered skirts
are usually handmade of satin-like, richly colored fabrics.

I have been asked, "Does a Navajo woman sometimes wear as many as 200 silver buttons on her blouse?" This seems to be almost an impossibility, but not long ago I counted close to one hundred on one. It looked as if she had placed buttons in all available spaces on her collar and sleeves.

People also ask if there are not several thousand styles, shapes, and sizes of silver buttons, ranging in diameter from one-quarter inch to three inches in size. The latter is practically true, but the first part is impossible. Two or three hundred would probably cover the range. Many handmade silver buttons are concave and cannot be sewed on a garment unless the needle is unthreaded each time the thread is passed through the eye of the button. Buttons made of dimes, quarters, and half dollars are not concave, and sewing them on a garment is simple. But the process of sewing seventy-five or eighty concave buttons on a blouse is a very tedious operation.

When hard times arrive, I notice the disappearance of silver buttons from Navajo clothing. After a selection is made and the price announced, the decision to make the purchase is followed by a request for the loan of a pocket knife, then off come the buttons to pay for the article. This money is later resold to a Navajo. The men give up their buttons first, with the women hanging on to theirs as long as possible; but if times get tight, the buttons are reluctantly removed.

Nowadays many Navajo women carry handbags. In the past, because there were no pockets, they tied small packages with things, like a pocket knife and comb, to the fringes of their belts. Other times they carried these items in a Ute-made beaded buckskin bag pinned or tied to a shirt waistband or belt.

During a recent ceremonial, I noticed Navajos, Utes, Hopis, and Zunis in tribal clothing, wearing woven cotton belts. These are usually about three inches wide with colored designs. In the old days they were woven by Hopi men and purchased by Navajos. Later, Navajo women learned to weave them and used them for abdominal support during pregnancy and ceremonies.

When I first met the Navajo, the native style of dress for men was simple. First, there was a homemade pair of white muslin pants or "manta." These were split in the crotch and the vacancy filled with a G-string, the ends of which were lapped over a strip of leather or belt holding up the pants. The ends of the G-string hung in the front and back. The sides of the pant legs were slit upwards at the bottom about six or eight inches, which gave them a somewhat bell-bottom effect. A very plain, handmade blouse of calico covered the torso and hung outside the pants. The head

Harding Yazhi with his wife and child in Shiprock. His clothing reflects dress style at the turn of the century: velveteen blouse, turquoise necklace, white muslin trousers, deer or cowhide moccasins, and headband. The woman has a more contemporary style. Design for the cradle board came from the Holy Beings and has significant teachings associated with it. Photo by Richard P. Evans.

Chéchi'il Yah Tó (Water Under Oak Tree), from Oak Springs, south of Beclabito, New Mexico. His dress, from headband to vest to jewelry, illustrates Evans's description of his customers visiting his post. Photo by Richard P. Evans.

opening was rounded at the neck with no collar but slit sufficiently to allow pulling it on and off.

Red buckskin moccasins covered the feet and a pair of hand-knit blue yarn footless stockings protected the calves of the legs and ankle. A knitted strip passed under the middle of the soles of the feet, preventing the stockings from working up. If the individual could afford a pair of red buckskin leggings, they covered the lower legs below the pants. A red bandanna or piece of colored cloth for a headband adorned the head, while coral, white shell, turquoise, and silver necklaces, rings, and bracelets showed a person's wealth. A large silver concho belt later became indispensable. To complete the ensemble when traveling and to furnish a bed covering at night, a Navajo wore a Pendleton robe, or if not available, a Navajo blanket.

Vests later became popular. The four pockets in the vests carried small articles such as combs, matches, cigarette papers—purchased at the post or made from corn shucks—and a pack of Duke's Mixture or Bull Durham tobacco. Indeed, the pockets were the main reason for the popularity of the men's vests or waistcoats.

Now, the young blades are addicted to Levi's with the cuffs rolled up three to six inches, bright modern shirts, mackinaws, fancy belts, black wide-brimmed hats turned up sharply at the sides, and half boots. Bright silk kerchiefs give a touch of color during festivals.

Hairstyles

Hairstyles on the reservation have changed dramatically in the last twenty years. In the early days the hair grew long, was folded into a five- or six-inch knob, and tied in the middle by a traditionally spun woolen cord with the short ends hanging loosely below the knob. The spun cord was generally white, although other colors could be used. Now [1951], only in isolated parts of Navajo country do men wear their hair bunched and tied at the back of the head. Elsewhere, young men and boys cut their hair like their white brothers.

Many of the women and girls, however, cling to the old hairdo, but changes among the younger women are on the way. The trend is to trim the hair when it starts to grow too long. It is then combed back from the forehead and worked in a curly roll fairly high on the shoulders. This is copied from their white sisters. Another style of the younger females, married or not, is to let the hair grow full length, put it in a single braid, then wind it around and around at the back and slightly atop of the pate.

Navajo men are seldom bald, but many older women are, just behind the forehead on the top of the head. Both men and women use the traditional hairbrush made from a bunch of coarse grass stems that are tapped on a log or rock until the lower part is even, then tied tightly with string two or three inches from the base. This makes a coarse but potent brush. It is frequently and roughly used on the top of the head, pulling the hair back and eventually causing partial baldness.

In the past, Navajos had little soap to wash their hair. Native shampoo came from dried yucca roots, which make a lively bunch of suds. Following its use, Navajo hair shines a blackish blue, like a raven's wing.

Tobacco, Alcohol, and Morality

Indians use tobacco sparingly. There were few smokers among the women, although occasionally one might see an older one smoking; she almost certainly was not smoking a commercial variety of tobacco, but rather the sacred tobacco called mountain smoke [Dził-Nát'oh] for medicinal purposes. Today, however, some are taking up the habit of smoking cigarettes.

Navajo men prefer cigarettes over pipes. Occasionally a younger Navajo wants to appear smart, so smokes a pipe for a time but soon discards it. As a rule, a pipe is only used in ceremonies. A Navajo-made pipe is a peculiar, cone-shaped, stemless object made of clay, from which the sacred smoke (mountain tobacco) is blown to the four points of the compass.[5] While younger Navajos use the prepackaged type of cigarettes, the older men prefer rolling their own and are partial to using fine corn husks called dá'átáá or "thin covering."

Chewing tobacco, however, is another story. Each post had a "bull pen," a square or rectangular area surrounded by high, wide counters, where the Navajos stood to trade. The floor was hard-packed adobe swept clean at the close of each day's business. In some stores, where the traders were not too particular, these earthen floors received many globs of tobacco-laden spittle before the last customer left.

Other traders were more fastidious and, with a thought for better sanitation, provided an old wooden box, ten or twelve inches square, to put cut plug chewing tobacco. They insisted that their customers spit in this box filled with sand or loose earth. Years later, concrete floors came along, and with much preaching and effort, the owners persuaded the Navajos to either stop spitting or do it outside. The "free tobacco" box on the counter and the sand box are now things of the past, relics of an old custom.

Alcohol was a different issue and a source of problems. One day I saddled my horse and took the trail from Two Grey Hills toward Sanostee. While I was traversing the flats west of Bennett's Peak, I saw a group of horsemen coming over the hill a few miles away. As I judged their actions, I could tell that they had been drinking. There had been a series of squaw dances, the Navajos moving to a new location by day then drinking and dancing at night. I had learned that they had been making alcohol or "gray water" [tó łibá], a corn liquor. This is created by allowing a quantity of fresh corn kernels to ferment in water. When the brew reaches a milky consistency, it is very potent. Since there were no stills to separate the liquid from the mash, the Navajos drank the "milk" or gray liquid and soon became intoxicated.

I was now in a spot. If I left the trail and fled down the flats, the approaching horsemen might discover that I was a lone, unarmed white man and follow me to have some "fun." If I rode straight ahead, they might have "fun" with me anyway. I quickly decided to ride straight and face the crowd, hoping I might see a friendly face or two in the party of about twenty.

Coming abreast, I realized that my apprehensions were unfounded. They were happily full of gray water, and I was relieved to find that I knew most of them. All were young fellows, some from the San Juan River area, others from Sanostee, and the rest from the surrounding region. To my greater relief they were not in a vicious mood; all were pleasant. Each one rode up singly to me and shook my hand. They insisted that I accompany them to the sing that afternoon, but I begged off, saying that I must get home. They rode away in a friendly mood after talking and joking for some time.

By way of speculation, what might have happened back in those days had a lone Navajo rider encountered a bunch of drunken white men on a lonely trail in white man's country? I shudder to think. Some time ago, a seventy-year-old Navajo friend came to town from Shiprock. He had no big wad of money, only two dollars. He visited me and told me how he came to town for the ride and to see some old friends. I fed and talked with him for about an hour. He later ran into a bootlegger, who sold him some cheap wine. In his aged condition and not being used to drink, he became intoxicated. I do not know if he went to sleep on the sidewalk or around some corner in an alley or if he was just staggering around; he did not tell me. But he was arrested, thrown in jail, then tried and fined sixty dollars or sixty days in jail.

This old fellow was harmless and good natured. He has an aged wife, a son, and several grandchildren to support on a small government pension. His fine meant that his dependents would be obliged to reduce an already meager ration and that the trader who extends him credit will have to carry him over until the fine is paid. I am disturbed by the inequity in our local laws. The current rules allow the white man to drink beyond his powers of perception and control, while the Indian is not allowed to drink at all. What is fair for the white man should be fair for the Indian.

Navajo women in public appear to be more modest than their white sisters. Most advances are usually made by the men, although women have a way of letting it be known that they are open to suggestions. In the old days it was fairly common for a man to start a conversation with a woman of his acquaintance or perhaps a relative, but never with strangers. Today, the younger people are freer in their social approach than their elders.

Navajos do not have double standards of morality. In fact, one might say that in the past there was little standard at all and that being found out was the only sin. In these situations, the woman was as free to go her way as was the man; however, most of the people lived good, honest, and moral lives, according to their standards.

Illegitimacy appears to carry no stigma or shame for either mother or child. I have often thought this attitude more sensible than ours. I believe that the mother paid whatever debt she may have owed society when she brought the child into the world. The baby is here through no fault of its own, so there should be no rejection or shame of any kind. I admire this attitude in such matters, although there are those who might say that acquiescence breeds further illegitimacy. Perhaps, but Navajos accept the situation, and the child is not handicapped because of the exigencies of its birth.

There is no word in their vocabulary for prostitute. The term they use is "kiyąąh si-zíní, meaning "She who stands by the side of the house." As far as I can learn, this name came about in the early days of Gallup and other railroad towns near the reservation, when loose women stood in the shadows of buildings and beckoned men to follow them.

There is some intermarriage among the Navajo and other tribes, mostly the Pueblo Indians on the eastern fringe of the reservation, giving the Navajos a strain of Pueblo blood in their veins. Very few Navajos have married whites or Mexicans. Although they are "over the fence neighbors" to the Utes, there is hardly any intermarriage between the two tribes, perhaps because the enmity of the old days smoulders yet.

Navajo Marriage Customs and Family Life

When a Navajo girl reaches the age of puberty, a four-day ceremony or Kinaaldá is held in her honor. This ceremony serves notice to others that she has attained womanhood, although it is usually some years before she is betrothed and married. There are few old maids in Navajo land. There are those without husbands who are raising families and doing well, supporting them to the best of their ability. In some instances, these may be polygamous wives married in the Navajo custom. The rest do not remain unmarried very long. Sooner or later some young man is ready to fill the vacancy.

Bachelors are as scarce as old maids. There are no tribal laws or taboos concerning the status of unmarried women and bachelors, but there seems to be an undertone of feeling against it. Married life is regarded as the ideal state of existence. I know one married woman, fairly young looking yet, who tells me that she has borne her husband twelve children, five of whom are still alive. The birthrate among the Indians is very high, and if it were not for the high infant mortality rate, they would have a huge population.

Navajo parents are choosy about whom their daughters marry. Marrying into a well-to-do family is considered good judgment. In the old days, daughters were not sold, but the parents of the groom did make an exchange of so many sheep and horses for the girl. There is not much bargaining done nowadays, although the custom is sometimes still observed. Many couples obtain a license from the county clerk; others meet and decide to live together, set up housekeeping, and are considered married by their neighbors.

The Navajo marriage ceremony is simple but looked upon with as much religious fervor as an Anglo wedding. Guests are not formally invited, but word is sent out that a wedding, sing, or other type of gathering will be given by a family on a certain day. Those who wish to attend appear.

The first part of the ceremony consists of sprinkling sacred corn pollen toward the four points of the compass within the hogan. The heads of the bride and groom are then anointed with pollen. There is much singing and praying led by the medicine man with guests joining in. During the main part of the ceremony, the bride and groom eat cornmeal from a ceremonial wedding basket that has been blessed. The pair do not reach for the sacred meal themselves; a pinch of it is placed between their lips by the medicine man. Later, everyone is given a taste of the meal.

When the singing ends, the group feasts on coffee, fried bread, roasted or broiled mutton or goat, and canned fruit. There is usually plenty since guests bring a good supply of food to contribute.

Navajos do not consider the relationship stronger on the mother's side than the father's, but the mother is the real head of the family. Children take their clan name from her, and she has an important say in the home. All clan names originate with the woman who is the head of the family.[6] The children belong to her clan and not the father's. A son may be called Tall Man's Son, to establish his parentage in the minds of others, but if his mother is a member of the Mud [Hashtł'ishnii] clan, he is a "Mud" too and not a "Salt" [Áshįįhí], from his father's clan. The People do not believe in marrying even distant blood relatives, no matter how remote the relationship may be. Marriage to members of the same clan is strictly forbidden. Even a marriage with a very distant clan member is taboo. This is, in my opinion, one of the major reasons why Navajos are a virile race today.

In the past, Navajos practiced polygamy, but seldom had more than two or three wives, and these were often sisters. The government maintained a constant vigil to suppress the practice. Young men sometimes married women with children older than themselves.

I know of many young men who marry an older woman because she has a good flock of sheep and perhaps a good-looking daughter in the bargain. Often her daughter becomes his wife as well. Financially, it was a fine thing for the man, as it provided two blanket weavers instead of one. In such cases, the young woman often had a flock of sheep and goats of her own as did the older woman, and the young groom had a more or less idle existence, freeing him to attend sings, dances, horse races, and card games. Even so, he had no claim on the wealth of the two women because the flocks and herds belonged to them. He may not have any personal resources except those passed on to him by his wives.

The dress of these Navajo children reflects the care of their parents and the process of enculturation of Navajo values.

It was taboo for a Navajo to speak to his mother-in-law or meet her face to face. This was sometimes overcome by marrying both mother and daughter as just mentioned. The mother-in-law taboo comes from antiquity from the legend of Big Snake Woman's first meeting with her prospective son-in-law.[7]

Childbirth, to a Navajo woman, does not seem to be the ordeal it is among white women. I recall when a woman camped at the hogan provided by the trading post for use of its customers. That night she gave birth to a stillborn child. The next morning she got on her horse and rode home several miles away. Most Navajo women were equally mobile following a delivery.

The pride of the Navajo people is their children. In sickness or in health, nothing within the means of the parents is too good for their offspring. I have known wealthy families to impoverish themselves by hiring medicine men to heal their sick children. Love for them is a marked characteristic.

Navajos seldom punish their children in the American way, but "spare the rod and spoil the child." This does not mean that they do not occasionally slap a child hard on the face or other parts of the head for misbehavior; but they seldom spank them, and so Navajo children are "spoiled" in this way. It is a common occurrence at a trading post that when a child wants candy, soda pop, or cookies, if he or she is insistent, the goodies are forthcoming.

The men, too, are fond of their offspring and will often carry them about when they are small, showing much affection. A father may be seen carrying his baby in public as often as the mother, which seems to give him great pleasure. However, this is a modern innovation. I have no recollection of having seen much of this in the old days. There were scenes of much fondling and petting of a little fellow in the hogan when the father was home, but on trips, the mother carried the cradle board on her back. I have never seen it carried by the father. It was unthinkable that a man should engage in such a feminine chore. Now [1951], few cradle boards are found in the homes of younger couples.

The cradle board was made from two pieces of board acquired at a white settlement or Indian agency.[8] The wood was from one-half to one-inch thick, five or six inches wide, thirty inches long, notched at the top, and fastened together with thongs of buckskin. At the base was a footboard and at the top a willow arc or bow fastened near the head, from which hung a curtain the length of the cradle. This fabric was usually made of light, white muslin. Under a layer of cloth on the backboard was a pad of inner cedar bark upon which the baby lay full length. The mother replaced the pad as necessary.

On each side of the board were flat buckskin ribbons from top to bottom. The mother fully wrapped the infant, placed it on the pad, and lashed the baby securely to the wooden frame. This was done with a third piece of buckskin ribbon woven back and forth through the side loops, in zigzag lightning pattern. When the child slept, the mother dropped the curtain over the entire carrier, insuring the child protection from winter draft or summer flies.

With the advent of the trader, a half section of a round wooden cheese box replaced the bent willow curtain holder, forming the bow or arc at the head of the baby carrier. This was about three to four inches wide and three-sixteenths of an inch thick. The circular cheese box, made of hardwood, has not been used for shipping cheese for a number of years, but the cheese-box head pieces are still in evidence. Some of them have lasted through two and three generations of families.

Navajos do not make public demonstration of their affection. I have never seen a Navajo man and woman kiss but have often seen a mother kiss her baby. After the children get beyond babyhood and into their teens, parents apparently do not kiss them. They do put their arms around them, draw them close, and say endearing words. The meeting of a father with a grown son or daughter is very formal but filled with feeling; he presses the hand and gives a low murmured "my son" or "my daughter." The greeting of a mother and grown daughter is similar. The greatest show of affection is made when a mother sees a young son who has been away at school for a few months. She pulls the little fellow into her arms and says, "My little one." This is a commonplace statement, but in the Navajo language it literally means "a part of me." When spoken with the yearning of a Navajo mother, it takes on a pathos and tenderness hard to express.

Divorce

A Navajo woman was just as free to divorce her husband as he was to divorce her, and she did so just as often. In many cases the wife was the breadwinner and owner of the flocks and herds. If she decided her husband was incompatible, she divorced him by simply setting his saddle and other belongings outside their hogan. If he divorced her, he simply left. Marriage vows were held somewhat lightly in those days, so divorce was common.

The old restrictions are being violated more; often a woman just walks off and leaves her husband, particularly if there is little property involved. When the matter is brought before the native courts, more often than not, the case is decided in her favor.

Once in a while such issues have a tragic ending. On the San Juan River above Shiprock, there lived an Indian whom I will just call Charlie. He was a shiftless, no-account character, lazy and mean to his wife. He also dallied with local belles and contracted a social disease. His wife contracted it too, sending them both to the local hospital. His meanness grew so she finally left him, going to her sister's home. He talked her into coming back to him, promising to mend his ways. But in a short while he was just as cruel as ever, so she returned to her sister's hogan.

This time Charlie went back to fetch her with an extra horse and a lariat. He did no pleading, just forcibly placed her on the spare pony, tied her with the rope, and led the captive to his home. That night, while

Navajo mother with baby wrapped in a traditional cradle board. Protection and security in both a physical and spiritual sense are part of the teachings that continue to encourage the use of this device today.

Charlie slept, his spouse picked up the family axe, bashed in his head, and with the help of her sister, dragged his carcass to the edge of the river and threw it in. Someone discovered the body the next day and had it tenderly buried in the agency cemetery.

The wife and her sister received accommodations in the federal jail in Santa Fe, where they did not object to the lodging, beds, and regular meals. Soon the sister returned home, and the federal court discharged Charlie's wife on a plea of justifiable homicide.

Tribal Traditions and Lore

As the elders die, it will only be a matter of time until the traditions and clan history of the Navajos are gone. The "records" are the minds and memories of the old medicine men, who are rapidly passing away. Several years ago, Mustache Smeller of Sanostee, an old medicine man who really understood the Yé'ii Bicheii and its sandpaintings, died, leaving only one Navajo residing north and east of the Chuska range who fully understood the rite; the other man also passed away a few years ago.

This left a former schoolboy who dabbled a little with ceremonies to become a self-appointed Yé'ii Bicheii "specialist." His efforts are somewhat dramatic but lack the true ritual depth performed by the older men. His sandpaintings of the Yé'ii Bicheii ceremony are just caricatures of the ancient ones. I was fortunate to get copies, in the old days, of the true sandpaintings.

Because of the educational advancements of the Navajo, the ancient rituals are gradually dying. The old-timers realized things would soon be lost, so one old medicine man and close friend told me a great deal. This gentleman, because of his upbringing, said, "I know this history as it was taught me by my father, who in turn was taught by his father, and so on back for generations. I am getting old and will soon return to the Land Beneath. All the older men are gradually passing away, and the government is sending our children to school. They are not acquiring the knowledge of their forefathers, and our legends will soon be lost. I want to give the stories to you so they can be written down and kept for our children, as well as their children, who will learn to read and write and keep these stories in that way."

The Navajos have two types of teachings, which for convenience I call legendary lore and folklore.[9] The former pertains to the Navajo religion and recounts the creation of the earth, animals, vegetation, and human

Storytelling is an integral part of Navajo life, as shown in this photo taken in the Teec Nos Pos area, near the Four Corners. Sleeping Ute Mountain, Colorado, is in the background; Mesa Verde plateau is to the far right. Evans wrote, "The Navajo is a natural born storyteller. His method of communication makes it necessary. The only newspaper the Navajo boasts is the occasional visitor from the other clans, who tells the story of recent happenings. The storyteller has the ear of the listener without interruption until the story is fully told, and then the teller becomes listener in turn and thus an exchange of news is made." Photo by William Pennington.

race. The boys and girls who attend government schools now know practically nothing of this legendary lore but do know some of the folklore. The legends had come down previously in an unbroken line through the elders. These traditions recount, in detail, the coming forth of the Holy Beings from what I call the Land Beneath. In this place, the People lived in three worlds, where various events took place.

According to tradition, the Holy Beings made a great effort to reach the earth's surface and bring forth life as part of the creation. There are stories about terrible creatures, the killing of these monsters, and the preparation of a peaceful habitation for man. During this time, the four sacred mountains, which bound Navajo land, came forth. To the east are the San Juan Mountains; the south, Mount Taylor; the west, San Francisco Peaks; and the north, the La Plata Mountains.

Navajo beliefs also tell how different branches of religious ritual developed their own chants and sandpaintings of the stories with their Holy Beings. With each branch of the ritual there is an oral record of its origin and ceremony, how it began, and what took place. A recital of these accounts takes a long time. I have not yet been able to connect the material from all of the branches of these rituals; to my limited knowledge, no white man or even any Navajo ever has. However, I have recorded the stories to the period of time where it branches off and have collected information pertaining to Navajo theology. Behind all of this is the Great One, called First Man, who was the leading spirit in the acts of creation and whose image is never depicted in the sandpaintings.[10]

Navajo folklore is separate from the traditions, although some features of it creep into the latter. Folklore deals with extraordinary individuals or the exploits of an animal or bird. These are the stories which give the members of the animal kingdom the power of thought and speech, sometimes crediting them with a cunning master mind. For instance, there is the story of Big God [Yé'iitsoh] and the Turkey. Big God is a mythical being who had considerably less sense than bulk, who sought Turkey for a dinner. Turkey, however, was too smart for the gullible Big God, who died because of his foolishness. There are other stories, such as how the White-haired One wrestled Bear for possession of a corn field; the story of how shrewd Coyote outsmarted the lumbering and foolish Big God; the tale of Owl, a bird of evil omen, who brought fear to the heart of the Navajo named Pinto Horses; and the story of Coyote, Horned Toad, and Turkey, in which the deer became wild, having once been tame.[11]

Sandpaintings

The Navajos are a deeply religious and spiritual people. I often hear of many spiritual manifestations—visits from a Holy Being or a dream or vision—that they receive. The faith of this people is sublime. If it were not for that faith, there could not possibly be the great number of cures wrought by "singers." Rituals are not all manipulation of fetishes and charms. Medicine men also understand the efficacy of numerous herbs, which, when joined by their great faith, often achieve wonderful results. I admire their fortitude and adherence to what they believe is right.

When I first came to Navajo country, I heard a lot about the beauty of sandpaintings, one of the interesting rituals of the Navajo. My first opportunity to see this unique form of art happened the second summer following

A medicine man making a sandpainting of the corn plant, using colored sand, crushed rock, and other natural materials on a smoothed floor of sand.

the Great Snow, while I was still at the Sanostee Trading Post. An old fellow who traded at our post and was friendly to us became very ill. His name was Tall Blacksmith ['Atsidi Nez ('atsidí means "to hammer")].

Tall Blacksmith lived on a small farm two or three miles from the store up Sanostee Wash. He specialized in making heavy, richly ornamented bridle bits, crude copies of the enormous bits used by early Spanish settlers. Most of the iron for making these bits came from the Fort Defiance smithy. Today these bits are only in museums or private collections.

One Saturday afternoon, our roustabout, Dan Pete, told me there would be a sandpainting for Tall Blacksmith the next day. Sunday morning I invested in a couple of packages of Arbuckles Coffee and some sugar to take along. Leaving Pete to guard the locked-up post, I started out on foot about 10:00 a.m. and followed the banks of the wash to Tall Blacksmith's home. Before I got close, I heard a sort of "whoo-whooing," as well as the chant of the singers. As I neared the hogan, I saw what was making the sound. Four Navajos stood on top of the hogan, each facing a cardinal direction and twirling a string about three and a half feet long with a short piece of whittled wood at one end. The wood was hollowed out the length of one side. As the Navajos swung the strings in a circle, the pieces of wood [called a bullroarer or tsinidi'ni'] spun, making the strange sound.[12]

Joe Redcap demonstrates the art of sandpainting behind the Shiprock Trading Company. Yé'ii figures are depicted above, while a coiled snake is depicted at right.

Four other Navajos stood in front of the hogan, rolling large willow hoops in the four directions, while at the same time the singers huddled together, chanting lustily and swaying in rhythm to the music. I watched until they finished, then followed them into the hogan.

I handed the coffee and sugar to the lady of the house. She received them with a word of thanks and a smile. Tall Blacksmith, drawn and pale and showing the effects of illness, lay on a sheepskin. He greeted me with a firm handclasp and faint smile, but I wasted little time in formalities. Next, I was drawn to what lay on a smoothed layer of sand in the center of the hogan floor. There was a single figure, seven feet in length, with a large square head of blue pigment with black spots for eyes and mouth. I did not know then that this represented a mask, and so thought it looked strange. From the top of the head, feathers branched out in beautiful tracery of white pigment with black tips. A skirt covered the long, narrow body and loins. The legs and feet were visible, and ornaments hung from the wrists, elbows, waist, corners of the skirt, and knees. Typical Navajo designs decorated the skirt.

The outstretched arms of the figure held a bow in one hand and an arrow in the other. The colors used to create the figure were black, white, blue, red, and yellow. This combination of colors and details of design

were exquisite. There it lay: a mere sprinkling of colored sand upon a floor of ordinary sand, but the product was a work of art, a source of joy and pleasure to look upon. My first view of a sandpainting was an incredible experience. I almost had to pinch myself to realize that I was still in what is sometimes called "The Sand Hills of New Mexico."

Once the medicine man completed the sandpainting, he sprinkled sacred corn pollen upon Tall Blacksmith's head, then to the four directions as a blessing upon the man and his house. The men then laid Tall Blacksmith, who was naked except for a loin cloth, full length on the "painted" figure. The medicine man chanted a song, the men in the hogan joining in, while a gourd rattle provided a steady rhythm.

My friends told me before the singing began that there would be four long songs. I was welcomed to stay, but if I did, then I could not leave until the four songs were completed. I elected to stay. The songs were indeed long, but I wanted to witness the entire ceremony. I did not understand their meaning at the time but learned afterwards that the chants addressed the god pictured on the floor. There was also a hymn of thanksgiving to the Holy Beings for the blessings of nature—the hills and mountains; trees, shrubs, grass, and flowers; sunshine, moonlight, and starlight; clouds, rain, snow, rivers, and fruits of the field.

When the ceremony ended, I walked back down the trail and picked up my first prehistoric flint arrowhead. I also thought a lot about what I had seen. Soon, I became an ardent fan of sandpaintings and attended all the sings I could, but it would be a few years before the medicine men allowed me to sketch their work. Through close acquaintance and sympathy for the aims and problems of the people, I have been allowed to quietly copy many designs. I am grateful that I was welcomed wherever I went. It seemed only natural that I begin to collect reproductions of these beautiful pictures and devote a lot of time to Navajo traditions.

I believe that if the Navajo religion were written, it would fill a book larger than the Bible. Their numerous chants and prayers have sandpaintings and songs connected together, the sandpaintings illustrating each phase of a ritual. A medicine man often uses one part of a larger body of knowledge, while another singer uses a different portion. This practice comes from the story Navajos tell about the origin of the sandpaintings.

One time during the Creation, a Holy Being was hunting, found no game, became tired, and sat under a cedar tree to rest. Four flashes of lightning picked him up as he slept and carried him onto a cloud where the Great Ones were making sandpaintings and singing the songs that accompanied them. The gods directed the hunter to commit the designs to memory so that he could take them back to earth for the benefit of the people. He slid back to earth on a rainbow and taught each medicine man the songs, sandpaintings, and rituals that accompany them.

Thus, each detail of the picture must be correctly drawn from memory. The general outline of a sandpainting should be the same, but some details may be changed as the medicine man directs. Usually four assistants help the medicine man, but on an unusually large sandpainting I have seen as many as twelve at work. Different healers who use the same song have different versions of that sandpainting. I have, in my collection, three different versions of the same picture, illustrating how the figures mean the same thing but are arranged differently. This has caused people to believe that there are a greater number of pictures than there really are. Navajos made much more use of these paintings in the old days. They are a beautiful work of art, a work requiring patience, skill, and love of mystery. They used to be drawn for many occasions, but now they are used primarily for healing.

Following the completion of a sandpainting, the medicine man chants around it. The songs sound melodic in the Navajo language and are poetic in translation. Here are some of my favorites.

War Chant
Lo, the Flint Youth, he am I,
    The Flint Youth.
Moccasins of black flint have I;

Lo, the Flint Youth, he am I,
  The Flint Youth.

Tunic of black flint have I;
Lo, the black flint am I,
  The Flint Youth.

Clearest, purest flint the heart,
Living strong within me—heart of flint.
Lo, the Flint Youth, he am I,
  The Flint Youth.

Living evermore,
Feared of all forevermore,
Lo, the Flint Youth, he am I,
  The Flint Youth.

Monster Slayer,
Lo, behold me, he am I,
  The Flint Youth.

Leggings of black flint have I;
Lo, the Flint Youth, he am I,
  The Flint Youth.

Headdress of black flint have I;
Lo, the black Flint Youth, he am I,
  The Flint Youth.

Now the zigzag lightning four
From me flash,
Striking and returning
From me flash;
Lo, the Flint Youth, he am I,
  The Flint Youth.

Lo, the Flint Youth, he am I,
  The Flint Youth.

Song of the Masked Dancers

The day broke with slender rain.
The place which is called "lightning's water stands,"

The place which is called "where the dawn strikes,"
Four places where it is called "it dawns with life,"
I landed there.
I went among the shy youths.
One came to me with long life.
When he talked over my body with the longest life
The voice of thunder spoke well four times,
He spoke to me four times with life.
Holy sky youth spoke to me four times,
When he talked to me my breath became.

Song of Monster Slayer and Born for Water
The slayer of alien gods.
    That now am I.
The bearer of the Sun
    Arises with me,
Journeys with me,
    Goes down with me,
Abides with me,
But sees me not.

Child of the Water
    That now am I.
The bearer of the moon
    Arises with me,
Journeys with me
    Goes down with me,
Abides with me,
    But sees me not.

Ka-Niga Song
The poor little bee that lives in
    the tree.
The poor little bee that lives in
    the tree.
Has only one arrow
    In his quiver.

There are patterns repeated throughout these songs. For instance, four is one of the sacred numbers in Navajo tradition. Most important events in their teachings happen in sequences of four. Parts of ceremo-

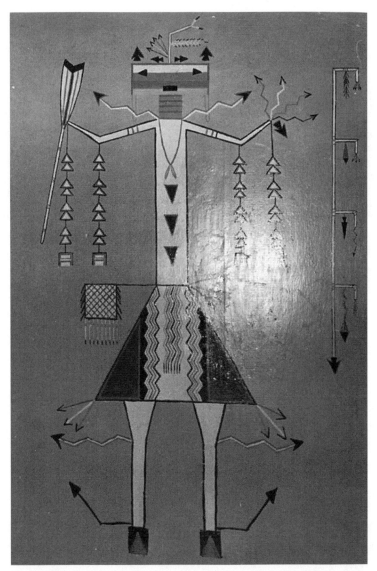

A mural painted by Evans depicting Monster Slayer, one of the holy twins of Changing Woman. He killed the monsters formed during the time of creation, making this world safe for the Navajos.

nies or activities are repeated four times, and certain characters in Navajo lore grew from babyhood to maturity in four days. When the Great Snake Man blew upon the Sun four times, it immediately went down; and four days of darkness followed. A great winged creature on Shiprock flew down four times before it grabbed Monster Slayer and carried him to the top of Shiprock, where he destroyed the creature; and there are four sacred colors used in sandpaintings, four sacred directions, and so on. I have asked several medicine men the meaning of these sequences of four. They tell me they do not know, only that the ancient ones told them that this was the way it should be.

There are other teachings about things such as why the sun travels a shorter distance across the sky in winter than in summer. According to medicine men, Sun Bearer [Jóhonaa'éí] carries the sun across the great dome of sky each day. Once it goes down, he takes it back to the east, as a special duty. In the east he has a large house, said to be twelve stories high—a type of pueblo built of turquoise.

The sun is hidden in a large room each night, covered by a number of black blankets. In the morning Sun Bearer sallies forth with his burden, following one of the many trails across the sky. In the winter, when the weather is cold and stormy, he takes the shorter trails to get back to the warmth of his home in the east as quickly as possible. When the warmer days of spring and summer arrive, he uses the longer sky trails.

Navajo First Daylight Song
The curtain of daylight is hanging
The Daylight Boy, it is hanging
From the land of day it is hanging
Before him at dawn, it is hanging
Behind him, as it dawns, it is hanging
Before him in beauty, it is hanging
Behind him in beauty, it is hanging
From his voice in beauty, it is hanging.

My First Fire Dance

I was still working at Sanostee Trading Post, when Dan Pete told me there was to be a Fire Dance [Dziłk'ijí Biką'jí (Mountainway)] several miles up Sawmill Road, in the foothills of the Chuska Mountain range.[13] There was plenty of timber on those slopes and so no shortage of wood for the great central fire or the smaller campfires. The beautiful starry night was cool, it being close to November. I saddled old Dobbin, tied on a heavy rolled blanket for protection against the cool night winds, and brought a good supply of oats for my horse. I climbed into the saddle and with an escort of Navajo friends made my way to the dance.

From my excellent vantage point provided for me by my companions, I was close to all that was going on. There was a great circular enclosure, formed of hewn cedar and pinyon trees, and a vast array of wagons, horses, mules, and saddle horses outside. The odors of hot coffee, mutton, and goat flesh broiling over fires inside the enclosure greeted my senses. Horses whinnied and mules brayed; a snarling dog jumped out on the pathway.

East of the enclosure was an opening about three paces wide, which provided an entrance for the different relays of dancers and spectators who sat within. I later learned that this spot was especially important to the fire dancers, who retreated through it to greet the first rays of dawn. In the center of the enclosure was a great fire. Skirting the inside edge at regular intervals were smaller fires around which onlookers sat or reclined and watched.

While I waited for the dance to begin, I had a fleeting impression that I had been carried back to prehistoric times. I stood and walked outside the enclosure. Reality jerked me back after I climbed a low hill and looked down upon the modern world with the ancient rituals behind me.

Near the entrance of the enclosure, there stood a "dressing room" of cedar and pinyon boughs. A low murmur surged through the crowd as the dance started. I returned to my post near the great central fire, sitting far enough away to keep from getting singed. I settled down to wait, a saddle blanket serving as buffer between me and the cold earth. As the night advanced, the air grew cooler, and my woolen blanket became a comfortable wrap.

A shrill, piping whistle sounded from the dressing lodge. In a few moments a dozen near-naked Navajo men came rushing and leaping through the opening, garbed in nothing but the traditional loin cloth. Their bodies were smeared with white clay, and their faces painted. They danced around the central fire, eight to ten feet in diameter and fed with large logs of cedar and pinyon. The flames shot twelve to fifteen feet into the air.

The dancers entered the arena uttering low growls and huskily singing a fierce song. Each dancer carried a slim, hollow wand about three feet long, on the end of which hung a small eagle feather. They circled the fire, dancing, growling, and singing, then gradually moved closer and closer toward the center. When it seemed they were close enough to roast, they plunged the ends of the rods into the flames, burning off the eagle feathers, then darted back a distance from the fire and pantomimed that they had destroyed the feathers.

The ceremony continued, as the wands whipped the air and the feathers miraculously reappeared. Dancing and singing in defiance of the fire, they disappeared through the opening of the enclosure with a great show of jubilance.

A couple of youths led the next group in. One young man was dressed as a woman, decorated in ribbons and silver ornaments. The other was nude except for his loincloth and body painted white. A large silver belt held his loincloth, while here and there were fastened small round pocket mirrors and a profusion of ribbons. The ribbons gave a modern touch and undoubtedly replaced the buckskin fringes of the past.

Following this couple came twenty or thirty Navajos wearing ordinary attire, singing and dancing in single file. The couple at the head of the group carried a sort of lattice work made of willows and branches of cedar, about twelve by eighteen inches in size, and decorated lavishly with evergreens and ribbons.

As the dancers reached each of the four cardinal directions on their trip around the fire, they paused for a moment, retreated, then advanced, dancing back and forth from the fire, each time presenting the lattice-work symbol to it four times. They then moved to the next direction, where they repeated their actions. After four trips around the fire, the dancers filed out of the enclosure and were followed by four groups of singers. They repeated the dance, with some variations, during the night.

At one point in the ceremony, four semi-naked dancers led a party into the enclosure; each of the four carried a wand with a wooden disk about six inches in diameter. The end of the wands extended three or four inches beyond the disks and were decorated with eagle feathers. Triangular black shapes were painted on each different colored disk, representing the eyes and mouth of a ceremonial mask. Each disk was painted one of four colors: blue represents Sun Bearer[Jóhonaa'éí]; white represents Moon Bearer [Tł'éé'honaa'éí]; yellow, Yellow Holy Wind [Níłch'i Łitsoii]; and black, Black Holy Wind [Níłch'i Łizhinii]. These are the four sacred colors used when creating sandpaintings.

While the rest of the group squatted on the ground and sang, the four dancers moved in a line, back and forth, to and from the fire on the west facing east. Each time they moved forward, they presented the symbols to the fire. At one point, the leader brought in the effigy of the sun and danced before the fire, offering the symbol each time he advanced and retreated, a total of four times.

On a number of occasions the semi-naked dance leaders carried the tsin dzilgiizh, a length of scissor-like lattice work. When the handles were pulled in opposite directions, the tsin dzilgiizh retracted toward the dancer. When they pulled the handles together, it shot forth toward the flames to a length of about two and one-half feet. Backing from, then advancing toward the fire four times, the dancers extended the tsin dzilgiizh close to the flames, while uttering shrill whoops. I was told that these objects represent lightning. The whole scene, hour after hour, was indescribably strange.

Toward morning a group of dancers entered, one of them carrying a shallow, concave "medicine basket" about fourteen inches in diameter. A tied bundle of six long, white-tipped eagle feathers lay in it. After circling the fire a couple of times, the group went into a huddle in front of the medicine man. The dancer who carried the basket stood in the center. All the time they were in this group, they rapidly repeated the word "dineh." In a few minutes the huddle ended, and the dancers sat in a group, off to one side, chanting. The basket contained a bundle of feathers, which was placed in front of the medicine man, in the center of a spread Navajo saddle blanket. An eagle feather lay in each of the four directions on the sides of the basket.

A little girl came to the medicine man, and he handed her the four feathers. With two in each hand, she began dancing to the group's singing. One of the singers pounded out a dull thumping rhythm with a short padded stick on an overturned medicine basket. The little girl waved the feather wands up and down, and soon the bundle of feathers in the basket stood and danced in perfect unison to the wands and singers' chant.[14]

The audience sat motionless as the medicine man showed his power. After several minutes of this performance there was another huddle over the dancing feathers. When the group dispersed, the singer who brought the basket picked it up, another man picked up the saddle blanket, and they all left the arena.

Later a different group of dancers entered. This time the basket held a small wooden disk representing the Sun. Two long eagle feathers were set in the edge of the disk to represent arms. A pair of feathers attached at the bottom edge of the disk was the legs. Again, there was the previous dancing to the fire, after which the men gathered. When they dispersed, the basket lay on a blanket in front of the medicine man. The little girl came forward again and picked up the feather wands. As she danced and waved the wands, the effigy slowly rose up in the basket and danced on its feather legs.

The Navajos laughed and marveled. The few whites present tried to explain it and talked of invisible strings, but only the medicine man and the men knew the secret. Here was the effigy of the Sun dancing before the fire and facing the East in anticipation of the coming of the great Sun to rule over the day.

A short time later another group entered the enclosure, danced before the fire, huddled before the medicine man, and laid a blanket on the ground before him. More dancing, another huddle over the blanket, so that when the group returned to the fire and pulled the blanket back, there were the green points of a yucca plant exposed a few inches above the ground. A repetition of these events, and each time the plant appeared to be in a more advanced stage of growth, until it finally emerged full grown with the central stalk bearing seed pods. This was the magic growth of hashk'aan, the fruit of the yucca plant, and a demonstration of the medicine man's power.

Next, a clown with a distorted painted face appeared, carrying a bow and arrow and making merriment for the crowd. He aimed an arrow at flying sparks or reached for the seed pods of the yucca, then in apparent sudden fear, changed his mind. Sometimes a spark popped out of the fire, making him jump with affected nervousness. Navajo crowds are always ready for fun; the people roared with laughter.

Soon an old woman with a rolled blanket upon her back began a pantomime conversation with the clown, much to the crowd's amusement. The clown tried to pick the seed pods from the magic yucca plant to feed her, but she refused to let him. Finally, despite her protests, he picked the pods, placed them in her basket, and together they hobbled out of the arena.

The growth of the yucca plant during the Fire Dance ['Ił náshjingo hatááł] ceremony is symbolic, illustrating the power of the sun, to whom the ceremony is directed, to bring plant life. The ceremony makes a profound impression on the people and is the crowning achievement of a medicine man.

Just as the first rays of sunrise appeared above the eastern hills, the climax of the night's activities began. The central fire had been built to gigantic proportions, and there was an air of expectancy. Soon there was a cry—"Here they come!"—and about a dozen breech-clouted Navajos trooped through the narrow opening of the enclosure. White mud smeared their bodies, and they danced wildly around the fire, bearing torches of twisted cedar bark, which they lit from the roaring flames.

They danced wildly, slapping themselves over the shoulders and back with the blazing torches, hitting each other, causing sparks to fly in every direction. Some of them swung their brands between their legs and rode them like stick horses. Strange chants, not heard in any other ceremonies, were accompanied by a sort of huff-huffing and strange growls. Shouts and war whoops mingled with laughter and shrieks of the spectators, and for a few minutes the excitement was indescribable. The people crowded back to escape the leaping men with brands and sparks; but as soon as the dancers left the arena, the Navajos rushed in and picked up the glowing, smoking fragments dropped by the dancers and washed their hands in the feeble flames and smoke.

This ritual gave them the smoking embers of a mysterious healing power, and by washing their hands in them, they believed that other parts of their anatomy were affected. Many of the Navajos preserved a small

Ceremonial gathering in Shiprock, 1910. In the background to the right is a ceremonial hogan. Front left near the wagon tongue, a photographer has a large wooden camera on a tripod, focused on two men and an individual mounted on a horse. Shiprock Trading Post was a short distance to the left of this scene.

portion of the charred cedar bark by placing it in small buckskin bags, to contain the unusual healing power.

The final scene with the intense earnestness of the dancers and bloodcurdling yells left an impression upon me which lasted for days. I was quietly aware that dawn had come and that soon the Sun, creator and author of all fire, would shine gloriously over the landscape. The great ceremonial fire, symbol of the Sun, began to smoulder and die. The performance of this ritual, close to the winter solstice, shows the connection between the sun and the fire. The Navajo Fire Dance is one of the two major, all-night ceremonies practiced by the Navajo people. It seems to outrank in popularity the Yé'ii Bicheii [Night Chant], the other major ceremony. The Fire Dance appeals to white visitors because of its diverse nature. I shall never forget the sights, sounds, and feelings the ceremony evoked in me.

Squaw Dance (Enemyway)

Another dance that I have attended is the Enemyway ['Anaa'jí] or Squaw Dance.[15] During this event, the women choose their partners. They do not face them but grasp the waistband of the men's trousers and dance backwards with a peculiar little shuffle, pulling their partners around and around. The woman makes the fellow pay for the dance and will not release him until she receives it. The girls (they are always unmarried women) take their places in the dancing space, which is encircled by visitors.

The young women dash into the crowd, seize a man, then drag him into the enclosure, and dance until he has had enough and pays. He gives her a nickel or a dime, very seldom more, unless he wants to make an impression. She hangs on to the same man if she thinks he has a good supply of money or until he drags himself away. Fifteen or twenty young fellows gather in a group to sing the dance songs, while one of them beats a small drum for rhythm. The dance usually breaks up at what the Navajos call Half of the Night [midnight].

This dance has changed over the years. It was sometimes called the corn dance because it was formerly held when the roasting ears of corn had ripened. It was a dance of thankfulness, an expression to the Holy Beings, who sponsor the fruitfulness of the corn fields. There was a form of stateliness and dignity befitting the occasion.

Now, squaw dances are held when the weather is warm enough in the spring and into the summer. These have degenerated into an arm-in-arm crow-hopping exhibition, to cadences of the singers and the tom-tom, à la Hollywood barn dances. The spirit and meaning has vanished with the changes.[16] Many of the other ceremonies are also not what they used to be. They are only caricatures of the old-time rituals.

Death, Witchcraft, and Skinwalkers

In the old days, Navajos had a great fear of the dead and would have a trader or missionary handle a burial whenever possible. But if a white man could not do it, then one person had the task of preparing the body. People also avoided the grave day or night. The burial place was usually a crack in the rocks where hills are easily accessed. The site was walled up with rocks or boulders to keep wild animals from disturbing the body. In flat country the burial was on level ground and the body covered with boughs, brush, and earth and the entire site covered with cedar or cottonwood poles. The Navajos who performed this necessary task became unclean, so they had to have a four-day purification ceremony performed by a medicine man before returning to society.

Often, as a last resort, when a patient was nearing the end, he or she would be taken to a government hospital, where agency employees were obliged to dispose of the body after death. If a Navajo died in his or her hogan, the body remained there and all the openings of the structure tightly sealed. The hogan was left strictly alone with no one taking even a stick of wood for a fire from it. It would be extremely unlucky to use any timber from this abandoned hogan as firewood for cooking food. Partakers of that food would be bothered by a malignant spirit. Thus, the timbers slowly rotted away, and after many years, the whole structure returned to Mother Earth.

One day several years ago, during a lull in trading, I listened to two old medicine men discussing some of their experiences. They talked of the weather and a recent rainfall, which was of great assistance after an extended period of drought.

"Do you know," said one, "I believe Hopi medicine is stronger than the Navajos'. Our elders have tried for months to get rain, and now in nine days the Snake Medicine [Tł'iish Bé'niih] has brought plenty of rain. We miss the days of Ugly Man and Bizhóshí, whose rain medicine was very strong. Even the witches had greater power in days gone by."

Thus they started discussing witchery. The taller of the two, Tall Man, remarked:

"When I was a boy my family lived near Tó Łeehchxǫǫn. In the neighborhood with his large family lived a peculiar fellow called Many Goats Uncle [Tłízí Łani Bida'í]. The neighbors whispered to each other that he was a witch. They said that he could turn himself into a skinwalker.[17] Of course, there was never any real proof; the Navajos just said that so and so happened. Someone would become ill. Failing with all sorts of medicine, sandpaintings, herbs, and chants, the medicine man would say, 'Well, Many Goats Uncle must have thrown one of his medicine darts.' Then he would cut the skin of the patient somewhere and suck out the terrible thing. Some of the excitable ones wanted to kill him, but wiser heads prevailed. They said, 'We shall make stronger medicine than his.'

"Soon people were saying terrible things about him. When a coyote howled at night, the young people cowered and shivered; and the older people would say, 'There goes Many Goats Uncle again. I wonder whose baby he'll get tonight.' There were whispers that this dreadful man transformed himself into a skinwalker, lurked about in the dark, and howled as he traveled. People told tales, in hushed tones, that this human wolf sneaked out to the grave of a babe that had recently died and ate its little body. This was when he gathered the material for his wicked darts—hairs, pieces of clothing, and the like. Everyone by this time was excited and afraid."

"Why," asked the other fellow, "did they not destroy this terrible person?"

"Well," answered Tall Man, "the Storm God saved the people this trouble. One day Many Goats Uncle was riding cross country. When he passed through an arroyo, a black cloud arose, and a Holy Being struck him off his horse with a bolt of lightning. After the thunder ceased, a torrent of rain and flood waters washed his body into a deep arroyo, where it still lies, covered with mud and trash."

Another time in the post, I noticed that an old customer seemed to hold himself aloof from the others, not talking to any of them. This seemed strange because all the other Navajos shook hands and carried on conversations. Not this man, whom I shall just call Hastiin. He drove to the post with his pony team and wagon, bumping and pounding his way down the road. He, his wife, and children all squatted on the bottom of the wagon box since there was no seat.

Once he arrived at the post, he was business-like, hurrying through his trading, paying no attention to anyone, and no one paying attention to him. With one exception: while Hastiin remained in the post, all trading ceased. Navajos leaned against the counter or wall, silently watching the quiet man. He was a good trader, never asked for credit, and had a nice flock of sheep and goats, which took care of his family's needs. He appeared to be such a quiet and harmless fellow that I naturally wondered about him.

Later, after all the other customers had gone, there remained one lone Navajo whom I questioned. "Why did Hastiin act so strangely, and why did the others treat him the way they did?" The Navajo seemed loath to answer, but with the gift of a bottle of pop and a candy bar he talked a little, but to the point. After looking around to see if anyone else was there, he told me almost in a whisper that Hastiin was a skinwalker and that people were afraid of him. They said he went forth in the dead of night desecrating graves, shooting bad medicine darts at people, and performing gruesome rites.

I asked why the Navajos did not investigate the fellow by following him on his nightly raids to discover if there was anything to the rumors. The man shook his head. That could not be done: it was forbidden and his medicine was very strong. He went on to tell about many strange things Hastiin was supposed to have done. But when I pinned him down, he had never seen any of these things happen, but other Navajos had. Such stories are only one form of native beliefs, but in the old days, they were common, creating a flurry of excitement and speculation among the people.

Another time, Small Man [Hastiin Yazzie] had not been to the post for two or three weeks. When he did come, I told him that I had missed him and wondered what had happened. He said, "I have been ill; Shits'ilí,

East side of Shiprock Trading Company, where Evans painted a rug design on the wall. *Left to right:* Mrs. Navijohn Begay and daughter, Sarah Evans, Will Evans, Sandoval girl, and Nita Pete Lee.

my younger brother, is very ill. I thought for some time that my turn to die had come. We could not find what ailed me. I had a pain beneath my heart and was afraid some witch had shot a medicine dart into my body. We tried the Evilway Ceremony but to no avail. We tried the Na'at'oyee chant but still no relief; finally I had them send for Navijohn—you know, the one who raised the woman from the dead and brought relief. So, here I am, glad to see you again."

Tall Man had been listening. He broke into the conversation at this point, saying, "I am sorry, my elder brother, but I am glad you are able to be with us again. Many things have happened since we last met. When you mentioned your fear about a witch, I remembered an incident which happened some years ago when I lived beyond Shiprock. We both recall the strange and frightening trial of the witches at the agency. Well, I must tell you what happened to my nearest neighbor. Good Singer's Grandson complained of a sharp pain in the right side of the back of his neck. The area was painfully swollen; he could not eat, lost weight, became very thin, and was about to give up. Tall Singer, who had been chanting over him, said one day, 'Perhaps you have been witched. I am going to find out.' So he took the sharpest arrowhead he had in his medicine bundle and cut a slit in the sick man's neck. The opening was almost as long as two joints of my finger.

"Then he sucked and sucked on the wound, at first getting nothing but blood and fluid, which he spat on the ground. Finally he got something, and what do you think it was? He pulled out a piece of charcoal with human hair wound around it. The object was about the size and length of half of the first joint of your little finger. Some witch had secured a piece of charcoal, not from an ordinary fire, but from the remains of a hogan which had been burned because someone had died in it, thus making it very bad medicine.

"Then this witch had gone to the resting place of a dead person and plucked hair from the decaying head. This long hair was what the witch had wrapped around the small piece of charcoal. Tall Man said it had been blown into the neck of Good Singer's Grandson, who became very ill. The patient mended rapidly once the dart was removed."

This happened long ago. Today, witches are scarcer. Still, several years ago a number of Navajos came up from the lower country, bringing tales to the Shiprock Agency that a certain Navajo had been shooting mysterious darts at other Navajos, causing much distress. Some of the men did not want to take the risk of killing him but asked the Superintendent to send him to the penitentiary for safekeeping, ridding them of his presence.

They argued the pros and cons of the case during a trial at the tribal court in Shiprock. There was a lot of heat from the accusations flying around, but there was no statute to prevent the shooting of his darts. Indeed, there was no proof of the act. So there sat the accused, facing the fact that the case would be thrown out of court, since the judge had no jurisdiction in such cases.

Then someone had a bright idea. The fellow was a polygamist, and polygamy was against the law; so why not report it? Not only did the culprit have two wives, but they were mother and daughter; and over and above the breach of law, the younger woman was not of age. The dart shooter was not only guilty of unlawful cohabitation but also a charge of rape of his younger wife. That fact sent him away for several years to Fort Leavenworth prison, even though it appeared that the court had railroaded him. The excitement subsided, and things returned to normal.

The accused returned from prison some years later, happy and talkative as before. He seemed to hold no grudge but was willing to talk of his experiences among the jailbirds. There was no rumor of witchery after that, and a steady decrease of witchcraft has taken place since that time.

Several years ago another strange rumor came out of the northwestern part of the reservation. People reported a Navajo woman who lived across the San Juan River from Bluff had given birth to a snake. This startled the inhabitants around Shiprock, and speculation ran rampant, even though no one had any details of the incident. Navajos are jittery regarding snakes.[18] Perhaps the mother in question was startled by the sudden appearance of a snake during her pregnancy, and in her mind, the child would arrive with a birthmark. In the process of transmitting the rumor, the story had grown from a birthmark to an actual serpent.

Some Navajos wear a piece of turquoise or shell in their hair or on their hatband to keep lightning from striking and snakes from biting them. Turquoise is often carried as a general good-luck charm to ward off evil influences. Most Navajos depend on their keen eyesight to avoid snakes. If bitten, they use an herb which grows in the foothills and prevents death. I have known of several Indians bitten by rattlesnakes, and none died. Their bodies swelled considerably and they suffered greatly, but the medicine man saved them.

Navajos and Animals

Most Navajos will not kill a wolf, coyote, bear, snake, frog, or lizard. They do not have a desire to kill any living creature which might cross their path. The wolf, coyote, bear, and snake have a prominent part in the traditions and had the power of speech in the beginning of time. Frogs are not killed because they are said to be responsible for the gift of moisture, while the lizard was helpful to the Holy Beings in the very beginning of life on earth.

The following story tells not only about the origin of the Navajo shoe game [Késhjéé], but also why bears' toes point inward like a human's. The shoe game is played by having teams choose sides. A pair of moccasins is placed on one side of the hogan and covered with a blanket or robe.

It is a game of chance, based on the members on each side providing themselves with short pieces of wood, perhaps sections of willows, as counters. The beginning team secretly places an object like a piece of wood or stone in one of the shoes. The robe or blanket serves as a temporary screen to keep the opposing side from seeing where it is placed.

The guessing side places sticks opposite the shoe they suppose contains the hidden object. The number of sticks laid down is regulated by the optimism of the players. If they guess right, the team is enriched that much. Each group takes turns until one side or the other goes broke; or, if a stalemate occurs, the game ends, and the side having the most sticks is declared winner.

The story about how this game first began is tied to the day and night creatures. Long ago when Bear walked like a man and all the animals used a universal language, the creatures of the night and those of the day got together. For some time the animals of the night had expressed a wish that there would be total darkness, while the creatures of the day desired the opposite. They decided to meet in the evening and play the shoe game, declaring that if the day animals won, there would be no more night, and vice versa. They played in the great hogan in which First Man and his assistants had performed the creation.

Bear's shoes were the only ones considered large enough to play the game properly, and so he offered their use. The day birds as well as the night birds were there, taking an active part in the proceedings. The animals started the game in the middle of the first half of the night. Since noon is considered the half, or middle, of the day, so is midnight called the middle, or half, of the night. They recognized midnight by the position of certain stars and other natural phenomena.

The game continued, punctuated by the grunts and growls of the animals and the squeaks and tweets of the birds. It was a close game; but as the night passed, there still was no winner. Once in a while Bear would let out a couple of grunts, indicating that he and the daylight boys had made a point. Then Owl would shout, "Whoo, whoo, whoo, whoo," revealing that the creatures of the night had scored. Thus it went on, all through the hours of the last half of the night. The day animals were sleepy and tired, but the night creatures were in fine shape, calling for a win so that their prowling in the darkness could continue uninterrupted.

Suddenly, Prairie Dog stumbled breathlessly through a hole in the wall, squealing as loudly as possible, "Daylight is coming, daylight is coming. You creatures of the night better get going, or you'll be caught outside before you reach the dens where you hide when the sun comes up." Streaks of dawn appeared in the east; confusion reigned amidst the animals. The night creatures were eager to get back to their usual haunts, as were the animals that prowled in the daytime. Bear was the last to get away, grabbing his shoes, turning them over to dump them out, and hurriedly placing them on his feet. In the confusion, he got the right shoe on his left foot and the left shoe on his right foot. That is why today bears' toes turn inward, as they did on that early morning after the shoe game held long ago.

Postscript
The Death of a Man, the End of an Era

As Evans prepared to celebrate his seventy-seventh Christmas, he passed
from this life. On December 6, 1954, the white community of Farmington and the Navajo community surrounding Shiprock became aware of
his death. His obituary announced that he had died quietly after several
months of failing health. But it was a peaceful farewell, as his wife, Sarah,
three sons—Ralph, Richard, and David—and daughter, Gwen, paid their
last respects.

To the Navajo community, Missing Tooth [Awóshk'al'ádin] had "gone
away." In Window Rock as the Navajo Tribal Council held session, Chairman Sam Akeah brought the news to many of the tribal advisors who had
known and worked with Will. He had often noted in his "Navajo Trails"
column, which he wrote right up to his death, the passing of another elderly Navajo with a piece of the tribe's history. He also mentioned that,
sometime, the two would meet again. That time had come.

The white community again recognized Will for his accomplishments—his authoritative study of the Beautiful Mountain uprising, his
knowledge of Navajo lore, his stint in the state legislature (1928), his service as police judge, and his presiding as justice of the peace, before retiring from public life. His artistic creations were another tangible means by
which he was remembered. Indeed, on August 30, 2002, an open house
at the Farmington Museum featured an exhibit entitled "Painting with a
Passion: Will Evans and the Navajo." There the public encountered his
close-to obsession in using Navajo symbols to beautify his home, on everything from lampshades and tables to vases and wall hangings. His art
has now become a collector's item.

Evans resting in the mountains near his home in Farmington, 1952.

But Evans's real legacy rests in what he has preserved in Navajo and trader history. At a time when there was comparatively little interest in the People, he set about to consciously capture the personalities, culture, and events of this isolated group living on the northern part of the Navajo Reservation. What could have been a passing fancy became a lifelong immersion to learn of a very different, when compared to his Welsh ancestry, group of people.

Will it make a difference to present and future generations? Hopefully so. As a personal example, when this manuscript was in various stages of preparation, Jim Benally of Provo, Utah, helped the authors with translation and spelling. During his assistance, he discovered that his grandfather, Slim Policeman, was featured in a lengthy section of the book. It is unnecessary to point out the personal nature the manuscript then assumed.

With Evans's passing, the era of trading posts and Navajo traditional lifestyle dependent upon them were also fading. He missed the turbulence of the 1960s and 1970s, culminating in the Federal Trade Commission hearings (1972–1973) and the closing of many posts because of changes in Navajo and white society. He also missed the conversion of many posts into convenience stores and the revolution in transportation that made going off reservation a normal, almost mandatory, way of life. And he missed the very controlled aspect, so prevalent in the twenty-first century, of collecting and preserving cultural knowledge on the reservation.

Perhaps it is just as well. Living at a time when everyone struggled to survive, Evans enjoyed personal relationships and activities that enriched

Will Evans as he appeared near the end of his "Trail," surrounded by his personal art pieces and the traditional artifacts he collected over a lifetime. His legacy continues.

his life. As mentioned previously, he had no regrets—only fond memories, even though times were often hard. He later rejoiced in the difficult experiences he encountered and was anxious to share with others the lessons that came from those trials. He did so sensitively for the era in which he wrote. Future generations can be thankful for what he has done in recording the past. May they live as well.

Evans at the Grand Canyon, 1926, around the time that he began to write "Navajo Trails."

Appendix
Publications by Will Evans

[Editors' note: This list is based on information available in the Will Evans Collection at Brigham Young University.]

The Corner Post, organ of the Four Corners Club, issued the 15th of each month; William Evans was editor and a member of the Board of Directors:
"The Four Corners," vol. 1, no. 9, February, 1926
"Pioneers Made Waste Places Fruitful," vol. 1, no. 11, April, 1926
"Progress" vol. 1, no. 12, May, 1926
"Four Corners Region Rich in Resources," no date or number
Farmington Daily Times:
"Wm. Evans of Shiprock Wants Historical-Scientific Society" May 24, 1923
"Early Day Missionaries to Indians Were True Pioneers and Peacemakers," August 23, 1950
"One Christmas Eve in Navajo Land Is Described Vividly," December 24, 1951
"Impact of Oil, Gas, Other Minerals Changes Navajo Outlook: Former Indian Trader Tells of Early Search," March 28, 1952
"Will Evans Describes His First Christmas in Navajo Land," December 24, 1952"
"Trader Tells How Gas Has Affected the Navajo," March 28, 1953
"Mysterious Toe-Koh-E Helps Navajos," March 27, 1954
"Fifty Years in Navajo Land," vol. 63, no. 95, no date
"Indian Trader Does Not Like 'Good Old Days,'" no date or number
"Navajo Ceremonial Art: Interesting Pottery of Ancient Times," no date or number

"Oil and Gas Wealth of Navajo Land," no date or number

"Voting Accord," letter to the editor, no date or number

"Why the Turkey Tail Feathers Are White, A Navajo Legend As Told by Mr. Will Evans, Indian Trader at Shiprock, N.M.," no date or number

The Farmington Quill Club, a monthly writer's group:

"A Navajo Recessional," December 10, 1934

"Timberline," sometime in 1939

"Old Trails," February 8, 1940

"Saint Patrick's Day," March 8, 1940

"Sand," March 30, 1940

"Portrait of a Pioneer," Poem, March 31, 1940

"Sunset," May 4, 1940

"Wild Flowers," May 1940

"Thanksgiving," November 6, 1940

"Words," November 16, 1940

"Superstition," December 7, 1940

"Nothing," January 18, 1941

"George Washington," February 22, 1941

"The New Year, Just a Few Random Thoughts," January 17, 1943

"Brief Sketch of a San Juan Pioneer," July 21, 1950

"Billy the Kid, an Episode of the Wayside," by Will Evans and John Arrington, February 14, 1953

"The Children on Christmas Eve," no date

Farmington Times Hustler,

"Ancient Peruvians Had Economic System That Gave All a Fair Deal," August 17, 1934

"A Tempest in a Teapot," March 22, 1938

"House Bill Introduced by Wm. Evans, J. M. McMath and Lloyd Ambrose," State of New Mexico House of Representatives, Ninth Legislature, Santa Fe, to amend the New Mexico School Code Chapter 148, Laws of 1923.

"'Jake Morgan, Pioneer Navajo Tribal Leader: Tribute to a Great Indian," no source.

Latter-day Saints' Millennial Star, the church organ in Great Britain, "The Origin of the American Indian" by William Evans, Shiprock, New Mexico, August 4, 1938.

Letters to the editors of the *Farmington Times Hustler* and *Farmington Daily Times* published the following dates:

February 11, 1938	February 27, 1950
January 29, 1951	February 5, 1951
April 5, 1951	April 11, 1951
February 25, 1952	September 2, 1952

Liahona: The Elders' Journal, organ of the missions of the Church of Jesus Christ of Latter-day Saints in the United States:
"The Necessity of Obedience," vol. 7, no. 22, November 20, 1909
"Mormonism to the Rescue," vol. 7, no. 31, January 22, 1910
"The Test of Reason," vol. 7, no. 47, May 14, 1910
"Origin of the American Indians," vol. 35, no. 19, March 8, 1938
Montezuma Valley Journal, "The Beautiful Mountain Rebellion," September 17, 1986.
"Our Neighbor the Navajo," talk given by Will Evans over KIUP radio station in Durango (songs by Richard Evans, such as "Waters of the Minnetonka" and others).
"Reminiscences and Comparisons," February 28, 1952, no source.
New Mexico Folklore Record, publication of the New Mexico Folklore Society, of which Will Evans was honorary vice president, "The Origin of Navajo Sandpainting," vol. 9, 1954–55.
San Juan Valley Sun, "Was Shiprock a Ship at Time of Noah's Ark," June 9, 1949.
Southwest Tourist News, "Venerable Hos-too-ee Discuss a Cure," vol. 7, no. 17, March 10, 1937.
Southwestern Lore, journal of the Colorado Archaeological Society:
"Navajo Folklore," vol. 1, 1935: 10–16
"The Venerable Hos-Too-E Discuss Owls," vol. 4, no. 2, 1938: 37–38
"Eclipse of Moon Mars Navajo Fire Dance," vol. 4, March 1940: 78–79
"How Jackrabbit Got His Long Ears," vol. 3, 1947: 41–42
"The White-Haired One Wrestles with Hosteen Bear, A Navajo Folk Story," vol. 13, no. 4, 1948: 53–54
"Hosteen Bear Loses the Second Fall, A Navajo Folk Story," vol. 14, no. 1, 1948: 3–4
"Navajo Folk Lore," vol. 14, no. 3, 1948: 48–68
"Sandpainting," vol. 17, no. 3, 1951:52–55
"The Winged Monsters on Shiprock," December Folklore no date or number
The Relief Society Magazine, "Indian Culture," vol. 25, no. 7, July 1938.
The Sunny San Juan Magazine, "The Land Beneath," 1939 Christmas edition, pp. 16–23.
The Utah Genealogical and Historical Magazine, "Shiprock," October 1912.
"Why I Am a Mormon," talk with the Indian Traders at Winslow, Arizona, no date.

Notes

Introduction

1. Frank McNitt, *The Indian Traders* (Norman: University of Oklahoma Press, 1962, 1989).
2. Richard D. Poll, Thomas G. Alexander, Eugene E. Campbell, and David E. Miller, eds., *Utah's History* (Provo, UT: Brigham Young University Press, 1978), 133.
3. For an excellent study of this era, see Charles S. Peterson, *Take Up Your Mission: Mormon Colonizing along the Little Colorado River, 1870–1900* (Tucson: University of Arizona Press, 1973). For a less scholarly approach, see James H. McClintock, *Mormon Settlement in Arizona* (Tucson: University of Arizona Press, 1921, 1985).
4. This information is derived from LaVerne Powell Tate, "A Family of Traders: History and Reminiscence," *Blue Mountain Shadows* 29 (Winter 2003–2004): 67–80; McNitt, *The Indian Traders,* 299–302 (see n.1).
5. Tate, "A Family of Traders," 69 (see n. 4).
6. Informal survey of family members by Susan Woods, February 17, 2004.
7. Franc Johnson Newcomb, *Navajo Neighbors* (Norman: University of Oklahoma Press, 1966), 22.
8. Rosetta Biggs, *Our Valley* (J. T. Biggs Family, privately printed, 1977).
9. For more information on Navajo trading customs and expectations, see Robert S. McPherson, "Naalyéhé Bá Hooghan, 'House of Merchandise': Navajo Trading Posts as an Institution of Cultural Change, 1900–1930," *American Indian Culture and Research Journal* 16, no.1 (1992): 23–43.

10. For a more complete explanation, see Dan Vogel, *Indian Origins and the Book of Mormon* (Salt Lake City: Signature Books, Inc., 1986).

11. The information about Evans's life, unless otherwise cited, is used with the permission of the Farmington Museum and comes from a publication written by Liesl Dees entitled *Painting with a Passion: Will Evans and the Navajo* (Albuquerque: Cottonwood Printing Company, 2001).

12. Thomas Evans, "Journal," Will Evans Papers, Special Collections, Brigham Young University Library, Provo, UT.

13. Evans's second Navajo name was "Chiishch'iłi" meaning "Curly Head."

14. Will Evans, "An Autobiography," BYU.

15. Ralph William Evans, *Life History of Ralph William Evans* (Salt Lake City: 1979), 25.

16. Sarah Walker Evans, Reminiscences, April 23–24, 1951, BYU; U.S. Post Office database information courtesy of Jim White; Ralph William Evans, *Life History,* 36 (see n. 15).

17. Frank Leland Noel and Mary Eliza Roberts Noel, manuscript, "Eighty Years in America," compiled by Jennie Noel Weeks, 1962, p. 81; Will Evans to Sarah Evans, June 24, 1907, BYU.

18. McNitt, *The Indian Traders,* 300 (see n. 1).

19. Ibid.

20. David Joseph Evans, *Life History of David Joseph Evans*, compiled by Bruce Evans (Farmington, March 1999), 14; manuscript, "Indian Country/Family History Tour, Evans Family Reunion, Cortez," 1984, Special Collections, Brigham Young University Library, Provo, UT.

21. Nancy J. Parezo, *Navajo Sandpainting: From Religious Act to Commercial Art* (Albuquerque: University of New Mexico Press, 1991), 44–45.

22. For an interesting discussion of some of the latest thinking on this topic and the influence of the well-known trader Dick Simpson, who is credited as being one of the first to introduce this art, see Jean-Paul and Rebecca M. Valette, "In Search of Yah-nah-pah: The Early Gallegos 'Yei' Blankets and Their Weavers," *American Indian Art Magazine* (Winter 1997): 56–69.

23. Will Evans's autobiographical information to John MacClary, September 25, 1937, Special Collections, Brigham Young University Library, Provo, UT.

24. Ibid.

25. Ralph William Evans, *Life History* 46 (see n. 15); Gwen Evans Jones, miscellaneous material in Special Collections, Brigham Young University Library, Provo, UT.

26. "Wm. Evans of Shiprock Wants Historical-Scientific Society," *Farmington Daily Times,* May 24, 1923, 8.

27. Records of the State of New Mexico, Library Legislative Council Service; information from the *New Mexico Blue Book, or State Official Register, 1929–30.*

28. Evans to MacClary, September 25, 1937 (see n. 23).

29. Beth Burt, wife of Richard Evans, remembers that by 1940, Will's painted furniture enlivened the family's living area at the trading post, but she didn't meet Will Evans until their marriage in 1945. Beth Burt Evans interview with Liesl Dees, April 29, 2001; Will Evans to M. K. Sniffen, October 31, 1938, Special Collections, Brigham Young University Library, Provo, UT.

30. Florence Walker Cluff, "Heaven with the Evans," March 1982, Special Collections, Brigham Young University Library, Provo, UT.

31. *Farmington Times Hustler,* April 25, 1941.

32. *Farmington Daily Times,* January 31, 1982; Sarah Walker Evans, Journal, booklet 1:3, 7, compiled by Susan Evans Woods, 1997, in possession of author (Woods).

33. Will Evans to David Evans, September 25, 1943, "Appendices to David J. Evans's Mission to Hawaii 1941–1943," compiled by Bruce Evans.

34. The trader-missionaries and their families were Will Evans, James B. Collyer, George R. Bloomfield, and William J. Walker. The fifth person, Paul Burnham Palmer, was from a trading family, while Oliver Stock was a farmer. David Kay Flake, "History of the Southwest Indian Mission" (master's thesis, Brigham Young University, July 1965), 111–113.

35. Will Evans to Levi Edgar Young, December 29, 1942, Special Collections, Brigham Young University Library, Provo, UT; Beth Burt Evans interview with Liesl Dees, April 29, 2001.

36. Family tradition recalled by coeditor Susan Woods.

37. "To Whom It May Concern," May 2, 1945, Will Evans legal document, Special Collections, Brigham Young University Library, Provo, UT.

38. Sarah Walker Evans, Journal, booklet 1:3 (see n. 32).

39. *Farmington Daily Times,* January 31, 1952.

40. *San Juan Valley Sun,* August 14, 1952.

41. "Navajos 'Pawn' Jewelry to Pay Fines," undated article, Special Collections, Brigham Young University Library, Provo, UT.

42. Sarah Walker Evans, Journal, booklet 1:12; booklet 5:16; booklet 6:33; booklet 7:4 (see n. 32).

43. William Evans, "Indian Culture," *The Relief Society Magazine* 25, no. 7 (July 1938): 438–441.

44. Ibid., 438.

45. William Evans, "The Origin of the American Indian," *Latter-day Saints' Millennial Star,* August 4, 1938, 483.

46. Ibid., 441.

47. William Evans, "Sand Paintings: Nature and Origin" (Talk before the San Juan Archeological Society, Farmington, NM, December 12, 1938).

William Evans Papers, Special Collections, Brigham Young University Library, Provo, UT.

48. William Evans, "Navajo Sandpaintings and the *Book of Mormon*" (Talk before the MIA, Kirtland, NM, January 3, 1938) Special Collections, Brigham Young University Library, Provo, UT.

49. William Evans to *Improvement Era,* December 12, 1937, Special Collections, Brigham Young University Library, Provo, UT.

50. Evans, "The Origin of the American Indian," 482–485 (see n. 45).

51. B. H. Reddy to Will Evans, July 18, 1939, Special Collections, Brigham Young University Library, Provo, UT.

52. Will Evans to B. H. Reddy, July 21, 1939, Special Collections, Brigham Young University Library, Provo, UT.

53. Maureen Trudelle Schwarz describes succinctly this phenomenon: "The principle of synecdoche holds that people, objects, and other entities that have contact may influence each other through the transfer of some or all of their properties. The part stands for the whole. Teeth, saliva, sweat, nails, hair represent a total person, in such a way that through these parts one can act directly on the individual concerned, either to bewitch or enchant him. Separation in no way disturbs the contiguity; a whole person can even be reconstituted or resuscitated with the aid of one of these parts: *totum ex parte*' (Mauss 1972[1902]: 64)." *Molded in the Image of Changing Woman: Navajo Views on the Human Body and Personhood* (Tucson: University of Arizona Press, 1997), 5.

54. B. H. Reddy to Will Evans, July 27, 1939, Special Collections, Brigham Young University Library, Provo, UT.

55. Will Evans to B. H. Reddy, August 1, 1939, Special Collections, Brigham Young University Library, Provo, UT.

56. B. H. Reddy to Will Evans, August 9, 1939, Special Collections, Brigham Young University Library, Provo, UT.

57. Sherry L. Smith, *Reimagining Indians: Native Americans through Anglo Eyes, 1880–1940* (New York: Oxford University Press, 2000).

58. Ibid., 5.

59. John Stewart MacClary, "He Links Stone Age with Steel Age," *The Desert Magazine* (December 1937): 18.

60. Will Evans to Richard Evans (son), October 16, 1938, Special Collections, Brigham Young University Library, Provo, UT.

61. Ibid.

62. Smith, *Reimagining Indians,* 13 (see n. 57).

63. Ibid., 14.

64. For a sampling of autobiographical and biographical writings about Navajo traders, see the following: Martha Blue, *Indian Trader: The Life and Times of J. L. Hubbell* (Walnut, CA: Kiva Press, 2000); Hilda Faunce, *Desert Wife* (Lincoln: University of Nebraska Press, 1928); Frances Gillmor and Louisa Wade Wetherill, *Traders to the Navajos:*

The Wetherills of Kayenta (Albuquerque: University of New Mexico Press, 1952); Laura Graves, *Thomas Varker Keam, Indian Trader* (Norman: University of Oklahoma Press, 1998); Alberta Hannum, *Spin a Silver Dollar* (New York: Ballantine Books, 1944); Elizabeth C. Hegemann, *Navaho Trading Days* (Albuquerque: University of New Mexico, 1963); Frank McNitt, *The Indian Traders* (Norman: University of Oklahoma Press, 1962); Frank McNitt, *Richard Wetherill: Anasazi* (Albuquerque: University of New Mexico Press, 1952); Samuel Moon, *Tall Sheep: Harry Goulding, Monument Valley Trader* (Norman: University of Oklahoma Press, 1992); Franc Johnson Newcomb, *Navaho Neighbors* (Norman: University of Oklahoma Press, 1966); Gladwell Richardson, *Navajo Trader* (Tucson: University of Arizona Press, 1986); and Willow Roberts, *Stokes Carson: Twentieth Century Trading on the Navajo Reservation* (Albuquerque: University of New Mexico Press, 1987).

65. Franc Johnson Newcomb, *Navaho Neighbors* (Norman: University of Oklahoma Press, 1966); *Hosteen Klah: Navaho Medicine Man and Sand Painter* (Norman: University of Oklahoma Press, 1964); *Navaho Folk Tales* (Albuquerque: University of New Mexico Press, 1967, 1990).

66. Will Evans to John Stewart MacClary, September 25, 1937, Special Collections, Brigham Young University Library, Provo, UT.

67. Ibid.

68. Leland C. Wyman, "Navajo Ceremonial System," in *Handbook of North American Indians: Southwest,* vol. 10, ed. Alfonso Ortiz (Washington, DC: Smithsonian Institute, 1983), 542.

69. Richard P. Evans to Sheldon Dustin, August 19, 1938, Special Collections, Brigham Young University Library, Provo, UT.

70. "To Whom It May Concern," signed affidavit, May 2, 1945, Brigham Young University Library, Provo, UT.

71. "Sanostee (6,000 ft.), San Juan County, New Mexico, . . . is located on the Sanostee Wash on the eastern slope of the Tunicha Mountains 20 miles south of Shiprock and eight miles west of U.S. Highway 666." Laurance D. Linford, *Navajo Places: History, Legend, Landscape* (Salt Lake City: University of Utah Press, 2000), 258.

72. Many traditional Navajos believe that objects associated with the dead, when used by the living, can attract the deceased's evil influence. Evans is referring to the problem of burning wood that would cause the dead to return and interact with those associating with the store.

73. The color system used by older Navajos to identify coins is derived from observation. A penny, because of its light brown copper color, is called a "red." Nickels in the old days were made of a gold material and so were known as "yellows." The silver in a dime, when it became tarnished, obtained a blue hue, hence the name "blue." John Holiday,

Navajo medicine man, conversation with author in Monument Valley, June 16, 2004.

Events

1. While this is certainly the white man's view, prevalent in the 1950s, many more-recent books and articles explain the Navajo view. Briefly, there were problems with broken treaties, infringement on their lands, military incursions against them, and little understanding of their culture and needs. The resulting series of conflicts, starting in 1858 and continuing through 1866, resulted in over 8,000 Navajos surrendering and being moved to Fort Sumner for incarceration (1864–1868), until the Navajos returned to their homeland and a new reservation. For the Navajos' perspective, see Broderick H. Johnson, ed., *Stories of the Long Walk Period* (Tsaile, AZ: Navajo Community College Press, 1973).

2. The Navajos signed the Treaty of 1868 with the federal government represented by William Tecumseh Sherman on June 1. Barboncito was the main spokesman of the Navajo delegates, all of whom placed their thumbprints next to their names. From this agreement, the Navajos received a reservation that straddled what is today the New Mexico-Arizona boundary.

3. Manuelito was born around the Bears Ears in southeastern Utah sometime in the 1840s. By the time of the Long Walk period, he was a war leader and the last of the well-known Navajos to surrender and go to Fort Sumner. A few years after his release (1868) and return to the new reservation, he accepted the position of head of the newly created Navajo police force (1872). He served effectively for some time but by 1884 had turned to alcoholism and spent the remainder of his life battling its effects.

4. Coyotes, wolves, and bears played an important role in traditional Navajo religious teachings because of their supernatural powers and the things they did for humans. Extensive teachings about these creatures are related through ceremonial knowledge. Respect must be shown for them by following prescribed procedures when one comes in contact with them. Medicine men who understand how to handle these animals' power may use objects related to them in ceremonies.

5. This was Mormon Tea or Brigham Tea: *Ephedra trifurca.* This herb was thought to be beneficial in treating syphilis, colds, and stomach ailments.

6. In Catron County, New Mexico, sixty miles south of Zuni Pueblo and eighteen miles northwest of Quemado, a bed of salt lies in the bottom of a volcanic bowl and is under the control of the Zuni. This

salt lake provides much-needed salt in the region. Navajos generally had to barter for it, while the Zunis took care of extracting it through evaporation. Note by Ralph Evans.

7. "Mancos Creek: Montezuma County, CO and San Juan County, NM. . . . At its headwaters, this creek is formed by three branches, East, Middle, and West which drain the La Plata Mountains in the vicinity of Sharks Tooth Mountain. The creek then passes through the Mesa Verde Country, traveling 67 miles before crossing into New Mexico, where it enters the San Juan River approximately five miles farther downstream." Laurance D. Linford, *Navajo Places: History, Legend, Landscape* (Salt Lake City: University of Utah Press, 2000), 158.

8. The Hay Stacks are rounded sandstone outcrops that stand a short distance south of Window Rock, Arizona.

9. Yellow Horse is mistaken in this aspect of his account. General William Tecumseh Sherman and Special Agent Samuel Tappan were the men who led the peace process and signing of the treaty on June 1, 1868. Indeed, Carson died on May 23, 1868, one week before the signing of the treaty. Prior to his terminal illness, he had been much more involved with the Utes than the Navajos. Yellow Horse's mistaken identity may be because Carson, to the Navajos, became the symbol of the entire Long Walk–Fort Sumner experience.

10. Will Evans first worked on the reservation for Joe Wilkins at Little Water and later at Sanostee, about eight miles west of Little Water. He wrote of the bitter north winds in winter; so the store was probably moved to Sanostee, where there was more shelter. For this same reason probably, more Indians lived at Sanostee. Thus the move was logical.

11. Traders often built a guest hogan and supplied wood, water, and cooking utensils for their customers who traveled long distances.

12. The Beautiful Mountain Uprising is an interesting piece of history, for which Will Evans has been proven to be knowledgeable. He had the opportunity to discuss with many of the participants—both Anglo and Navajo—some of the circumstances surrounding the incident and was present at the time. As an oral history, the following account gives a valuable perspective on a local level, particularly from the traders' point of view. Frank McNitt in *The Indian Traders* (Norman: University of Oklahoma Press, 1962, 1989), 347–358, provides a more complete rendering based on various written and oral sources. Together, the two versions give a wonderful sense of the complexity of events and personalities that made this incident such a dramatic story.

13. There is yet another view of this event, that of Bizhóshí. On November 1, 1913, Reservation Superintendent Peter Paquette and Father Anselm Weber interviewed Bizhóshí concerning the incident at the Shiprock Agency. Part of the transcript from that meeting follows. Bizhóshí began by telling of his return to his home after a twelve-day

absence only to find his family gone. Then, with a group of relatives and friends, he started out to retrieve his missing family members.

"We did not intend when we started to have war or have a fight. We camped on this side of the San Juan. I said we would go to the Superintendent and beg four times for the children and women before we would take any steps. Early in the morning we rode up to the San Juan School. All the young fellows were ahead. When I overtook the young men they were all in front of the police quarters but he [a policeman] did not answer me where they were. I asked the policeman why he had taken them to the Agency. . . .

"The Clerk would not let us take the women. I begged him to let us [have] the women. I told him we would camp before the store. We would take the women over there and get them something to eat. The Clerk said no. I asked him eight times. I told him we would go over by the store and wait for Mr. Shelton to come back but the Clerk would not listen to us. We got the women out. One of the women ran toward where we went to go. We put one of the women on a horse. We went out the same way we came in. It was the road toward the store. When we went out that way there were some white people and some school children blocking the way so we could not get out. Then I rode up and I asked them to let us pass on and stay in front of the store until Mr. Shelton got back, but they would [not] open the way for us. They blocked the way so I rode among the crowd and one of the white men (a farmer) got hold of my bridle rein. Another called 'Yellow Man' (Jensen) got hold of the rein on the other side and would not let us go. We found there were only two policemen there. All at once one of the policemen jumped one of our men. I got hold of this fellow. I got hold of the policeman's wrist and held the policeman's hand. I then began whipping my horse. One of the white men, a farmer, tried to stop me. He is just about as ugly as I am. I ran my horse through the crowd. Some of the young fellows whipped the policeman. The white people did not do anything at all. . . . I do not think we have done anything wrong. They came and stole the women, and we stole them back."
"For Our Navajo People": Diné Letters, Speeches, and Petitions, 1900–1960, ed. Peter Iverson (Albuquerque: University of New Mexico Press, 2002), 124, 127.

14. "Beautiful Mountain: (9400 ft.) San Juan County, NM. . . . This large, isolated mountain runs northeast from the Tunicha Range on the Arizona State line 24 miles southwest of Shiprock. . . . In Navajo mythology, this mountain is the feet of Goods of Value Mountain, a male anthropomorphic figure, the head of which is Chuska Peak, the body the Chuska Mountains, and the feet the Carrizo Mountains. Shiprock is a medicine pouch or bow that he carries." Linford, 174–175 (see n. 7).

15. General Hugh Scott was the commandant of West Point at this time, while the soldiers were Troops A, B, C, and D, 12th Cavalry, from Fort Robinson, Nebraska.

16. Chee Dodge began his political career at a young age as a translator. He eventually became the first Chairman (now called President) of the Navajo Nation from 1922 to 1928 and later 1942 to 1946. A sharp business man, Dodge combined wealth with a lifestyle that rivaled that of some of the most affluent whites living in New Mexico in his day. He died in 1946.

17. While Will is certainly reflecting the Navajos' and many of the traders' attitudes toward John Collier, this Commissioner of Indian Affairs (1933–1945) did not implement programs to intentionally hurt the People. His New Deal legislation focused on providing Indians with self-determination, economic prosperity, effective tribal government, cultural pride, and positive educational reform. On the Navajo Reservation, because of the livestock reduction issues, some of these programs were not accepted; and all of them were tinged by the economic, cultural, and social tragedy engendered in the government's reduction of sheep, goats, cattle, and horses.

   From the Navajos' perspective, he was an evil man, who destroyed their economy, attempted to enslave them through economic means, and was deceitful in his dealings. The traders were also greatly affected by his policies. Wool production was a central aspect to the trading-post economy. Decreasing Navajo flocks by as much as one half had its effect on what transpired over the counters as well as in the culture of the livestock economy. The end result would eventually push Navajos off the reservation in search of a different form of livelihood. For more on the Navajo perspective, see Robert S. McPherson, *Navajo Land, Navajo Culture: The Utah Experience in the Twentieth Century* (Norman: University of Oklahoma Press, 2001), 102–120. For a brief but excellent treatment on the environmental impact of this program, see Richard White, *The Roots of Dependency: Subsistence, Environment, and Social Change among Choctaws, Pawnees, and Navajos* (Lincoln: University of Nebraska Press, 1983).

18. Window Rock is located twenty-five miles northwest of Gallup, Arizona. In 1933, Collier selected this site as a place where consolidation of the six different agencies on the reservation could be achieved in one central location. During 1936–1937, the Tribal Council was formed and has served as the governing body of the Navajo Nation ever since.

19. This is a reference to the teachings about the Navajo Twins, Monster Slayer and Born for Water, who cleansed the earth of monsters preying on the People. Two large monster birds called Tsé'náhalééh, lived on a flat outcrop of Shiprock, where they built a nest for their young. The

birds would sally forth, find a human, fly back to the nest, and feed the babies. One of the birds picked up Monster Slayer and tried to dash him against the rocks, but he was protected by supernatural powers. He then destroyed the evil birds and turned the offspring into more useful creatures that would serve mankind.

20. The exploration and exploitation of oil in the northern part of the reservation has been in two phases. The initial development occurred in 1921–1922, when four oil companies signed agreements with the tribal business council. The areas around the Hogback, Tocito Dome, Table Mesa, Rattlesnake (near Shiprock), and Beautiful Mountain——all of which Will was familiar with——were developed. By 1927, there were twenty-nine producing wells, but with the advent of the Great Depression, pumping came to an end.

Starting in the mid 1950s, oil exploration started anew. The Greater Aneth, Utah, area rivaled those around Shiprock, as oil production assumed a large scale. It has been a source of tribal revenue and controversy ever since. Although both fields are still producing large quantities of petroleum, the resource is decreasing. Bill P. Acrey, *Navajo History: The Land and the People* (Shiprock, NM: Central Consolidated School District No. 22, 1988), 2:198–200, 287–288.

21. Will died prior to the large-scale development starting in the 1950s. He also missed the protests and takeovers of oil facilities in the 1970s and the issues of environmental degradation and intratribe political unrest of the 1980s and 1990s. Still, production has provided the tribe with much needed revenue and a source of employment.

People

1. Frank McNitt gives the following account of the establishment of the Two Grey Hills Post: "In the spring of 1897, . . . [Joe] Wilkin[s] joined with the Noel brothers [Henry and Frank] to start a new trading post in the Chuska Valley. The place they chose was at the eastern base of the Chuskas eighteen miles north of Crystal by airline . . . . The partners set up a tent in a treeless valley on the Tuntsa (Big Tree) Wash, sheltered to the south by a low flat-topped peninsula of land that extended eastward several miles, its surface littered by the fallen walls and potsherds of an Anasazi village. . . . Within a year Wilkin[s] felt restless again and sold out his interests to the Noel brothers, moving north to build a trading post at Sanostee." *The Indian Traders* (Norman: University of Oklahoma Press, 1962, 1989), 257–258.

2. Westwater was located east of the Hogback Ridge, which at that point is rather low and not steep as at the San Juan River. The old Mormon Trail from Bluff and Blanding, Utah, skirted the Mesa Verde

bluffs, crossed the Hogback and descended into a sandstone canyon, where the store stood on a point facing the wash on its eastern side. Westwater was a resting place for the pioneers who came into the Fruitland area.

High on the sandstone outcrops, on a smooth surface of rock facing south and across the wash from the old store location, is a carved and ornamented inscription, "Hatch and Thurland." According to Stewart Hatch of Hatch Brothers Trading Post of Fruitland, this Hatch was his father, Joe Hatch. Son of Ira Hatch and early friend of many Indian tribes of the Southwest, Joe Hatch was a Mormon missionary sent by Brigham Young to live among the Indians. Edgar Thurland was a native of England, who at one time in his life found a thick bed of ancient oyster shells in The Meadows and built a furnace in which the shells were burned to make lime for mortar in many of the old brick buildings of the San Juan Valley. Joe Hatch and Edgar Thurland built the Westwater Store in 1897 or 1898. When it was closed, no one else took the business over. In time, many individuals took building materials from it and now only a bare outline of the building's foundation remains. Across the oil field road, which runs very close to the point on which the store stood, lie the circular remains of Navajo hogans, clustered close together.

Edgar Thurland married one of Costiano's widows. After this woman's death, Thurland married into a prominent Mormon family at Kirtland and raised a family. He and his wife died many years ago, but some of his children survive and still live in the area. (Richard Evans, Will Evans's son)

3.   Some traditional Navajos believed that by talking about the dead, by going to a burial site, or by thinking too much about a person who has died, the deceased will return and bother that individual. The afterlife is often seen as an unpleasant place, and so the deceased wants to have another's company to make the difficult more palatable.

4.   Black Horse is best known for this incident, although it was more involved than just a handful of lost whiskers. Agent David Shipley went to the Round Rock Trading Post in 1892 to demand that Navajo children be sent to the Fort Defiance Boarding School, a place notorious for mistreatment and unhealthy conditions. Black Horse listened to the agent's orders then angrily refused, even when threatened with punishment. The argument became heated, Black Horse insisting the agent and all traders be driven from the reservation. A fight ensued. Black Horse dragged Shipley out of the post, broke his nose, and threatened to throw him off a cliff into a dry wash below. Eventually Chee Dodge, who would later become Tribal Chairman, a Navajo policeman, and trader Charles Hubbell managed to get Shipley back into the post, where they remained until a military

detachment arrived thirty-six hours later. In a matter of months, Lieutenant Edward Plummer replaced Shipley as Navajo agent. For further details, see Bill P. Acrey, *Navajo History: The Land and the People* (Shiprock, NM: Central Consolidated School District No. 22, 1988), 2:108–110; also McNitt, *The Indian Traders*, 278–281 (see n. 1).

5. Navajo traditional beliefs varied by individual and family. Navajos often had a number of names simultaneously: one that was sacred and used only for ceremonies; one received as a child; nicknames given for physical characteristics, an experience, where one lived, one's clan, or ownership of an object; and a name used in white society. In each case, it was considered impolite to speak of oneself using one's name.

6. Shootingway and the Chiricahua Windway are part of the Holyway Chantways subgroup. Leland C. Wyman, a noted expert on Navajo ceremonial classification, wrote of these chants: "They are used to alleviate troubles attributed to the effects of thunder and lightning or to their cognate earth symbols, snakes and arrows. Chest and lung troubles and gastrointestinal diseases are often ascribed to these factors." "Navajo Ceremonial System," *Handbook of North American Indians: Southwest,* vol. 10, ed. Alfonso Ortiz (Washington, DC: Smithsonian Institution, 1983), 545. Thus, the Chiricahua Windway deals with sinus problems, fever, rashes, troubled eyesight, aches, sores, and dizziness. Whirlwinds are also believed to bring on these symptoms. Either a two- or five-day ceremony with sandpaintings of the Sun and Moon is part of the cure, along with the use of cactus prayer sticks.

7. For another version of this event, made into a story, see Frances Gillmor, *Windsinger* (Albuquerque: University of New Mexico Press, 1976).

8. Mary Eldredge came to New Mexico from New York in 1891 as the Field Matron of the Methodist Ladies Home Missionary Society. She served well into the first quarter of the twentieth century, helping the Navajo people in the general Shiprock area with health, agricultural, and domestic needs. Will had high respect for her and her assistance.

9. For additional information and photographs of Sandoval, see Earle R. Forrest, *With a Camera in Old Navajoland* (Norman: University of Oklahoma Press, 1970). In November, 1928, Aileen O'Bryan interviewed him about traditional Navajo teachings. From this came a publication rich in Navajo lore, entitled *Navaho Indian Myths* (New York: Dover Publications, 1993).

10. Navajo tradition dictates that while both a mother's and father's clan is important, the predominant claim of ancestry by an individual is that of the mother's. Thus there is the differentiation between the father's and the "family" clan.

11. The U.S. military officially established Fort Lewis in July 1880, after having been in the general vicinity for the previous year and a half. For eleven years the post served as a military fort, after which it was turned over to the Department of the Interior and became a school for Indian children—primarily Ute and Navajo. In 1910, the State of Colorado received it and made it a branch of the state agricultural college. See Robert W. Frazer, *Forts of the West: Military Forts and Presidios and Posts Commonly Called Forts West of the Mississippi River to 1898* (Norman: University of Oklahoma Press, 1965, 1980), 38–39.

12. William M. Peterson served as Superintendent of the Ute school at Fort Lewis between 1903 and 1906. In 1905, the average enrollment was 183 students. Boys learned the trades, such as blacksmithing, farming, carpentry, and leather working, while the girls learned domestic skills. The students also received rudimentary English and math instruction. W. M. Peterson, "Report of School at Fort Lewis, Colorado," August 3, 1905, *Report of the Commissioner of Indian Affairs,* vol. 1, 417.

13. While Evans may have had a guilty conscience over this event, Slim Policeman may not have been as surprised as the trader believed. There are well-established Navajo traditions associated with an eclipse. These include stopping all work and sitting quietly, ceasing travel, awakening anyone asleep, and avoiding talk. Evans's sincerity is not doubted, but his interpretation of the event may say more about him than it did his "victim."

14. "The blankets woven by the women on the reservation in the early days were quite rough of weave. They spun the yarn in a loose, knotted way, hence their weaving was thick, coarse, and bumpy. It was Pete's job to spread such a piece across the counter, comb out the bumps, and clip them with scissors if they were stubborn. The product is vastly improved today; weavers use more skill in spinning the yarn and in weaving, so that the finished blanket is a beautiful work of art." (Richard Evans, pers. comm.)

15. Begochidi, with his conflicting characteristics, is not a clearly defined Navajo deity. He is a type of trickster god involved with vulgarities. Gladys Reichard states: "[Begochidi] is described as the son of Sun, who had intercourse with everything in the world. That is the reason so many monsters were born. . . . He was Sun's youngest son, spoiled by his father, who put him in control of many things, such as game and domesticated animals. He was a transvestite and the first pottery maker. He could move without being seen, and change into different forms at will—into a rainbow, wind, sand, water, or anything else." *Navaho Religion: A Study of Symbolism* (Princeton, NJ: Princeton University Press, 1950), 386–390.

16. Compare this version with that of Washington Matthews, "The Origin of the Utes," *The American Antiquarian* 7 (September 1885): 271–274.

17. There are certain times of the year when particular stories, teachings, and ceremonies can be discussed and other times when it is forbidden. Most of this information is shared during the winter. However, there are some that can be related during the summer. Dan Pete, as a practicing medicine man, has determined to share this story with Evans based on this practice.

18. In Navajo culture, the Holy Beings established the pattern that if something—a favor, request for an object, or plea—were asked four times, it should be granted on the fourth request.

19. Owls are the harbingers of death and have connections with the dead. The "come, come" is beckoning Pinto Horses to the land of the dead, an undesirable place in many Navajo teachings.

20. During the time of creation, Monster Slayer and Born for Water cleansed the world of monsters that had been created because of wrongdoings. Among those creatures that needed to be destroyed were the Tsé'náhalééh, two large birds that fed Navajo victims to their young, whose nest was located on Shiprock. The male bird picked up Monster Slayer and tried to dash him against the rock formation, but a life feather allowed him to land softly. Monster Slayer waited for both birds to eventually return, then killed them with lightning arrows. The young birds in the nest started to cry and so he spared two—the eagle and the owl, both of which he gave specific instructions concerning the Navajo. To the owl he directed that man would listen to its voice and learn of the future. From Robert S. McPherson, *Sacred Land, Sacred View: Navajo Perceptions of the Four Corners Region* (Provo: Brigham Young University, 1992), 33.

Culture

1. These two different types of hogans are classified as female (the one Will just described) and male (the conical shaped one he is about to explain). In Navajo thought, everything is either male or female, which has nothing to do with whether men or women use the edifice, but rather how the structures are designated in the mythology. Holy Beings made the first hogans, establishing how they were to be built, proper etiquette, and religious teachings about them. Preferably, ceremonies today are performed in a hogan, since the Holy Beings recognize it as the home of a Navajo.

2. Navajos explain that gentleness in a handshake shows respect and affection. A forceful grasp suggests power and dominance, not friendship.

3. While the majority of anthropologists may agree with Will's belief that the Navajos learned weaving from the Pueblos, others do not. The generally accepted theory is that, following the Pueblo Revolt of

1680 and the subsequent reconquest of New Mexico by the Spanish, extensive mixing of the Pueblo and Navajo cultures provided great impetus to the spread of weaving. The minority who do not accept this view say that the Navajos entered the Southwest already possessing this skill, suggesting that they obtained it while living in the Northwest. To the Navajo, both ideas are wrong, since they learned weaving from the Holy Beings before they ever emerged from the worlds beneath this one. For a brief explanation, see Ruth Roessel, "Navajo Arts and Crafts," *Handbook of North American Indians: Southwest,* vol. 10, ed. Alfonso Ortiz (Washington, DC: Smithsonian Institute, 1983), 592.

4.   The sweat lodge, like the hogan, was first created by the Holy Beings, who established the pattern. It is conical like the male hogan and is also classified as male. Proper etiquette and the songs used in the sweat lodge have been provided by the gods. Either men or women may take a sweat but not together. It is used to purify a person, to prepare for or to conclude a ceremony, or simply to clean oneself and relax.

5.   These pipes, called by the Pueblo peoples "cloud blowers," have been found in Anasazi ruins and are often used in ceremonies. The Franciscan Fathers describe this use: "A pipe is filled with [mountain tobacco] and lighted with punk made of corncob pith. The pipe is stemless, conical in shape, and provided with a hole in the bottom to draw the smoke. When necessary they are made of clay mixed with crushed broken pottery, though frequently pipes found in old ruins are made to answer. The singer smokes this pipe facing east, and blows the smoke first downward to the earth; then to the sky in front of himself, to his right, rear and left side and finally from above downward. This is repeated in turn by the patient and all present." Franciscan Fathers, *An Ethnologic Dictionary of the Navajo Language* (Saint Michaels, AZ: Saint Michaels Press, 1910, 1968), 395.

6.   While Will's emphasis on the maternal clan is correct, offspring also pay attention to the father's (patrilineal) descent. One is "born into" the mother's clan and "born for" the father's clan. Paternal relations can play an important role in a child's upbringing and training, while memorization of relatives on the father's side is done just as much as it is on the mother's side.

7.   The traditional description given of a son-in-law who sees his mother-in-law is that he will act as a moth who carelessly burns itself in a fire, because it ventured too close. The belief that there will be psychological harm and inappropriate actions encourage those who practice this belief to stay away. If necessity warrants that mother-in-law and son-in-law have seen each other or that they must interact, there is a ceremony that can be performed to allow this restriction with its accompanying effects to be lifted.

8. As with many other aspects of traditional Navajo culture, the cradle board came from the Holy Beings, Changing Woman being the first to have been found in one. Each aspect of the cradle, from the type of tree and other materials to its actual structure, is imbued with meaning. The backboard represents Mother Earth, the two holes at the top its eyes, the footrest a short rainbow, the wooden canopy a longer rainbow, the loops zigzag lightning, the thongs sun rays, and the baby's blankets the clouds. Evans, in his description, has bypassed much of this significance.

9. Evans's characterization of legendary lore and folklore is his simple way of classifying a very complex oral tradition that does not fit nearly as cleanly as he may have supposed. Anthropologists have attempted to be much more exacting, placing each type of myth, legend, and tale into specific categories based as much upon how they function in the culture as upon their motifs and content.

10. This is not entirely accurate. While First Man and First Woman do play a prominent part during the creation story, they are not all-powerful and do make mistakes. They are assisted by other Holy Beings, without whose help they could have failed. Evans may be searching for the one omnipotent God or Heavenly Father that he found in Mormon beliefs.

11. Evans published these stories in *Southwestern Lore* 14, no.3 (December 1948): 48–68.

12. A bullroarer is made from lightning-struck wood and covered with pitch from a lightning-struck tree, which, when combined with its noise, is a powerful force to keep evil away from the patient. It may also be pressed against the patient's limbs and places of pain to drive the evil away. See Franciscan Fathers, *An Ethnologic Dictionary of the Navajo Language* (Saint Michaels, AZ: Saint Michaels Press, 1910, 1968), 415.

13. The name Fire Dance is given because of the last and most dramatic part of the five-day Mountainway ceremony. "The [Mountain Chant is] often stated to be particularly applicable to cases of mental illness, fainting spells, delirium, and the like. Animals are mentioned as etiological factors. . . . Indeed, snakes, bears, or porcupines are almost invariably mentioned in the legends, sandpaintings, the songs, the making of cut stick offerings." Leland C. Wyman and Clyde Kluckhohn, "Navajo Classification of their Song Ceremonials," *Memoirs of the American Anthropological Association,* 1938, no. 50:24. For a detailed explanation of the various facets of the ceremony, see Leland C. Wyman, *The Mountainway of the Navajo* (Tucson: University of Arizona Press, 1975).

14. This and other seemingly magical elements of the ceremony are based upon the power of the animals who first performed these rites in

the myths. Confidence and a sense of well-being for the patients are evoked by both the ceremony and the medicine men performing it.

15. The Enemyway ceremony was formerly used to protect warriors from ghosts of the enemy killed in battle. Today it is used as "a cure for sickness thought to be caused by ghosts of non-Navajos. It is classed with the other Ghostway (Evilway) ceremonials" and may last either three or five nights. From Leland C. Wyman, "Navajo Ceremonial System," *Handbook of North American Indians: Southwest,* vol. 10, ed. Alfonso Ortiz (Washington, DC: Smithsonian Institution, 1983), 541. The ritual is based on a myth in which Monster Slayer is cleansed from evil influences after killing monsters inhabiting the earth. The ceremony is often called a squaw dance because of a social feature in the evenings where a woman chooses her partner for a dance.

16. This is definitely Will's interpretation of how Navajos view this ceremony and dance. While Navajo elders often bemoan the fact that there have been changes and that the orderliness that used to be a part of the activities is disappearing, the Enemyway is still an important and sacred ceremony of the Navajo people.

17. Skinwalkers participate in one of a number of forms of Navajo witchcraft. The name comes from the belief that the witch practitioner actually puts on the skin of a wolf, coyote, or some other such animal and, by doing so, assumes supernatural qualities used against an individual. Through prayer, ritual, and knowledge of evil, the skinwalker performs antisocial acts shunned by a "normal" person. See Clyde Kluckhohn, *Navaho Witchcraft* (Boston: Beacon Press, 1944).

18. Snakes are considered powerful creatures, based on their role in Navajo mythology. Big Snake, a Holy Being, is sometimes treacherous and can cause illness or death if not shown proper respect. The sight of one may cause birth defects in an unborn baby. Snakes and lightning, because of their crooked shapes, are often associated with each other. Snakes are not handled, and both snakes and lightning-struck objects are avoided, unless a medicine man understands how to negate the evil and utilize the power from them.

Index

Acoma, 118
Agapito, 5, 53–58
Akeah, Sam, 235
alcohol, 204–5
Aldrich, Stephen E., 75
Algert Trading Company, 13, 50
Allen, Frank, *137*
'Anaa'jí. *See* Enemyway, Squaw Dance
Anasazi ruins, 251, 256
animals, Navajo relationship to, 233–34, 247, 255, 258
'Anísts'óózí. *See* Thin Man
Apaches, 58–59
Arbuckles Coffee, 37, 45, 75, 81, 189
Arrington, John, 7, 56
arrowheads, 182, 217
Ashcroft, Charles, 7, *8*
astronomy, 64–65
'Atsídí Nez. *See* Tall Blacksmith
Awóshk'al'ádin. *See* Evans, Will
Ayres, James, 95, 101
Ayres, Willard and Mrs., *95*

Baker, Robert S., 81
Baldwin, Harry C. (Hunter, Naalzhééhii), 77–79, 81, *82*–85
Barber, Frank, 76
Barboncito, 247
Be Dugal Chun. *See* Mustache Smeller
Beautiful Mountain Uprising, 31, 53, 79, 91–104, 248–49
Beclabito (Bitł ááhbito'), 155
Beesh łigaii. *See* Peshlakai, Boyd
Begochidi, 166, 254
Benally, Jim, 236
Benito, 172
Bernard, Bruce, 6
Beyal, Clyde, *19*

Big God (Yé'iitsoh), 171–72
Big Sheep. *See* Mount Hesperus
Biggs, Rosetta, *Our Valley*, 7
Bilįį Néiltihígíí. *See* Fast Running Horses
birth, 66–67, 208, 258
Bitł ááhbito'. *See* Beclabito
Bitter Water Clan (Tó dích'íi'nii), 152
Bizhóshí, 31, 40, 79, 91, 126–32, *127*, *131*, 135, 154, 162, 229, 248–49; Beautiful Mountain uprising, 93, 96, 97, 100, 103; sons of, 130, 131
Black Horse, 84, 88–89, 122–26, *123*, 135, 154, 252
Black Whiskers, *93*
blacksmith, 215
Blair family, 7
blankets. *See* rugs, Navajo; sandpainting, blankets
Bloomfield, George R. and Lucy, *6*, 7, *19*, 29, 244
Blue Canyon trading post, 5
Bluff, UT, 5, 10, 74, 149, 251–52
Book of Mormon, 8, 10
Born for Water, 250
Boy Raised by Owls, 171–72
bridles and bits, 129, 215
Bryan, Tom, 79, 81
buffalo, 57, 61, 69–71, 118
bull pen, 37, 81, 102, 124, 130, 165, 203
bullroarer (tsinidi'ni'), 215, 257
Burnham, Roy R., 7, *8*, 17–18
buttons, 83, 124, 164, 200, 259

C. H. Algert Trading Company, 13, 50, 87
Cambridge, Louis, *93*
Canyon de Chelly, 136, 182
Captain Tom's Wash Post, 79, 80, 101
card playing, 76, 84

Carlisle (PA) Indian Institute, 150, *151*
Carson, Kit, 6, 72–73, 136, 248
ceremonies, 142–43, 257; gathering, *227*; healing, 137–38, 154, 160–62, 215–17, 253, 257. *See also* chants and songs
Chaco Canyon, 54, 182
chanters, 62, 126, 132, 134, 135, 137, 177, 218, 220
chants and songs, 72, 104, 119–20, 126, 133–35, 137, 138, 154, 159–60, 161–62, 166, 214, 215–20, 222, 225, 227, 231, 253; chantways, 33, 257. *See also* ceremonies; *names of specific chants and ways*
Chatterer (Ha'diłch'ałí), 144–45
Chéchi'il Yah Tó. *See* Water Under Oak Tree
Chee-Kent-De-Ghunnie, 174
ch'įįdii 'atiin. *See* Devil's Road
Chiisheh'ili. *See* Evans, Will
Child of the Wind, 166
Chinaman (Shawl, Hastiin Dáábalí), 140–43, *141*
Chiricahua Windway, 136, 253, 269
Christmas, 43–45, 110–13
clans, 119, 152, 207, 256
Cly, Ella, 56–57
coal, 16, 110, 148
Cole, Mrs. Henrietta G., 13, 77–78
Collier, John, 53, 82, 104–7, *105*, 250
Collyer, Cyril J., *80*
Collyer, James B. "Jim," 112, 244
Comanches, 57, 68–71
corn: dance, 228; food, 57, 59, 62, 76, 81, 143; husk cigarette papers, 132, 164, 202, 203; pollen, 23, 134, 138, 162, 207, 217
Costiano (The Talker, Adiits'a'í), 117–22, *118*, 154, 252
cradle boards, *201*, 209, *211*, 257
Crystal trading post, 19, 75, 79, 110, 112
cultural bias, 30–33
Curley Jim, *93*, 108, *120*
Curly Head. *See* Evans, Will
Currie, Hugh, 80

Dághaa' Chin. *See* Mustache Smeller
Davies, Ed, Mrs., and Mary, 6
Dawn Boy. *See* Talking God
Dayish, John, 98–100
death, 228–29, 232, 246, 252
deer and antelope, 58, 61
Dees, Liesl, research efforts, 10
Deshna Clah, 8
Devil's Road (ch'įįdii 'atiin), 194
Dibé Ntsaa. *See* Mount Hesperus
Dilóshí Begay, 90
Diné Tsosie, 90
divorce, 210, 212
Dodge, Chee, 75, 96, 100, 101, 108, 150, 250, 252

Dooda'Ólta' (No School), 149
Dustin, Bert, 6, *8*, 13
Dustin, Edwin Seth, 12, 39, 40, 41, 45, 128
Dustin, Sheldon, 6, 14
Dził' łíí'íní. *See* Prayer to the Mountains
Dził-Hanáádlį́. *See* Huerfano Mesa/Peak
Dziłk'ijí Biką'jí. *See* Mountainway

eclipse, 30–31, 158, 254
economy, 4, 53, 76, 82, 104–8, 147, 250
Eddie Lake trading post, *18*
Eldredge, Ruth, 83
Eldridge, Mrs. Mary, 13, 77, 83, 149, 253
Enemyway ('Anaa'jí), 136, 227, 258. *See also* Squaw Dance
Escavada Wash and Pueblo Bonito, 33–58
Estep, Evan W., *8*
ethnocentricism, 30–33, 254
Evans, David, 13
Evans, Edwin (Ted) C., *9*
Evans, Gwendolin, 13, 15
Evans, Jane Ann Coles, 9–11
Evans, John, *9*, 149
Evans, Ralph, *13*, *15*
Evans, Richard, *8*, 13, 19, 33–34, 252
Evans, Sarah Luella Walker, 12–13, *13*, 21, 75, *142*, *231*
Evans, Thomas, *9*, 10–11, 149
Evans, Wilford, *9*
Evans, Will: Beautiful Mountain Uprising, 30–31; beginnings as trader, 12–13; biography, 10–21; contributions to historiography, 26–27; Curly Head (Chiisheh'ili), 243; ethnocentricism of, 30–33, 254; Missing Tooth in Front (Awóshk'al'ádin), 11, 37, 235; missionary, 13, 17, 19, 244; Mormon/Navajo belief correlations, 19, 21–26; "Navajo trails" manuscript, 19, 20, 27, 33–35; obituary, 235–37; photographs, *6*, *9*, *12*, *13*, *15*, *18*, *19*, *28*, *32*, *38*, *39*, *46*, *50*, *80*, *231*, *236*, *237*, *238*; preservationist, 14–16, 27–30, 33
Evilway (Ghostway), 58, 136, 176, 231, 258

farming, 57, 62, 76, 89, 90, 144, 146, 187
Farmington, NM, 7, 56, 80, 83; Will Evans at, 13, 19, 82
Fast Running Horses (Bilį́į Néiltihígíí), 160
Fat One (Fat Medicine Man, Neesk'áhí), 136–37, *137*
Fat One's Son (Neesk'áhí Biye'), 136–40
Father Sky (Yá'aash), 168–70
feathers, dancing, 134, 225
fire, starting, 63
Fire Dance, 133, 222–26, 257. *See also* Mountainway
First Man, 214, 257
food, 61–63, 76, 81, 190–91, 207, 247; taboos, 174

Fort Defiance, AZ, 58, 75, 106, 148, 150; trading post, 13
Fort Defiance Boarding School, 252
Fort Lewis Indian school, 155–56, 254
Fort Sumner, NM, 56, 66, 74, 132; life at, 57, 71–73, 147. *See also* Long Walk
four: sacred colors, 224; sacred mountains, 213; significance, 220–22, 224
Four Corners region: Mormon expansion into, 4–5; Navajo trade in, 13
Four Corners trading post, 82
Foutz, Al, 6, 14
Foutz, Jesse, 6
Foutz, Joseph Lehi, 4–6, 10
Foutz, Junius (June), 6, 13, 14
Foutz, Luff, 8
Frank, 99
Fruitland, NM, 11, 13, 80, 81, 120, 252
Fruitland Trading Company, 5
Fryer, E. R., 105

Ghostway. *See* Evilway
Gibson, Walter, 8
Goldsmith, Ike, 6
Good Singer's Grandson, 231
Goodman, Loncy Tanner, 96
Great Snake Man, 221

Ha'dilch'alí. *See* Chatterer
hairstyles, 125, 202–3
Haltsooí Dine'é. *See* Meadow People
Hamblin, Jacob, 3, 4, 6, 10, 21
handshaking, 190, 255
Hans Aspaas, 145, 150, 151
Hard Belly, 93
Hashch'eelti'i (Talking God), 166
Hashtł'ishnii. *See* Mud People
Haskell, Thales, 10
Hastiin Bicheii, 78
Hastiin Chxó'í. *See* Ugly Man
Hastiin Dáábalí. *See* Chinaman
Hastiin Dághaa'. *See* Mister Mustache
Hastiin Deshnod and family, 64
Hastiin Dóola. *See* Mister Bull
Hastiin Házhó'ógo Nahanání. *See* Walker, John L.
Hastiin Łįįłkizhí. *See* Pinto Horses
Hastiin Nez. *See* Tall Man
Hastiin Tapaha, 165
Hastiin Tó Niłchxon. *See* Smelly Water
Hastiin Washburn's daughter, 144–45
Hastiin Yazzie. *See* Small Man
Hataałii Nez. *See* Tall Singer
Hataałii Yazzie. *See* Little Singer
Hatch Brothers Trading Post, 252
Hatch, Ira, 6, 10, 252
Hatch, Joe, Sr., 12, 252
Hatch, Lude Kirk, 12
Hatch, Stewart, 252

Hay Stacks, 65, 248
Hinds, Mr., 94
hogans, 42, 54, 63, 63, 124, 183–86, 184, 248, 255
Hogback, 126
Hogback Canal, 83–84
Hogback Mission, 77, 83
Hogback trading post, 66, 77, 81, 83, 84
Holly, (James M.?), 6
Holy Beings (Yé'ii), 126, 176, 192, 213, 214, 217, 255, 257
Holy Young Man, 119
Holyway Chantways, 253
hospitality, 187–90
Hubbard, Matt and Harry, 81, 86, 88
Hubbell, Charles, 252
Hubbell, Roman, 25
Huerfano Mesa/Peak (Dził-Hanáádlí, "Place of Creation"), 126, 171
Hull and Baldwin trading post, 81, 121
Hull, Henry (Hank), 77, 81, 83
Hunt, John, 6, 7
Hunter. *See* Baldwin, Harry C.
hunting, 58–59, 61–62, 132, 145–46, 172, 173–74

illegitimacy, 205
Indian agencies centralized, 106
intermarriage, 152, 206
ironwood people, 172
irrigation, 62, 83–84, 146, 150

Jack, Vernon W., 19
Jensen, Sephus, 94
Jewett Valley, 81, 149
John Walker's trading post, 75
Johnny Cow, 132
Jóhonaa'éí. *See* Sun Bearer
Judge Clah (Tł'ah, "Left-Handed"), 192
Junction City, 80

Kinaaldá (female puberty) ceremony, 206
Kirtland, NM, 5, 81, 252

Lame One (Na'nishhod), 94
Lee, John D., 3, 5
Lee, Joseph, 5, 80
Lee, Nita Pete, 231
Left-Handed. *See* Judge Clah
Lewis, Rhoda, 113
Little Singer (Hataałii Yazzie), 79, 90, 91–104, 92, 130, 130, 131, 131
Little Water, 40, 121, 258
livestock: losses, 76–78; reduction, 53, 104–8
Long Walk, 65–85, 132, 146–47, 152–53; period, 52, 59–74, 247. *See also* Fort Sumner
Luce, 94
Lukachukai Mountains, 40, 128, 140

Index

MacClary, John Stewart, 27, 190
magic in ceremonies, 134, 225–26, 257–58
Man Who Moves Slowly. *See* Walker, John L.
Mancos Creek, 65
Manuelito, 58, 135, 247
Many Goats (Tł'ízí Łáni), 135, 142, 162, 175–76
Many Goats Uncle (Tł'ízí Łani Bida'í), 229
Mapel, Edith and Frank, *6*
marriage customs, 206–8
Martin, Robert and Asenebá, *8*, *102*, 103
Maupin, Buke, 79
Mayer, Mr., 82
McGee, Roscoe, *8*
McNitt, Frank, 2–3, 7
Meadow People (Haltsooí Dine'é), 152
medicine men, 119, 133–35, 136–40, 142–43, 160–62, 175–76, 186, 214
Mesa Verde National Park, 150–51
Methodist: Church, 11, 13; Mission, 83
Mexican Clan (Naakaii Dine'é), 86, 88, 90
Mexican Water, AZ, 74; trading post, 80
military, 94, 98–100
Missing Link. *See* Bizhóshí
Missing Tooth. *See* Evans, Will
Mister Bull (Hastiin Dóola), 161, 162
Mister Mustache (Hastiin Dághaa'), *66*
monster birds of Shiprock (Tsé'náhalééh), 250, 255
Monster Slayer, 173, 176, 221, 250, 258
Moore, Guy and Ruth, 112
morality, 205–6
Morgan, Jacob C., *105*
Mormon: beliefs, 8, 10, 19, 21–26; expansion, 3–4, 147; trader networks, 4–8, 14
Mother Earth (Nahasdzáán), 168–70
mother-in-law, seeing, 208, 256
Mount Hesperus (Big Sheep, Dibé Ntsaa), 171
mountains, four sacred, 65, 103–4, 213
Mountainway (Dziłk'ijí Bika'jí, Mountain Chant), 119, 133, 134, 166, 222–26, 257
Mud People (Hashtł'ishnii), 152
Mustache Smeller (Dághaa' Chin, Be Dugal Chun), 77, 162, 212

Naalzhééhii. *See* Baldwin, Harry C.
Náasht'ézhí dine'é. *See* Zuni Clan
Nah O Kanh Gahilgiih (Nihookáá' Yigałígíí), 166
Nahasdzáán. *See* Mother Earth
names, 129, 253
Na'nishhod. *See* Lame One
Naschitti trading post, 75, 79
Nava, NM, 94, 101; trading post, 80
Navajo: art as decoration, 16–21, *17–18*, 31–32, *32*, *81*, *183*; children, *28*, 193, 208, 209–10, *211*; clothing, 61, 124–25, *193*, 199–202, *201*, *202*, *208*, *211*, *231*; life

before/after traders, 63–64; pastimes, 76, 84, 233; photographs, *61*, *111*, *184*, *188*, *231*; preservation of culture, 14–16, 27–30, 33; prosperity, 82, 104–10, 147; ways contrasted with white ways, 126–27; ways old and new, 157–58
Navajo blankets. *See* rugs, Navajo; sandpainting, blankets
Navajo John, 195
Navajo police, 85, *93*, 120, 146, 149–50, 152, 156, 247
"Navajo Trails" manuscript, 19, *20*, 27, 33–35
Navajo Tribal Council, 105, 108, 149, 250
Navajo Twins, 250
Navijohn, 231
Navijohn Begay, Mrs., *231*
Neesk'áhí. *See* Fat One
Neesk'áhí Biye'. *See* Fat One's Son
Nelson, Alphonso (Fonnie), *6*, *95*
Nelson, Charles, 7, 80, 94
Nelson family, *95*
Nelson, Mrs. Roswell, and family, 101
New Deal, 104, 107
Newcomb, Arthur J. and Franc, *6*, 7, *8*, 29
Newcomb Trading Post, 80
Nez, Josephine Salow (Siláo, policeman), 112
Nez, Mrs., 112
Night Chant (Yé'ii Bicheii), 119, 212, 227
Nihookáá' Yigałígíí. *See* Nah O Kanh Gahilgiih
No School (Dooda'Ólta'), 149
Noel, Edmund, *80*
Noel family, *95*
Noel, Frank L., 5, *6*, 41, 77, 79, *80*, 88, 94–96, *95*, 100, 251
Noel, Hambleton B. (Hamp), 88
Noel, Henry R., 77, 79, *80*, 251

oil and gas, 73, 108–10, 150, 251
Old Fat Medicine Man, 28
Old School Boy (Ólta'í Sání), 94, 103
Olio, NM, 81
owls, 175, 255

Palmer, Asa, *8*
Paquette, Peter, 248
Peshlakai, Boyd (Beesh łigaii, silver), 98
Pete, Dan, 31, 131, 162–77, *163*, 215, 255
Peterson, George, 84–85
Peterson, William M., 156
Pinto Horses (Hastiin Łįįłkizhí), 174–75
pipes (cloud blowers), 203, 256, 259
Place of Creation. *See* Huerfano Mesa/Peak
Plummer, Lt. Edward, 252
Polacca, Howela and Ruth, *112*, *113*
polygamy, 93, 144, 206–7
pottery, 195

Prayer to the Mountains (Zilth Neyani, Dził' łíí'íní), 159–60
Progressive Mercantile Company, 14

raiding parties, 65, 67, 68–71, 132–33
rainmaking, 133–35
"Red Clothes (Shirt)", 72
Red Lake trading post, 5
Red Mesa trading post, 80
Red Rock trading post, 79, 80, 86–91, 88, 94–95, 97, 98
Red Running into the Water Clan (Táchii'nii), 119
Redcap, Joe, 216, 217
Reddy, B. H., 24–26
Redshaw, Herbert, 6
Reitz, Joe, 79
Richardson, Gladwell, 29
Roanhorse, Rose, 112
Robinson, Eliza, 95
Round Rock, AZ, 125; trading post, 75, 80
rugs, Navajo, 14, 193–95, 254. See also Yé'ii rugs

sacred images, appropriated or preserved, 14, 16–21, 31–33
Salow-Elt-Socie. See Slim Policeman
Salow Nez, Mrs. Josephine (Siláo, policeman), 112
salt, 247–48
Salt Water Clan (Tó dík'ǫzhí), 152
San Juan River, 74, 79, 81, 121, 140, 148, 149, 156
Sand-hogan Clan (Séí bee hooghanii), 124
Sandoval Begay, 150–52
Sandoval (Tall Grass, Tłóh Nineezígíí), 145–52
sandpainting, 14–16, 29, 31–32, 120, 137, 138, 162, 168–69, 169, 175–76, 183, 212, 215–17, 218, 220–22, 221, 224, 253; blankets, 14, 138–40, 139; ceremony, 215–18
Sanostee, NM, 135, 246; trading post, 12, 36–45, 41, 79, 88–89, 94–95, 128, 131, 248, 251
sawmill, 101
school building, 158–60
schools, Indian, 150–51, 155–56
Scooped Water Clan (Tó Káán), 152
Scott, General Hugh, 94, 100–103, 101, 250
Séí bee hooghanii. See Sand-hogan Clan
Shawl. See Chinaman
sheep: raising, 194; upgraded herd quality, 82. See also livestock, losses
Sheep Springs, NM, 14, 75
Shelton, William T., 6, 7, 8, 84, 85, 93–94, 93, 96–98, 156
Sherman, William Tecumseh, 247, 248
Shipley, David, 252–53

Shiprock, NM, 14–15, 86–87, 93, 108, 150, 156, 227
Shiprock Agency, 61, 82, 149, 182
Shiprock formation (Rock with Wings On It, Tse'bit'a'í), 154, 165–68, 167
Shiprock Trading Company, 14, 15, 19, 21, 81, 86, 89, 182, 231
Shootingway, 136, 176, 253
sickness, 57, 72, 137, 138, 258
Siláo Ałts'ózí. See Slim Policeman
silversmithing, 146, 197–98, 197
Simpson, Richard, 81, 243
skinwalkers, 177, 186, 229–30, 258
Sky (Yá'aash), 168
Slim Policeman (Siláo Ałts'ózí, Salow-Elt-Socie, Tall Edge of the Water People's Son), 28, 30–31, 93, 152–58, 153, 236, 254
Small Man (Hastiin Yazzie), 230–31
Smelly Water (Hastiin Tó Niłchxon), 135
Smith, Evan, 17, 19
Smith, Merritt, 80
Smith, R. G., 80
Smith, Sherry L., 26–27
Smouse, Don, 8
Snake Medicine (Tł'iish Bé'niih), 229
snowstorms, 40–45, 76–78, 128
Soil Conservation Service, 82, 104–7
Song People, 176
songs and chants, 134–35, 218–20, 222
Squaw Dance (Enemyway, 'Anaa'jí), 15, 31, 136, 227–28. See also Enemyway
Squeezer (Taiyoonihi), 123
Stacher, Samuel B., 6
Steele, Milton and Jennie, 95
Stolworthy, Carlos, 7, 8
Storm God, 132
storytelling, 172, 213–14, 255; Big God and the Turkey, 214; creation of the world, 126; how Shiprock moved, 165–67; how the deer became wild, 172–73; monster birds on Shiprock, 250–51, 255; Mother Earth and Father Sky, 168–70; origin of sandpaintings, 119, 218; origin of the Utes, 170–72; seasons for, 172, 255; why bears' toes point inward, 233–34; why Navajos are afraid to go out at night, 177; why Navajos don't eat fish, fowl, or eggs, 174; why owls can tell people things, 176
Sun Bearer (Jóhonaa'éí), 177, 222
sweat lodges, 199, 256
Sweet Water trading post, 74, 80

Tábąąhá Nez. See Tall Water's Edge People
Table Mesa, 64, 73
Táchii'nii. See Red Running into the Water Clan
Taiyoonihi. See Squeezer
Talking God (Hashch'eelti'i), 166

Tall Blacksmith ('Atsidi Nez), 215–17
Tall Edge of the Water People's Son. *See* Slim Policeman
Tall Grass. *See* Sandoval
Tall Man (Hastiin Nez), 68, 85, 88, 160–62, 229–31
Tall Singer (Hataałii Nez), 135, 231
Tall Water's Edge People (Tábąąhá Nez), 152
Tanner, Joe M., 5, 6, 94–96, 100
Tanner, Loncy (Goodman), 96
Tappan, Samuel, 248
Taylor, Elmer A., 8
Teec Nos Pos, AZ, 74, 135, 192, *213*; trading post, 80
The Talker. *See* Costiano
Theodore, 143–44
Thin Man ('Anísts'óózí), 97
Thurland, Edgar, 252
Tł'ah Begay, 93
Tł'ah "Left Handed". *See* Judge Clah
Tł'iish Bé'niih. *See* Snake Medicine
Tł'ízí Łani. *See* Many Goats
Tł'ízí Łani Bida'í. *See* Many Goats Uncle
Tłóh Nineezígíí. *See* Sandoval
Tó dích'íí'nii. *See* Bitter Water Clan
Tó dík'ǫzhí. *See* Salt Water Clan
Tó Káán. *See* Scooped Water Clan
Toadlena, NM, 135, 142, 174; trading post, 29, 75, 77, 80
tobacco, 162, 164, 165, 203–4
Tocito, NM, 75
Tohatchi, NM, 74, 75, 79, 132, 158, 187
traders: Mormon beliefs and, 8, 10; Mormon families, 4–8, 244; Mormon/non-Mormon, 7–8; preservation of Navajo culture by, 29; writings about, 245–46
trading posts: color system of coins, 246; establishment of, 12, 36–45, 74–82; of Foutz family, 5; keeping books, 129; pawn, 75, 129, 191; prices, 75; trade tokens, *47*; transactions, 45–50, 89, 90, 190–93
traditions and lore, 212–14
Treaty of 1868, 57, 147, 247
Tse'bit'a'í. *See* Shiprock
Tsé'náhalééh. *See* monster birds
tsin dzilgiizh, 224
tsinidi'ni'. *See* bullroarer
Tuba City, AZ, 3, 5
turquoise, 191–93, 233
Two Grey Hills trading post, 13, 75, 77, 78, 79, 91, 121, *121*, 251

Ugly Man (Hastiin Chxó'í), 132–36, 154, 162, 229

Utes, 65, 67, 79, 170–172

Wade, John, 80
Walker, Claude, 86
Walker family, *142*
Walker, John L. (Man Who Moves Slowly, Hastiin Házhó'ógo Nahananí), 6, 75, 142, *142*
Walker, Olin C., 6, 80, 86–91, 94–95, 97–100
Walker, William J. "Will", 142, *142*, 244
Wallace, Dr. William N., 83, *118*
Washburn, Mrs., 144–45
Water Under Oak Tree (Chéchi'il Yah Tó), *202*
water wells, 54, 186
Waterway, 133–35
weavers, 138, 147, 193–96, *194*, *196*, 254, 255–56
Weber, Father Anselm, 248
Welch, Colonel, 83
Welch, Mr., 81
Westwater, NM, 120, 251; trading post, 122, 252
Wetherill, Louisa and John, 6, 29
Wheeler, Wilford, 66
Whitcroft, Mr., 86–87
White, Tom, 81
Wilkins, Joseph (J. R.), 12, 39, 40, 41, 45, 79, 128, 248, 251
William Meadows's trading post, 60
Window Rock, AZ, 105–6, 250
winter of 1898, 121, 148, 248
witchcraft, 137, 229–33, 258. *See also* skinwalkers
wool, *50*, *131*, 147, 193

Yá'aash. *See* Father Sky
Yazhi, Harding, and wife, *201*
Yé'ii Bicheii. *See* Night Chant
Yé'ii rugs, 14, 138, *139*
Yé'iitsoh. *See* Big God
Yellow Horse, 59–74, *60*, 154, 248
Young, John R., 11
Young Stake Mission, 17, 19, 29
Youngblood, Claude, *38*
yucca (hashk'aan), magical growth of, 134, 226

Zilth Neyani [Dził Líf'íní]. *See* Prayer to the Mountains
Zuni Clan (Náasht'ézhí dine'é), 119